CREATIVITY AND SCIENCE

LATIN AMERICAN AND CARIBBEAN SERIES

Hendrik Kraay, General Editor
ISSN 1498-2366 (Print), ISSN 1925-9638 (Online)

This series sheds light on historical and cultural topics in Latin America and the Caribbean by publishing works that challenge the canon in history, literature, and postcolonial studies. It seeks to print cutting-edge studies and research that redefine our understanding of historical and current issues in Latin America and the Caribbean.

No. 1 · Waking the Dictator: Veracruz, the Struggle for Federalism and the Mexican Revolution Karl B. Koth

No. 2 · The Spirit of Hidalgo: The Mexican Revolution in Coahuila Suzanne B. Pasztor · Copublished with Michigan State University Press

No. 3 · Clerical Ideology in a Revolutionary Age: The Guadalajara Church and the Idea of the Mexican Nation, 1788–1853 Brian F. Connaughton, translated by Mark Allan Healey · Copublished with University Press of Colorado

No. 4 · Monuments of Progress: Modernization and Public Health in Mexico City, 1876–1910 Claudia Agostoni · Copublished with University Press of Colorado

No. 5 · Madness in Buenos Aires: Patients, Psychiatrists and the Argentine State, 1880–1983 Jonathan Ablard · Copublished with Ohio University Press

No. 6 · Patrons, Partisans, and Palace Intrigues: The Court Society of Colonial Mexico, 1702–1710 Christoph Rosenmüller

No. 7 · From Many, One: Indians, Peasants, Borders, and Education in Callista Mexico, 1924–1935 Andrae Marak

No. 8 · Violence in Argentine Literature and Film (1989–2005) Edited by Carolina Rocha and Elizabeth Montes Garcés

No. 9 · Latin American Cinemas: Local Views and Transnational Connections Edited by Nayibe Bermúdez Barrios

No. 10 · Creativity and Science in Contemporary Argentine Literature: Between Romanticism and Formalism Joanna Page

CREATIVITY AND SCIENCE
IN CONTEMPORARY ARGENTINE LITERATURE
Between Romanticism and Formalism

Joanna Page

UNIVERSITY OF CALGARY PRESS

UNIVERSITY OF CALGARY LATIN AMERICAN RESEARCH CENTRE

Latin American and Caribbean Series
ISSN 1498-2366 (Print) ISSN 1925-9638 (Online)

© 2014 Joanna Page

University of Calgary Press
2500 University Drive NW
Calgary, Alberta
Canada T2N 1N4
www.uofcpress.com

This book is available as an ebook which is licensed under a Creative Commons license. The publisher should be contacted for any commercial use which falls outside the terms of that license.

LIBRARY AND ARCHIVES CANADA CATALOGUING IN PUBLICATION

Page, Joanna, 1974-, author
    Creativity and science in contemporary Argentine literature : between Romanticism and Formalism / Joanna Page.

(Latin American and Caribbean series ; no. 10)
Includes bibliographical references and index.
Issued in print and electronic formats.
ISBN 978-1-55238-732-0 (pbk.).—ISBN 978-1-55238-771-9 (pdf).—
ISBN 978-1-55238-772-6 (epub).—ISBN 978-1-55238-773-3 (mobi).—
ISBN 978-1-55238-770-2 (open access pdf)

    1. Argentine literature—20th century—Themes, motives—History and criticism. 2. Martínez, Guillermo, 1962- —Criticism and interpretation. 3. Piglia, Ricardo—Criticism and interpretation. 4. Cohen, Marcelo—Criticism and interpretation. 5. Science in literature. 6. Technology in literature. 7. Mathematics in literature. 8. Creative ability in literature. 9. Romanticism—Argentina. 10. Formalism (Literature)—Argentina. I. Title. II. Series: Latin American and Caribbean series ; no. 10

PQ7655.P34 2014   860.9'36   C2014-900037-5
                                            C2014-900038-3

The University of Calgary Press acknowledges the support of the Government of Alberta through the Alberta Media Fund for our publications. We acknowledge the financial support of the Government of Canada through the Canada Book Fund for our publishing activities. We acknowledge the financial support of the Canada Council for the Arts for our publishing program.

Printed and bound in Canada by Marquis
♻ This book is printed on FSC Enviro 100 paper

Cover image: #2703885 (colourbox.com)
Cover design, page design, and typesetting by Melina Cusano

To my father, who opened up the world to me

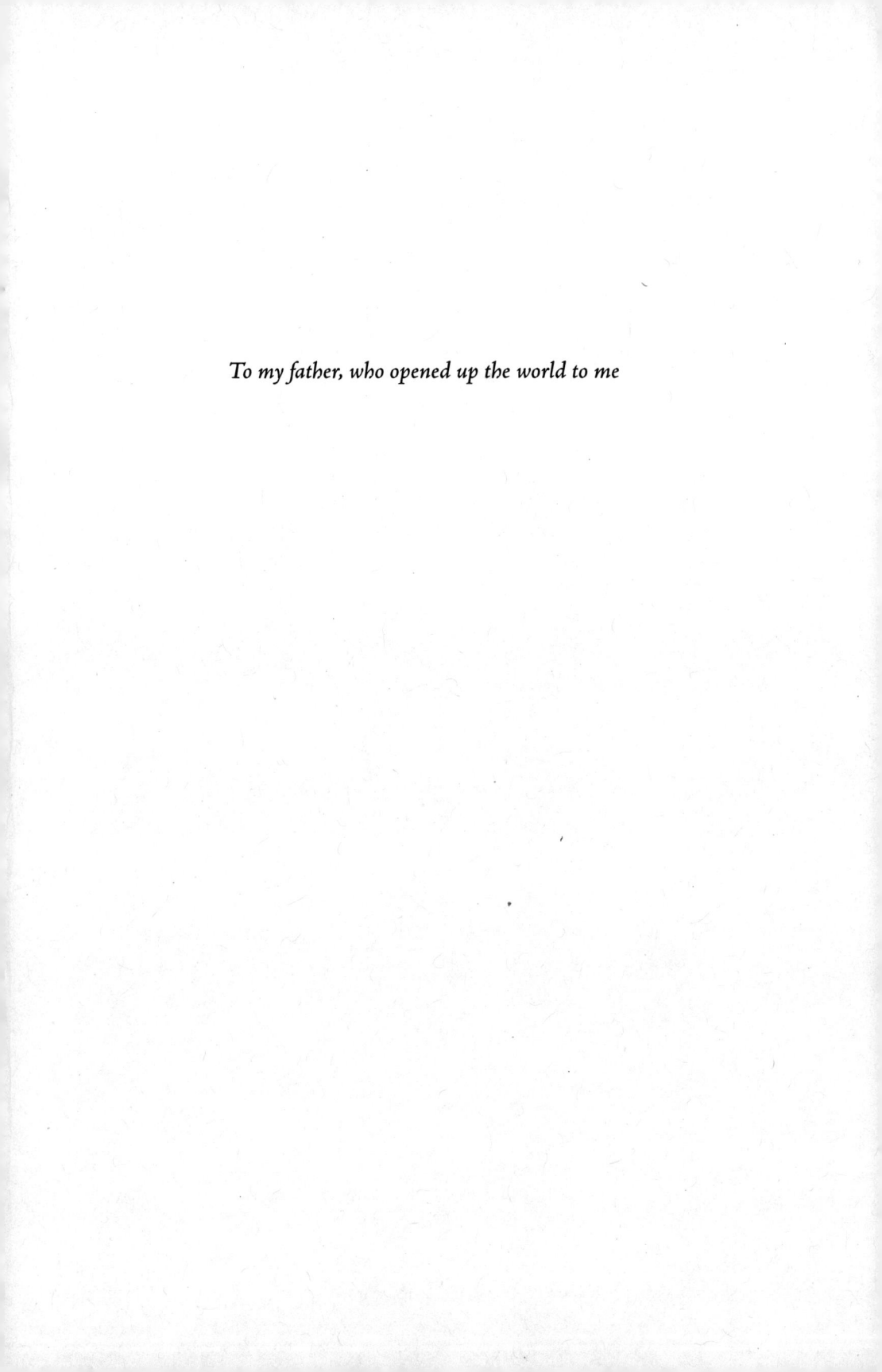

What is required […] is to stop courageously at the surface, the fold, the skin, to adore appearance, to believe in forms, tones, words, in the whole Olympus of appearance.
—Friedrich Nietzsche

CONTENTS

Acknowledgments — xi

Introduction: Countering Postmodern Apocalypticism — 1

1. The Science of Literary Evolution: Between Romanticism and Formalism — 27

    A postmodern Prometheus: innovation and tradition in literature / Martínez — 28

    Non-linearity, topology, turbulence, and other (Formalist) models of literary renewal / Piglia — 42

2. Allegories of Reading in an Age of Immanence and Uncertainty — 69

    Serial polysemia: crimes of logic / Martínez — 70

    Interpretation and interpretosis in an immanent world / Cohen — 81

    Literature: the laboratory of the future / Piglia — 95

3. Mathematics and Creativity — 115

    Creative contradictions and the mathematics of postmodern thought / Martínez — 116

    Post-Romantic principles of creativity in a self-organizing universe / Cohen — 133

4. Machines, Metaphors, and Multiplicity: Creativity beyond the Individual	*161*
Post-Romantic writing machines / Piglia	*163*
Entropy and metaphor / Cohen	*184*
Conclusion: Literature and Science, Neither One Culture nor Two	*223*
Bibliography	*245*
Notes	*259*
Index	*275*

ACKNOWLEDGMENTS

From start to finish, this book has been an immense pleasure to write. I owe an enormous debt of gratitude to the British Academy, whose award of a Mid-Career Fellowship gave me a wonderful year of quiet and productive time in which to complete the manuscript. I would also like to thank my colleagues at the Centre of Latin American Studies and the Department of Spanish and Portuguese, University of Cambridge, for their support, and particularly those (Geoffrey Kantaris, Rory O'Bryen, Steven Boldy, Erica Segre, Ed King, and Charles Jones) who stepped in to cover some of my responsibilities during that period. I am also very appreciative of the financial and practical support extended to me by Robinson College and the encouragement, friendship, and sound advice I have received from the Warden and Fellows there.

In Buenos Aires, numerous people have generously given their time and expertise to help me find materials or to suggest possible lines of investigation, and I am extremely grateful for their assistance. I would particularly like to thank Clara Kriger, Federico Lorenz, Carlos Gamerro, and Cristina Reigadas for their help over several years, as well as their warm friendship. Cecilia Gil Marino acted as my research assistant on several trips to Buenos Aires; she demonstrated an uncanny ability to hunt down elusive texts and pursued my project as enthusiastically and doggedly as if it had been her own. Back home, I am thankful for the support of my husband, Geoff, who is always ready to share in the highs and lows of bringing a book to publication.

Finally, I would like to thank the authors studied in the book – Ricardo Piglia, Guillermo Martínez, Marcelo Cohen – for the enormously rewarding intellectual adventure that their work has inspired for me. If the figure of the literary critic is often represented in their fiction and essays as self-deluded or (worse) parasitical, I suspect I will have avoided neither fault in their view. But their texts have done nothing less than open my eyes to an enthralling vision of the continually self-renewing and self-transforming capacity of literature, and its role in an endlessly creative universe. This book is an expression of a new faith, and of my desire to participate in that creativity: by extending these wonderfully rich fictions to new readers and new contexts, and by amplifying and broadening their resonance through new syntheses.

Introduction: Countering Postmodern Apocalypticism

In British and North American literature since the 1960s, models and theories from mathematics and science – incompleteness, uncertainty, entropy, chaos, and complexity – have most often been put to use in forging apocalyptic visions of social and cultural decay or of an incomprehensible universe that lies beyond the limits of our science. These theories seem to speak to a postmodern skepticism concerning any genuine advance in knowledge and, at the same time, any possibility of artistic regeneration. They have lent force to the postmodern sense of an ending, or impasse, bringing to a halt the drive of modernist progress towards greater knowledge, freedom, and creativity. This is the vision assembled in the fiction of Thomas Pynchon and J. G. Ballard, for example, in which the uncertainty principle renders futile all human efforts to understand the unhomely universe in which we are trapped, and the thermodynamic process of entropy seems to command an inexorable decline in every area of psychological, social, and cultural experience.

Against the grain of much anglophone literature since the 1960s, and the skepticism of many postmodern theorists, recent Argentine fiction does not call upon theories of chaos, entropy, and uncertainty to bolster proclamations of the futility of all epistemological and artistic enterprises. In the work of the three contemporary Argentine writers chosen for this study, Marcelo Cohen, Guillermo Martínez, and Ricardo Piglia, models and theories from mathematics and science are put to a very different use: to defend intellectual activity and to testify to the endless capacity of literature for self-renewal. The relationship these authors construct between chaos, complexity, and uncertainty, on the one hand, and literary creativity and evolution, on the other, allows them to counter postmodern claims of the exhaustion of artistic innovation. In different ways, their work mounts a vigorous challenge to the more apocalyptic strains of postmodernism that proclaim the end of epistemology and consign artistic creativity to mere bricolage, parody, or the endless production of simulacra. Instead, the visions that emerge are ones of anticipation, of new forms and new subjectivities to be shaped through a literature that does not merely survive crisis but thrives upon it. It is this book's contention that focussing on how mathematical and scientific theories are appropriated in these texts affords us greater insight into key tensions within postmodern thought, many of which demonstrate the contradictory persistence of both Romantic and Formalist conceptions of how newness enters the world.

ROMANTIC-POSTMODERN NOTIONS OF SCIENCE

Romanticism, in Hans Eichner's definition, is "perhaps predominantly, a desperate rearguard action against the spirit and the implications of modern science."[1] As a counter-movement to Enlightenment thought, Romanticism rejected the mechanistic models of the universe advanced by Newton and others in favour of more organic ones. Under attack were the Enlightenment beliefs that the universe could be reduced to a series of mechanical principles determining the function of any one part. Nature, the Romantics insisted, was not something to be dissected by Man as a superior observer of its forms; instead, greater knowledge – both physical and spiritual – of the universe would emerge through a dual contemplation of Nature and Man's role within it: not above it but co-existing harmoniously as part of it. Romantic *Naturphilosophie*, first emerging from work by Friedrich Schelling in the last few years of the eighteenth century, propounded an organicist view of the universe and advocated the re-uniting of Man with Nature as the foundation of true scientific enquiry.

The theories of Schelling and his contemporaries, immensely influential on the science of their time (particularly in the new field of biology), did not survive the positivist turn to empirical evidence in nineteenth-century science. Their influence on cultural values and discourses, on the other hand, has endured through to the present. Indeed, the "Science Wars" of the 1990s have provided ample evidence of the continuing legacy of Romantic ideas of science within postmodern thought.

The infamous Sokal Affair of 1996 was ignited by the publication of a spoof essay in a major cultural studies journal in the United States, proposing that quantum gravity should be understood as a linguistic and social construct.[2] That the editors of *Social Text* did not grasp that the essay was designed to parody the wildly metaphorical and imprecise use of science in postmodern theory was taken as further evidence of postmodern sloppiness. The hoax stirred up an unholy mud-slinging match in which both sides have, for the greater part, remained steadfastly committed to their ignorance of the other and their determination to reduce the diversity of views on each side to a single (outdated or inaccurate) one. The rhetoric had already been on the rise in the early nineties: in their book *Higher Superstition: The Academic Left and Its Quarrels with Science* (1994), Paul R. Gross and Norman Levitt claimed that the "moral blankness" of postmodern skepticism is akin to that which gave rise to fascism in the first half of the twentieth century.[3] They deride postmodernism's belief in its own "omnicompetence" to pronounce "with supreme confidence on all aspects of human history, politics, and culture"[4] and seek to discredit cultural theorists and social scientists who have dared to comment on science. Derrida, Foucault, Baudrillard, Lyotard, and their "clones" come in for unwavering censure. Gross and Levitt have, in turn, been accused of crude caricatures and ignorance of the positions they attack. Steven Best and Douglas Kellner devote several pages of their *The Postmodern Turn* (1997) to a detailed exposition of their claim that Gross and Levitt are guilty of precisely the same "deadly theoretical sins," blatant misreadings, and half-baked argumentation that the latter charge to critical theorists.[5]

Although intransigence and misunderstanding have characterized the positions of both postmodernists and scientists in these debates, the responses of postmodern theorists often reveal the extent to which they are operating with an outdated model of science. As if locked into replaying an earlier struggle between Enlightenment and Romantic approaches to science, postmodernists have often confused science with positivism and mechanicist rationalism, accusing scientists of adhering to naive notions of objective truth. Taking up the Romantic sword, theorists of the postmodern often go out to do battle against the champions of Newtonian absolutes without realizing that their adversaries have long since decamped. Scientists, for their part, have caricatured postmodernists as trapped in an idealism that cannot accept the existence of anything beyond language. Thus, in the view of many cultural theorists in the humanities, as Ira Livingston suggests, "science naively mistakes the thinly veiled projection of its own ideologies for universal and unmediated truth";[6] at the other pole, meanwhile, "scientists tend to think that their cultural critics mistake the world for language," turning material nature into "a frictionless fiction."[7]

For many commentators, the "Science Wars" of the mid-1990s were proof of the intransigence of the ever-widening gap that C. P. Snow famously found in 1959 to divide the "two cultures" of the sciences and the humanities.[8] Indeed, that gap is evident, not only in postmodernists' rejection of science as an obsolete remnant of positivism dating back to the Enlightenment, but also in their over-enthusiastic embrace of the "new science" of uncertainty and chaos theory. A number of thinkers have certainly demonstrated a belief in the "omnicompetence" of postmodernism by insisting that there are now no longer two cultures but one, as science has finally come round to postmodernism's own view on truth as inaccessible or constructed by the human observer. Best and Kellner even attempt to subsume recent scientific directions within "an *emerging postmodern paradigm*" and claim that, at the very least, we are witnessing "the construction of a new transdisciplinary paradigm."[9] This is evidenced by the coming-to-prominence of "a family of concepts" that "abandon mechanical and deterministic schemes in favor of new principles of chaos, contingency, spontaneity, and organism."[10]

It is clear that certain notions of contingency, the complex interaction between order and disorder in physical and biological systems, and the inseparability of the observing subject from the object of observation have shaped both scientific and artistic practice since the early twentieth century and into the twenty-first. It is not a question, however, of science belatedly acknowledging what (post)modernists always knew to be true about the universe. Postmodernists' celebration of the triumph of the "good new" science of chaos and complexity over the "bad old" science of Newtonian absolutes demonstrates a good deal of misunderstanding. Both "old" and "new" sciences have emerged from the rigorous, dialectical tradition of scientific methodology, and chaos theory does not prove the superiority of subjective intuition over objective measurement. What is often called "chaos theory," we should remember, embraces attempts to account for two different phenomena: firstly, the surprising presence of order within apparently disordered systems, and secondly, the capacity of disorder to stimulate the creation of new kinds of order. As Alan Sokal and Jean Bricmont point out, "chaos" is a misnomer; they accuse Baudrillard, Deleuze, and Guattari in particular of using the term as synonymous for "disorder," while an accurate definition would be "sensitive dependence on initial conditions."[11]

As N. Katherine Hayles puts it, "the science of chaos is not opposed to normal science. It *is* normal science."[12] Best and Kellner do acknowledge that "the older views of reality are not necessarily demolished" in scientists' attempt to account for a range of phenomena, including "reversibility and irreversibility, chance and necessity, dynamics and thermodynamics, entropy and evolution, natural selection and self-organization."[13] It is, of course, the case that science now explores probabilistic and statistical truths as well as the certainties of classical Newtonian mechanics, but one approach has not replaced the other: as scientists often feel the need to point out, Newton's law of universal gravitation still pertains in the majority of cases, and no theory of relativity or quantum mechanics will stop an apple falling on your head. In sketching out the "family of concepts" that link postmodernism to contemporary science, Best and Kellner move too quickly from the recent interest in stochastic systems rather than deterministic ones, or forms of statistical rather than absolute truth, to state that what they call "postmodern science"[14] seeks to "challenge all beliefs in foundations, absolutes, truth, and objectivity, often to embrace a radical skepticism, relativism, and nihilism."[15]

However grievously inaccurate, the correlation between the scenario of chaos and unpredictability, on the one hand, and epistemological failure, on the other, is continually reinforced in postmodern theory and literature. "Chaos" has become a particularly prevalent metaphor across the arts and social sciences: its wildfire spread signals, as John A. McCarthy acknowledges, "a growing sense that we have discovered a new tool for mapping our image of reality."[16] However, this new tool is often misused and regularly maps an image of reality that is not new at all but a rearticulation of Romantic views of science. We find ourselves still very much enmeshed in a Romantic set of oppositions between the subjective, the sublime, the experienced, the inner and the spiritual, on the one hand, and the objective, the measurable, the abstract, the visible, and the material, on the other. Paul Hamilton recognizes the stubborn presence of this framework when he reflects that "Sublimity, then, is deconstructed by Postmodernism into indeterminacy."[17]

For Lance Schachterle, "One sign of the inadequacy of C. P. Snow's thesis of 'The Two Cultures' is how frequently present-day writers turn to contemporary physics for underlying metaphors."[18] However, it is precisely the metaphorical use of scientific ideas that has irritated scientists most in postmodernism's fascination for theories of incompleteness, uncertainty, chaos, and complexity. Nowhere is this more evident than in the frequent references to the work of Kurt Gödel in postmodern literature and theory. Published in 1931, Gödel's incompleteness theorems demonstrate the limitations of axiomatic reasoning in proving mathematical truth. The first theorem maintains that every formal system will contain statements that cannot be proved or refuted, while the second goes further to state that no formal system can prove its own consistency. These theorems have frequently been wrenched from their context for use in other fields – by Régis Debray in sociology, for example – or simply to denote the failure of logic *tout court*. Whether the ungrounded use of such theorems in postmodern theory and the social sciences is denounced bitterly as a misapplication or welcomed as evidence of "creative misprision," in Gillian Beer's more receptive phrase,[19] depends largely, of course, on which side of the disciplinary divide one is situated. The impressionistic use of Gödel's theorems by theorists such as Kristeva, Irigaray, Lacan, Latour, Debray, Baudrillard, Deleuze, and Virilio has been catalogued in extensive and rancorous detail in a series of books published following the Sokal Affair, including Alan Sokal and Jean Bricmont's *Intellectual Impostures* (1998) and Jacques Bouveresse's *Prodiges et vertiges de l'analogie* (1999). The Argentine writer and erstwhile mathematician Guillermo Martínez has also entered the fray – see his *Gödel para todos* (2009), co-written with Gustavo Piñeiro – to add his voice to those scientists objecting to the use of Gödel's theorem as an analogy for an ever-increasing array of linguistic and sociological phenomena. On what basis, Martínez asks, should a very specific theory – on the incompleteness of formal systems – be chosen as an analogy, rather than the many other mathematical theories that *do* allow for axiomatic completeness?[20]

Where Gödel is referenced in postmodern theory and literature, he is often credited with the complete demolition of the foundations of mathematical thought. Incautious theorists have declared that "el Teorema de Gödel representa un límite absoluto para el pensamiento lógico, o un golpe mortal a la razón clásica, o el fin de la certidumbre en el terreno de la matemática, etcétera" (Gödel's theorem represents an absolute limit to logical thought, or a fatal blow to classical reason, or the end of certainty in the field of mathematics, et cetera).[21] As Martínez insists, in company with many mathematicians, Gödel's theorems do not invalidate any existing mathematical findings but simply demonstrate the limitations of a specific method.[22] The eager incorporation of Gödel's theorems as metaphors in so many literary, analytical, and theoretical texts bears witness to the chasm of understanding that continues to separate the humanities from the sciences. This divide is also evident in critical responses to such uses: the policing of disciplinary borders clearly demarcates different categories for artistic imagination and a metaphorical use of language, on the one side, and for scientific reason, on the other.

ROMANTIC-POSTMODERN NOTIONS OF ARTISTIC CREATIVITY

If the view of science held by many theorists of the postmodern is largely inherited from Romanticism, so, it would appear, is their understanding of creativity. The spectre of the divinely inspired Romantic genius haunts the present, a constant reminder of that spirit of genuine originality and creativity that we presume to have abandoned contemporary art. Postmodern techniques of collage, sampling, or other arts of revitalizing the past or constructing surprising connections between different fields are somehow always taken to be "less than" real originality, or "all that's left" when everything has already been said and done. As Zygmunt Bauman suggests, "The postmodern mind seems to condemn everything, propose nothing,"[23] erasing in its skepticism all hope of authentic creativity. By the 1960s, the notion that artistic innovation was no longer possible was widespread; a sense of coming to an end dominated cultural and critical discourse. The only thing now left for the postmodern artist to do, as Best and Kellner suggest, is "to play with the pieces of the past and to reassemble them in different forms."[24] The artist, no longer the unique, expressive self of Romantic literature, has become "a *bricoleur* who just rearranges the debris of the cultural past."[25]

In the inaugural issue of the online journal *Rhizomes*, editors Ellen E. Berry and Carol Siegel venture to account in some ways for this overwhelming "postmodern sense of an ending, of living after the future or suspended in a perpetual present."[26] They cite the widespread nature of the challenges mounted by postmodernism to Western rationalism and universalism, challenges that are "impossible to ignore if not utterly devastating"; in part, they maintain, "these critiques have emerged from a recognition that some of the bloodiest carnage of the 20th C was carried out in the name of bringing newness into the world." Utopian thinking is now indissolubly wedded to a series of catastrophic events. For Berry and Siegel, this suspicion concerning the possibility of radical change is reinforced by the commodification of newness by postmodern consumer culture, which substitutes an unprecedented proliferation of consumer choice – "a repetition of the idea of newness" – for genuine innovation.

This ennui, translated into fiction, has often been labelled the "literature of exhaustion," after John Barth's seminal essay. In fact, Barth is considerably less pessimistic than his essay's title might suggest, and certainly less cynical about the possibility for regeneration than many of the myriad postmodern theorists and critics who have cited him. Barth does find a form of creativity in reflexivity: Borges's "Tlön, Uqbar, Orbis Tertius" is taken to illustrate "how an artist may paradoxically turn the felt ultimacies of our time into material and means for his work – *paradoxically* because by doing so he transcends what had appeared to be his refutation."[27] This paradox was equally evident, of course, in the many Romantic poems that took as their subject matter the impossibility of writing poetry. As Hamilton suggests, in these cases, the "failure of the self to achieve its goal is recuperated as autobiography" and the inability to create is in fact creatively expressed, thereby fulfilling Romantic criteria for creativity.[28] In our own times, it would appear, reflexivity is not often recognized as sufficiently creative: it is far more likely to be associated with a lack of authenticity, a clichéd trick played on the weary reader, and with the more ludic practices of postmodern art, which flaunt their non-originality through parody, plagiarism, and simulation. For Raymond Federman, for example, reflexivity reveals that "there is nothing original about literary creation, and that the creator's imagination is not unlimited and endless, but that, indeed, the creator merely imitates, parodies, mimics, repeats, plagiarizes."[29]

Reflexivity has, according to Federman, alerted us to the fact that literature is about nothing other than itself; it has also dismantled two (Romantic) "myths" about literature, these being the author as the "sovereign consciousness which is the origin of the work," and "the idea of originality":

> the day ART in general (and LITERATURE in particular) began to reflect upon itself, to turn inward so to speak, and even to mock itself, in order to question, examine, undermine, challenge, and even, at times, demolish its purpose, its intentionality,

and its own means of production and communication, it began to abolish these two myths.[30]

That genuine innovation and revolution are always signified as an absence and a lack in postmodern culture, however, and that the latter has not invented competing ideas of real creativity, suggests on the contrary the degree to which postmodern thinking remains firmly locked within Romantic paradigms of creativity. Rob Pope considers that "Perhaps the greatest obstacles to a genuinely critical and historical understanding of creativity is the persistent stereotype of the 'Romantic writer' and the 'Romantic artist.'"[31] If the vision of the Romantic genius flowed from the divine inspiration of gods and muses (or from the more mortal temptations of opium), Pope suggests that creativity today still retains much of the mystique arising from its association with unconscious processes, although these are now expressed in psychological terms as "the unseen promptings and subterranean eruptions of unconscious desires, hopes, fears."[32] That Romantic notions of the creative self – together with the Romantic practice of literature as a reflexive and philosophical project – still underpin our understanding of literature and critical theory is the central argument put forward in Philippe Lacoue-Labarthe and Jean-Luc Nancy's *The Literary Absolute: The Theory of Literature in German Romanticism*. The discussions presented here of texts by Martínez, Piglia, and Cohen will often converge around the question of the extent to which they reinforce or deviate from this Romantic legacy; a more explicit engagement with Lacoue-Labarthe and Nancy's argument is reserved for the Conclusion.

SCIENCE AND CREATIVITY IN ARGENTINE LITERATURE

This book joins in an ongoing discussion of the different ways in which literature may engage with science, a topic that has attracted particular interest in recent decades following the publication of seminal studies by Hayles, Livingston, William R. Paulson, and David Porush, among others.[33] Most of this work has referenced anglophone literature; I aim to explore some key differences in the ways that science has been imagined in contemporary literature from Argentina. These differences, as I will show, shed new light on the role of literary engagements with science in postmodern thought and fiction.

A fertile interest in scientific ideas has characterized much Argentine literature since the mid-nineteenth century, and this has inspired some noteworthy scholarship. Roberto González Echevarría's *Myth and Archive: A Theory of Latin American Narrative* (1990), focussing principally on the nineteenth century, explores (among other trends) the influence of scientific travel writing on Latin American literature. In Sarmiento's foundational text, *Facundo* (1845), he finds classificatory gestures and tropes proper to scientific modes of travel writing, and above all an intent to mix natural and social science, responding to a belief that the instruments and methods of each were alike in their ability to penetrate realities and to expose them to observation.[34] In his *Test Tube Envy: Science and Power in Argentine Narrative*, J. Andrew Brown finds an appeal to "scientific" discourses such as phrenology to underpin the narratives of many writers associated with the Generation of 1837, including Sarmiento and José Mármol, bolstering the authority of their texts as political and social treatises.[35] Indeed, he finds that writers of a later generation, such as Lucio V. Mansilla, continue to draw on science (and indeed, phrenology) to support their rhetoric, this time wielding it as a weapon in a battle against the political values of their predecessors.[36] Brown notes perceptively that the legitimizing exercise works both ways: while the appeal to scientific discourse and the self-fashioning of the writer as objective observer effectively appropriate the cultural authority of science, they also act to construct that same authority.[37]

The decades bridging the nineteenth and twentieth centuries provide the context for an examination of the interplay between literature, medical discourse, and nationalism in *Ficciones somáticas: Naturalismo, nacionalismo y políticas médicas del cuerpo (Argentina 1880–1910)* by Gabriela Nouzeilles (2000). In her corpus of naturalist novels by Eugenio Cambaceres and others, Nouzeilles traces ways in which medical discourse ultimately provides writers with "un criterio de autoridad para legitimar ciertos prejuicios sociales" (normative criteria in order to legitimize certain social prejudices), particularly in relation to Argentina's experience of mass immigration.[38] In her study of early science fiction in Latin America, Rachel Ferreira Haywood also notes the importance of scientific discourse in the nation-building projects of nineteenth-century texts. Even in proto-science fiction novels such as Eduardo Holmberg's *Viaje maravilloso del Señor Nic-Nac al Planeta Marte* (1875), for example, literature and science are presented as "natural partners" in the process of developing a modern, scientifically informed nation.[39]

What marks the narratives of the Generation of 1880 more broadly, however, is a crucial ambivalence towards the science that appeared to make their modernizing projects possible. Eduardo Ezcurra's futuristic *En el siglo XXX* (1891) imagines a series of technological advances but demonstrates little confidence in the social benefits of scientific modernization. Oscar Terán observes that what is unusual about the modernizing process in Argentina is that its most zealous promoters were also those who expressed the deepest doubts about the consequences of their reforms. Thus Vicente Quesada laments the disappearance of the old farms and tall cypresses to make room for the railway in *Memorias de un viejo* (1889)[40] but at the same time envisions a future society enriched by European goods and customs.[41]

This ambivalence carries through to the twentieth century, even while – as Brown argues – we witness a continued strategic use of scientific discourse to bolster the authority of the literary text. A dystopian vision of science starts to emerge clearly in the work of writers such as Lugones, Quiroga, and Arlt. Beatriz Sarlo observes that the proliferation of stories about monkeys, such as "Yzur" (1906) by Lugones and "El mono ahorcado" (1907) by Quiroga, owes much to the ideas of Darwin and Haeckel that were circulating freely in intellectual circles at the time.[42] The discovery of the shared heritage of man and monkey fuelled a series of fantastical tales of cultural regression and barbarism. Arlt's novels of the 1920s and 1930s bring into the sphere of literature a heterogeneous collection of non-literary images and discourses, including metallurgy, aviation technology, and electricity. As Sarlo points out, there is nothing particularly new about his dystopian visions of an alliance between science and authoritarianism.[43] The genre of dystopian science fiction was already rapidly taking form, following novels such as Yevgeny Zamyatin's *We* (1924) and Aldous Huxley's *Brave New World* (1932). What is unusual in Arlt's fiction, however, Sarlo suggests, is that "Lo que es instrumento de una sociedad autoritaria (y enloquecida en su autoritarismo), es al mismo tiempo material de ensoñación y fuente de belleza" (that which is an instrument of an authoritarian society [authoritarian to the point of insanity], is at the same time the material of dreams and a source of beauty).[44]

Several recent studies have been published on the mathematical and scientific paradigms that may have informed stories by Jorge Luis Borges or may be retrospectively read in relation to his work. Of these, the most extended is Floyd Merrell's *Unthinking Thinking: Jorge Luis Borges, Mathematics, and the New Physics* (1991). Brown points out a central irony in this critical approach, as Borges's work – which rejects science as an explanatory framework, alongside all systems of human knowledge – appears to be valued in certain critical approaches precisely for its ability to anticipate new explanations deriving from chaos theory or quantum mechanics.[45] However, as Hayles argues (and Brown concedes), Borges's work certainly provides evidence for the "field model," a term used by Hayles both to describe the development of parallel interests in science and literature and to define an important transformation in thought over the twentieth century that approaches the universe through networks, relationships, and dynamic change rather than attempting to isolate its workings in time and space from the detached position of an observer.[46]

This study differs from those of González Echevarría, Brown, Nouzeilles, and Sarlo, cited above, not only in its closer focus on contemporary literature, but also in its approach: my primary interest is in the way that the writers discussed here engage with scientific notions and paradigms within a highly reflexive approach to fiction-writing. In other words, I argue that their texts do not simply register, or even reshape, imaginaries that derive in part from the dissemination of scientific ideas within culture, but instead experiment with those ideas as models for creating fictions and for evolution and innovation in literature. Thus this book moves beyond a discussion of how scientific ideas are reproduced and refracted in literature to explore how such concepts may be used to reflect on the creative practice of literature itself. In some ways, it may be considered an extension of Brown's work in *Test Tube Envy,* which begins in the final chapter to discuss more recent developments in Argentine literature. Brown observes a key shift in the use of science in narratives between the nineteenth century, where science is very much in the employ of politics, to the twentieth, when it becomes caught up in explorations of a metaphysical or philosophical nature.[47] Here, I discuss uses of science in literature since the 1980s that could be seen to mark a third iteration: to explore the metaliterary, or, more generally, the nature of human creativity.

A number of Argentine authors of recent years have drawn on scientific ideas in their work or experimented with modes of science fiction. Angélica Gorodischer is the nation's most well-known contemporary writer associated with the genre, although her fiction contains little "hard" science and focusses instead on exploring issues of gender in imaginary or futuristic worlds. Ana María Shua (*La muerte como efecto secundario*, 1997) and Eduardo Blaustein (*Cruz diablo*, 1997) have made incursions into the science fiction genre, as has César Aira (*Los misterios de Rosario*, 1994; *El congreso de literatura*, 1999; *El juego de los mundos*, 2000). However, the three writers chosen for this study – Piglia, Cohen, and Martínez – stand out from these in their sustained and explicit treatment of scientific theories as tropes and motors for literary innovation.

Science, mathematics, and the nature of creativity become central concerns in the work of all three. Cohen's fiction often approaches the genres of science fiction and the fantastic, creating worlds that are broadly familiar to us but in which certain trends are hyberbolized, from neoliberalism and monopoly capitalism to plastic surgery and robotics. Written in an apparently realist style, Cohen's fiction continually disarms the reader by slipping in neologisms (such as *flaytaxi* or *pantallátor*) that often evoke the technological landscape of a future society, or one that is organized in subtly different ways to our own. Cohen refers to his own use of neologisms as "un juego y una manera más de escapar de la realidad a la que nuestro lenguaje nos sujeta" (a game and another way of escaping the reality to which our language subjects us).[48] Placed within a richly suggestive prose that often blurs the distinction between metaphorical and literal meaning, they help to generate the effect of a virtual space that is somehow borne of, or connected to, our world but operates in a different dimension, as indeed it does: that of literature. Many of Cohen's narratives are located in an invented place, the Delta Panorámico, that references the real Argentine delta to the north of Buenos Aires and bears some social and cultural resemblances to present-day Buenos Aires and Argentina but evades direct interpretations of this kind. His characters live in hypermediatized societies in which they – and we as readers – often find it difficult to ground the many projections that surround them and to distinguish reality from simulation.

Cohen's literary work demonstrates a prominent interest in exploring realms of the intersubjective. Characters in many of his texts have access to the *Panconciencia*, a kind of virtual network that allows them to access other people's memories and experiences; in *Donde yo no estaba* (2006) he pursues a highly fluid understanding of subjectivity as a series of interpenetrations that take place between the self and the other, and he radicalizes the idea in *Casa de Ottro* (2009) by including technological objects in such exchanges. Throughout his fiction, subjectivity is consistently de-individuated, and he draws attention to the illusions of continuity that govern the use of the first-person in narration, or the construction of an authorial style.

Cohen often chooses to explore such concerns through the lens of scientific discourses on chaos theory, emergence, and complexity. His work abounds in references to waterfalls, fractals, turbulence, and a range of other forms and metaphors that have been used in chaos theory to understand a particular kind of order that emerges from apparently random systems. Indeed, much of Cohen's fiction, as I will show, can be read as a kind of literary experiment with principles of narrative construction suggested by the dynamics of complex systems in biology and physics. The theory of "realismo inseguro" (unstable realism) he develops in his critical work owes a considerable debt to the dissipative structures described by the physical chemist Ilya Prigogine, whose theory led to new research into self-organizing systems while earning him the Nobel Prize in Chemistry in 1977.

While apparently less well versed in these particular developments, Piglia also turns to mathematical and scientific theories in his exploration of the nature of literary creativity. His narratives also brush with science fiction where, like Cohen, he demonstrates an interest in de-individuated subjectivities and in the virtual experiences offered by literature. Artificial memory implantation, for example, becomes a trope in his fiction for the way in which literature inserts the memories and experiences of another into our own, through the experience of reading. Just as the many diaries, letters, sacred texts, and artefacts of Piglia's texts are not clues to be deciphered, pointing us to some meaning originating in the past, but are consistently mined for their capacity to predict and shape the future, so literature for Piglia becomes not a way of registering past or present realities but a "laboratory of the possible," a tool for generating new potential meanings for the future.[49]

This vision unites the apparently very different texts that make up Piglia's *oeuvre* to date. This includes his densely citational first novel, *Respiración artificial* (1980), which sets up a series of shifting and interchanging perspectives between the mid-nineteenth century and the present in its exploration of utopian ideals, betrayal, and political repression, *La ciudad ausente* (1995), a collection of short stories linked by a paratext that borrows from detective and science-fiction genres, and *Blanco nocturno* (2010), a rather Arltian crime narrative with a mad inventor at its heart. Piglia's writing embraces a vocabulary of microscopic observation and biological experimentation, tracing the continually dynamic interchanges between an organism and its environment that underpin autopoietic, or self-renewing, systems. Literature for Piglia becomes a combinatory art that works much in the same way as the endless variations produced by genetic recombination.

Martínez trained as a mathematician before turning to fiction-writing and has continued to publish and lecture on mathematical ideas in literature and critical theory. His *Borges y la matemática* (2006) presents a relatively light-hearted discussion of some of Borges's most well-known short stories in the light of concepts of infinity, Cantor's set theory, and other mathematical hypotheses, setting himself the challenge of explaining the links to a general public with no greater knowledge of mathematics than the ability to count to ten. The later and more heavyweight *Gödel (para todos)* (2009) again attempts to explain Gödel's theorems to non-mathematicians and – as mentioned above – to expose its inaccurate use by theorists such as Kristeva, Lacan, Debray, Deleuze, and Lyotard. As well as critical essays on Argentine and world literature, he has published several novels and short stories for a more popular market in Argentina and abroad; his *Crímenes imperceptibles* (2003) has been translated into over thirty languages and adapted for the cinema (*The Oxford Murders*, dir. Alex de la Iglesia, 2008). Most of his fiction draws on mathematics in some way: his characters are often mathematicians, and his plots frequently hinge on a fatal misunderstanding, ignorance, or belated discovery of a mathematical principle or hypothesis, such as Wittgenstein's rule-following paradox (*Crímenes imperceptibles*), the nature of chance (*La muerte lenta de Luciana B.* (2007), or an imagined alternative to the law of excluded middle (*Acerca de Roderer*, 1992). Martínez is also deeply interested in questions of artistic creativity and evolution, the major themes of his novel *La mujer del maestro* (1998) and of several of his critical essays.

The approaches of these three writers to science diverges radically from those of their predecessors in Argentine literature. There is nothing here of the attempt by Sarmiento, Mármol, or Mansilla to use scientific discourses to shore up the authority of their understanding of Argentine society or to promote a modernizing project. Neither do we detect a clear critique of science's baleful influence on modern society; nor is science marshalled to explain the essentially barbaric nature of a humanity descended from apes, in the way that it would in a short story by Lugones or Quiroga. Nor yet again do we witness the kind of emptying-out of science's claims as a metanarrative to explain the universe that is evident in Borges's fictions. Instead, science is reclaimed for its ability to tell a particular story about human creativity: the creative power of dialectical thought and artistic practice (Martínez), of textuality as an open system, constantly renewing itself through complex exchanges with its environment (Piglia), and of human innovation as a joyously indissoluble part of a self-organizing, creative universe (Cohen).

Alongside Borges, it might be tempting to posit Julio Cortázar as a precursor to the fiction of Martínez, Piglia, and Cohen. A number of critical studies have explored the shifting and provisional nature of subjectivity in Cortázar's fiction and the indeterminacy at the heart of *Rayuela*'s structure in the light of quantum physics, cybernetics, and other scientific advances of the twentieth century.[50] The breakdown of conventional boundaries between observer and observed in short stories such as "La noche boca arriba" and "Axolotl" and Cortázar's notion of the "figura" – a form of patterning that brings individuals or actions into a relationship despite separation in time and space – would seem to justify this kind of analytical approach. However, however eagerly they are seized upon by critics, there are just a few passing references in Cortázar's fiction and critical work to theories such as Heisenberg's uncertainty principle, and scientific theories never play a foundational role in his theory of literary creativity, as they do in the work of the three writers studied here.[51] Further, it is clear that Cortázar's appeal to quantum realities is an attempt to drive a wedge between rational and irrational approaches to the universe (and to give weight to his own anti-rational view of reality), and that this becomes part of a quasi-Romantic attack on Cartesian certainties. Thus Cortázar, rather like Borges in his appropriation of Cantor, draws on science in order to undermine its premise of rationalism. This binaristic vision, pitting rationalism/science against anti-rationalism/literature is emphatically not one that is pursued in the work of Piglia, Cohen, or Martínez.

Their texts' reflexive use of scientific paradigms often produces an entirely different perspective on the relationship between science and creativity when compared to previous generations of Argentine writers. As an example, we might compare Arlt's appropriation of the science of evolution as a metaphor for social struggle with Piglia's appeal to the role of genetic recombination in evolution as a metaphor for literary innovation, explored in Chapter 4. As Brown observes, while questioning the value and power of science in society, Arlt continues to draw on scientific paradigms (and particularly Darwinian ones) in the construction of his plots: thus, *El juguete rabioso* (1926) imagines a society that is governed by the rules of Darwinian natural selection and the survival of the fittest and constructs a narrative arc that fits the model.[52] The novel becomes a lament on the erosion of individual creativity and humanity in a rapidly modernizing, capitalist world. By contrast, Piglia, who also draws in his work on evolutionary models developed in biology, does not primarily do so to construct metaphors for social and cultural phenomena, but for the process of writing itself. This opens up a wholly different reading of the relationship between creativity and the science of evolution: rather than mourning the crushing of individual creative talent in a brutal battle for supremacy, Piglia celebrates the ever-changing, infinitely varied work of genetic recombination that guarantees the survival and flourishing of literature.

DIALOGUES AND DIVERGENCES WITH EUROPEAN AND NORTH AMERICAN LITERATURE

Indeed, in their exploration of scientific ideas, these authors dialogue most clearly not with national literary traditions but with European and North American writers: specifically, those authors whose work in the 1960s and 1970s formed part of a new wave of speculative literary interest in "new" scientific hypotheses, such as cybernetics, self-similarity (fractals), entropy, and chaos, and the popularization of older ones, such as Heisenberg's uncertainty principle and Gödel's incompleteness theorems. It is clear from Cohen's fictional and critical narratives that he understands his own work to engage to a significant extent with the 1960s and 1970s novels and stories published by Thomas Pynchon, William Burroughs, and J. G. Ballard. Piglia's main referent – in his exploration of mathematical and scientific ideas at least – is Ítalo Calvino, whose most relevant works were published between 1967 and 1972. Martínez's literary influences are eclectic and cannot be tied down to a particular period (they include Thomas Mann and Henry James as well as Borges and Piglia himself), but his principal frames of reference are the transnational genres of the crime thriller and the detective story.

In placing the work of Piglia and Cohen in dialogue with fiction by Pynchon, Ballard, Calvino, and others in this book, then, my first aim is to probe more deeply into an already existing critical and literary engagement on their part with this earlier generation of European and North American writers and to expose some key differences in the way that they appropriate scientific ideas. These differences are not replicated in more contemporary U.S. fiction, although a number of writers – including Lewis Shiner and Bruce Sterling – continue to engage with theories of entropy and complexity, for example. I return in the Conclusion to contrast Piglia and Cohen more directly with their contemporaries in North America. In the meantime, investigating the relationship they forge with a previous generation also allows us to trace the dynamics of literary change, a very prominent theme in the work of Piglia, Cohen, and Martínez and one that is often expressed with reference to scientific models of evolution.

In contrast to the more apocalyptic strains of British and North American fiction, the work of these Argentine writers presents a strikingly different vision of human creativity, marshalling scientific ideas, not as tropes for social, moral, or cultural decline, but as evidence of quite the reverse: of the endless, self-renewing capacity of literature. This crucial difference can partly be attributed to the particular interpretation given to certain scientific theories in these texts. Cohen, for example, follows the much more positive version of entropy developed by Erwin Schrödinger and Ilya Prigogine, who emphasize (in consonance with more recent developments in theories of complexity, self-organization, and emergence) the order that may be hidden within chaos or arises from it, and that may yield statistical truths, if not absolute ones. As Norbert Wiener observes, the second law of thermodynamics, while it may accurately describe what takes place within a closed system, is not valid with respect to a part of this system that is not wholly isolated; hence, "There are local and temporary islands of decreasing entropy in a world in which the entropy as a whole tends to increase."[53] Self-organization does not contradict the laws of thermodynamics discovered in the nineteenth century but essentially posits an open system rather than a closed one. This makes all the difference as, until we have found its limits, we can exchange a view of the universe as running down towards stasis and heat-death for one of the universe as an endlessly self-renewing entity.

However, it is perhaps these authors' interest in innovation of the literary rather than the scientific variety that provides the principal motivation for their unusual appropriation of scientific theories as metaphors for creativity rather than for decay or dissolution. If in Pynchon, Ballard, Burroughs, or Philip K. Dick, for example, scientific theories are set to work to bolster a particular vision of the world beyond the text as heading towards global disaster or decline, in the fiction of Martínez, Piglia, and Cohen, they are primarily mobilized in a reflexive manner to explore the continually creative and self-renewing capacity of literature. The literary text becomes a paradigmatic instance of how newness is generated through a series of processes observed by science, including autopoiesis (Piglia), complexity (Cohen), and through the dialectical evolution of scientific knowledge (Martínez). For a similar reason, machines and automatic processes in Piglia's texts, which often account for the transubjective nature of literary praxis, rarely become ciphers for the loss of human creativity, but instead for its continual self-renewal.

ROMANTICISM AND FORMALISM

This book diverges from existing studies of the inscription of scientific ideas in Argentine and Latin American literature in its explicit focus on notions of creativity in science and the arts. It also pursues a specific argument regarding the contradictory persistence of both Romantic and Formalist ideas of literary creation and evolution in postmodern thought. As I will show, Martínez, Piglia, and Cohen explore post-Romantic notions of creativity that take seriously the possibility of artistic innovation in our age and question our continued self-subjection to Romantic notions of authorship and originality, often expressed in postmodern culture as a lack. Paradoxically, this new direction (as we will see) involves a selective return to, or a reworking of, certain forms of subjectivity and ideas of newness that are also associated with Romanticism. However, it consistently maintains a critical distance from a Romantic-postmodern rejection of science and technology as over-rigid, alienating, and inhuman.

Of the three writers explored here, it is Martínez, with his mathematician's training, who presents the most direct challenge to common, Romantic-inspired, misconceptions of science as dogmatically empiricist. The relationship between science and literature cannot be reduced for Martínez to a tension between rationalism and irrationalism, dialectical rigour and creative inspiration. Both literature and science evolve by means of all of these, and his work expresses a reasoned belief in the continued potential for innovation in both science and literature, as each battles against tradition to find new forms and syntheses according to a dialectical principle. Piglia also steers well away from the usual Romantic-postmodern critique of mechanistic science: while the great majority of other fictional works that cite Gödel's theorems do so in order to puncture science's perceived complacency, in Piglia, Gödelian self-reference is not presented as a calamitous threat to logic and epistemological enterprise but becomes a point of entry into multiple worlds that enrich our understanding of the complex relationship between the real and the imagined, the material and the virtual.

However, as Hayles points out, there are a number of continuities between Romanticism and what she variously calls the "cosmic dance," "the cosmic web," or a field model of the universe. These share with the Romantic metaphor of the "organism" an understanding that "the whole cannot be adequately represented as the sum of its parts," together with "an emphasis on the dynamic, fluid nature of reality."[54] The work of Piglia and Cohen in particular allows us to reconstruct part of the Romantic heritage of the "new" science of chaos, emergence, and uncertainty.

In their exploration of the nature of creativity, Piglia and Martínez also return to certain ideas propounded by the Russian Formalists. These ideas may, in many ways, be understood as antithetical to Romantic ideas of art and creativity. Formalist theories of literature bypass the individual author, the hallowed genius of Romanticism, to focus on the self-renewing power of literature and the generation of new ideas and forms through the combination and recombination of different elements and devices. Literature does not emerge from divine inspiration or communion with nature, as it did for the Romantics; nor is its worth measured by its ability to throw up original insights. Instead, literary change for the Formalists is the effect of a dialectical struggle of forms, in which the individual writer plays only an accidental part.

Among the analyses of novels, short stories, and critical essays presented here is a new reading of *Respiración artificial*, developed in the light of Piglia's debt to Formalist theory, an influence that has gone all but unperceived in critical work on the novel. A focus on this debt, which leads Piglia to explore and advocate forms of writing that might be described as "anti-testimonial," allows us to grasp just how radical Piglia's literary project was in the context of the 1970s in Argentina; it also lays the groundwork for an understanding of his use of tropes from science and technology to explore the nature of creativity in literature.

Both Piglia and Cohen distance themselves from psychoanalytical approaches to subjectivity and literary interpretation, which elevate the author as the centre of meaning of his or her work, however deep in their unconscious such meanings may be buried. For Piglia and Cohen, literature does not *manifest* a series of symptoms to be analyzed and interpreted; instead, it *constructs* experience and affect. The framework within which Cohen pursues these ideas is not Formalist, however, but primarily a Deleuzean one. Examining these three writers' appropriation of scientific models and theories in their exploration of literary creativity allows us to glimpse an unexpected continuity between Formalist literary theories and Deleuzean thought, a connection – among others – that is explored further in the Conclusion.

SCIENCE AND LITERATURE: BEYOND TWO CULTURES VS. ONE CULTURE

In giving this book the subtitle "Between Romanticism and Formalism," my intention is to suggest a particular way that we might understand the tensions emerging in these texts between different ideas of science and creativity but also to emphasize that, while they explore concepts borrowed from mathematics and sciences, their primary field of intervention remains that of literary history and theory. New paths emerge through these writers' alternative – and more productive – recombination of the Romantic and Formalist legacies that underpin some of the contradictions of postmodern thought. These texts function as machines that bring other "machines" – texts, theories, discourses, images – into contact with each other to produce often surprising combinations. In place of conventional hermeneutics, Martínez, Piglia, and Cohen develop and practise an alternative, non-hierarchical, rhizomatic method of approaching texts that – very much in a Formalist vein in the case of Martínez and Piglia, and with closer reference to Deleuze and Guattari's thought in that of Cohen – focusses on construction rather than decoding, surface rather than depth, and resonance rather than meaning.

Like Deleuze and Guattari, Piglia and Cohen in particular develop a theory of literature that emphasizes its role in *creating* experience and affects rather than representing them. This approach distances us from an understanding of literature as a potentially deceptive medium that emerges both in the kind of symptomatic readings of postmodernism delivered by Fredric Jameson (combining Freudian and Marxist approaches to literary criticism) and in the many schools of criticism that have drawn attention to the hidden ideological investments lurking beneath the surface of the text. For Cohen, the task of the contemporary novel is to "re-enchant the world" and to dissolve the false dichotomy between reason and imagination: deception is wrought not by the construction of fiction and illusions but by an overly rigid use of language as a referential system, while the ambiguity of literature prevents it from being reduced to a single logic.[55] For both Cohen and Piglia, it is in literature's irreducibility to straightforward communication, its preference for recursion rather than referentiality, and in its marginality from mainstream culture, that its greatest potential for meaningful intervention may be found, a paradox also inherent to Deleuze and Guattari's concept of a "minor literature."

However, while their primary interest is in the workings of literature, these writers' appropriation of scientific models and theories also carves out alternative ways of thinking more generally about the relationship between literature and science. If these texts largely reject postmodernism's Romantic suspicion of science, they articulate another, somewhat contradictory, aspect of Romantic discourse: the hoped-for synthesis of science and literature. As Joel Black reminds us, it would be misleading to categorize the Romantics as "scientific rebels," as "The leading figures of romanticism were transgressing visionaries who aspired to achieve a grand synthesis of poetry and science."[56] This appears more achievable as an aim if science is depicted as a source of creative contradiction, of emerging hypothesis rather than monolithic absolutism, a vision that emerges most clearly in Martínez's work.

Black points out that at the time Wordsworth and Schlegel were writing, "the modern sciences of biology and psychology did not exist as such; the romantic project was precisely to formulate a science of life and a science of mind."[57] Furthermore, Black suggests that "Far from having negligible scientific value, as Eichner claimed, romanticism may be regarded as having provided the culture (in both the bacteriological and humanistic senses) necessary for the concept of life itself to come into being."[58] It would not be an overstatement to consider the work of Piglia and Cohen in particular as contributing to this project of formulating a science of life, in which literature does not take up a transcendent position of distanced observation but is wholly immanent to the flows of energy and matter that shape and renew life and all material processes in the biological and physical worlds. If social scientists and cultural theorists have been criticized for misappropriating entropy, complexity, autopoiesis, and self-organization to construct dubious analogies, several literary critics have insisted that the use of such models in literature, and particularly postmodern, reflexive literature, is *not* metaphorical. Peter Stoicheff, for example, argues:

> The crucial purpose in exposing the chaos and complexity of metafiction is not to provide another vocabulary through which to speak of a text; nor is it to suggest that the dynamics of metafiction are *like* those of chaos or of complex systems. Instead, it is to show that metafiction displays the properties located in what science calls chaos, and that a metafiction text *is* a complex system.[59]

Literary texts are not mimetic representations of a phenomenon occurring somewhere beyond them but participants in a series of creative and self-organizing processes that shape, and are shaped by, them. This view of creativity is not antithetical to that held by a number of scientists: the theoretical physicist David Bohm, for example, argues that the creativity of the human mind does not simply mimic the creativity of nature but is of exactly the same order.[60] Similarly, Erich Jantsch suggests that "In a dualistic world view it used to be the muse of divine inspiration which used the artist as instrument. In the non-dualistic world view, however, the creative process appears as an aspect of evolutionary self-organization."[61] To this, as we will see, Piglia and Cohen would add the creativity of machinic or inanimate processes, which often become indistinguishable in their work from organic ones. Indeed, in the growing "connectionism" that Sadie Plant observes to have arisen from the study of complex systems, "Distinctions between the human, the natural and the artificial are scrambled, and whatever was once said to belong to each of them finds a new basis on which to connect in the dispersed and connective processes which link them all."[62]

Ultimately at stake in our evaluation of literature's borrowings from science is the question of how literature should be read in relation to the world beyond it: as a textual representation of systems described by science, or as a system in and of itself, operating in conjunction with other, non-literary systems, but according to the same principles of life, movement, and growth that govern them. As Hayles, Brown and many others have pointed out, "Literature is not simply a place where you see scientific and technological ideas replicate themselves."[63] Brown identifies as damaging to serious interdisciplinary work what he calls a "show-and-tell criticism" that suddenly "discovers" in Borges's "El jardín de senderos que se bifurcan" an anticipation of Hugh Everett's many-worlds theory.[64] In different ways, the writers I focus on in this book ask a more far-reaching question: if literature is a system, what kind of system is it? How does it function with other systems around it? How does it create newness rather than simply represent or recycle the already-existing?

Although Martínez, Piglia, and Cohen write with close reference to European and North American literary theory and praxis, their highly reflexive and metafictional approach to the question of the relationship between literature, mathematics, science, and technology often reconfigures the forms and terms of existing debates. The syntheses these writers imagine between literature and science – and that they allow us to imagine in turn – are, I will suggest, more productive and nuanced than many of those that have shaped recent debates in European and North American academies, so often polarized around the "two cultures" and "one culture" perspectives.

1 | The Science of Literary Evolution: Between Romanticism and Formalism

Guillermo Martínez's *La mujer del maestro* (1998) is not particularly representative of his fiction in general: no mathematicians figure among the characters, and formal systems, logic, and the operations of chance are not prominent in the diegesis. The novel does, however, explore in depth two of his recurrent concerns: the nature of creativity and the figure of the genius in the contemporary world. This chapter focusses on the themes of artistic exhaustion and renewal that are central to both *La mujer del maestro* and *Respiración artificial* (Piglia, 1980). Piglia's first novel explores the difficulty and the necessity of writing in the context of military repression in Argentina, finding in the distanced perspectives of history a way to overcome the seeming impasse of the present. Both novels create a powerful and paradoxical dialogue between Romantic ideas of artistic creativity and Formalist notions of literary evolution. In Piglia, narrative figurations such as alienation, exile, utopia, and betrayal, taken from episodes in the political and cultural history of Argentine Romanticism, are used to articulate the displacements, estrangements, and anachronisms that underpin the Formalist vision of literary renewal. Martínez's novel bears witness to the demise of the Romantic artistic genius in the modern world; however, he draws on Formalist theories of literary succession, and on the dialectical tradition of science, to carve out the possibility of artistic innovation in an age of epistemological and aesthetic crisis. Both writers demonstrate how Formalist ideas of literary evolution can be mobilized to combat postmodern pronouncements of the "exhaustion" of literature.

A POSTMODERN PROMETHEUS: INNOVATION AND TRADITION IN LITERATURE / MARTÍNEZ

> The possession of originality cannot make an artist unconventional; it drives him further into convention, obeying the law of the art itself, which seeks constantly to reshape itself from its own depths.—Northrop Frye[1]

Set in the unscrupulous, feud-riven literary circles of Buenos Aires – Martínez suspects that a change of name may not have been sufficient disguise for some of his characters[2] – *La mujer del maestro* becomes the author's most direct enquiry into originality and literary evolution. The novel follows the struggle of a young writer who becomes locked in rivalry, both sexual and literary, with an older, more established author. The counterpoint between youthful inexperience and weary cynicism allows Martínez to stage several conflicting ideas about creativity: to ask, for example, whether originality arises from a close engagement with literary tradition or from a deliberate disregard of it, what value should be ascribed to a commercially successful author measured against the lonely pursuer of artistic originality, and whether reflexivity should be considered as a form of innovation or a signal of its exhaustion.

We could identify these conflicts in Martínez's novel as belonging to a central tension between Formalist concepts of literary creativity and those of recognizably Romantic stock. The staging of the struggle against literary inheritance, the novel's principal theme, draws on the Formalist understanding that "Every literary trend represents a crisscrossing, a complex interplay between elements of tradition and innovation."[3] For the Formalists, this interplay is characterized by dialectical struggle and discontinuity, in contrast to the classical idea of literary history as proceeding in a linear fashion through epochs, each united by a particular style and spirit. Apparently removed from Martínez's mathematical concerns, this novel establishes a crucial correlation that recurs throughout his fiction and critical essays between artistic innovation and logical reasoning, and between the battle of the individual against the literary canon and the dialectical progress of scientific thought. Martínez's novel brings into the light the cynicism that feeds, and is fed by, postmodern discourses on the "exhaustion" of art; with much greater ambivalence, it sketches out what genuine creativity might look like in our times. Although the novel charts a journey that takes its characters from enthusiasm, creativity, and love of literature to cynicism, parody, and self-serving ambition, it also reveals the dialectical processes that underpin literature's continual self-renewal, and that for Martínez render specious the now-familiar postmodern discourses of artistic exhaustion.

Avatars of Romantic creativity: Prometheus and Faust

In the invocation of three mythical figures in *La mujer del maestro* – Prometheus, Faust, and Daedalus – we can trace three contrasting conceptions of creativity. Since Aeschylus, Prometheus has been cast as the giver of writing and other civilizing skills to humankind, in defiance of Zeus; in later versions of the myth, he becomes involved in the very act of creating humankind. For Shelley (*Prometheus Unbound*, 1820) and others in the Romantic period, he became a symbol for rebellion against the tyranny of the established order. The novelists in *La mujer del maestro* – the young, unnamed protagonist starting his second novel and Jordán, the older, established author working on his life's masterpiece – discover that they are both writing versions of the Prometheus myth. The protagonist's plan is to insert the mythological character into the contemporary world, letting his young Prometheus loose in the midst of a huge city. His intention is to pose the question of whether any of the Romantic notions of heroism have survived his cynical century, and on this score he begins to have real doubts:

había empezado a preguntarse si todo el asunto tenía sentido, si era posible reconocer todavía en algún pliegue de la época contemporánea los elementos del mito, si no habría habido un corte definitivo, la pérdida de una fe, o de un grado de profundidad, que prohibía definitivamente resucitar al héroe después de Shelley.[4]

he had begun to ask himself whether the whole thing made any sense, if it were possible still to recognize any element of the myth in some hidden crease of the contemporary world, if there hadn't been a definitive rupture, a loss of faith or of depth, that prohibited, once and for all, the possibility of resuscitating the hero after Shelley.

Jordán's own novel-in-progress appears to draw on classical rather than Romantic versions of the myth, and specifically on Aeschylus's *Prometheus Bound*. It explores the idea that fire is not the first gift that Prometheus gives to man, but the ignorance of his end, the inability to predict the number of his days. As he cannot grant man the immortality reserved for the gods, Prometheus puts within his heart the "esperanza ciega" (blind hope) that Jordán describes as "Esa confianza absurda que nos hace dormir a la noche, creyendo que siempre veremos de nuevo la salida del sol [...] la condición que debe anteceder a todas, la única capaz de darle sentido a las empresas humanas" (that absurd confidence that sends us to sleep at night, believing that we will always see the next sunrise [...] the condition that has to come before all others, the only one able to lend meaning to human enterprise).[5] In his novel, however, Jordán imagines the experience of a man to whom this gift is *not* given: who struggles to complete his great work, robbed of meaning by the knowledge of exactly when he is going to die. Jordán therefore reworks the classical myth from a Romantic perspective: that of the tragedy of finitude, as explored by Fichte, Schlegel, and others.

Hope and cynicism, heroism and nihilism, creative life and finitude: these are also the themes of the framing story of *La mujer del maestro*. The struggle between Prometheus and Zeus is mirrored in the relationship between the young writer battling to define a path of his own against the supremacy of an older author. It is a struggle that allows Martínez to explore several ways of figuring the relationship between an individual writer and the literary canon. The protagonist finds his second novel impossible to write, as "lo paralizaban las voces superpuestas de la tradición, el peso abrumador de lo que ya estaba escrito" (he was paralyzed by the superimposed voices of tradition, the overwhelming weight of what had already been written).[6] His first book is admired by Jordán, who is moved by the reverent belief in literature that emanates from each page and sees something of his younger, naïve self in such zeal. He warns him that writing from within literary tradition means that "para entender a fondo su libro hay que cargarse encima una biblioteca entera" (to really understand your book, you'd have to carry a whole library on your shoulders) and that battling against the canon will inevitably result in his work being swallowed up into that same tradition.[7]

For his part, the protagonist recognizes instantly that Jordán's new book is crushingly original, laying waste to literary tradition and his earlier concerns and styles, banishing irony altogether. It is different from anything he has ever read, "un libro desolado y arrasador" (a desolate, devastating book).[8] The protagonist suspects that the books piled high in Jordán's study, once the objects of fervent study, have lain unopened and unread for some time; while young authors, as Jordán rather dismissively observes, are always interested in the subject of literary succession, it is a question that seems to have become irrelevant for writers of Jordán's stature and experience.

Thus far, Martínez's novel would seem to allow for the possibility of a kind of originality that represents a complete rupture with tradition: a Romantic creativity born of reclusion from the world and rebellion against its norms. And yet Jordán is deeply cynical about his achievement, attributing his success to his scorn for words: like women, he says, they flee from you if you adore them; humiliated and disparaged, they will never deny themselves to you. His reclusion, which once inspired the protagonist's Romanticized view of him as a lone genius, is eventually suspected to be nothing more than a publicity stunt.

It is not Prometheus who provides the most accurate model for the kind of creativity ultimately pursued by both Jordán and the protagonist, but Faust. Jordán's wife describes a character from one of his novels as "un Dorian Gray invertido" (an inverted Dorian Gray):[9] unlike in Wilde's *The Picture of Dorian Gray* (1890), in this case the moral degradation of the Jordán's Faustian composer results in the ever-greater perfection of the musical score. Martínez returns to the image of Dorian Gray at the book launch at the end of the novel, at which the previously youthful Jordán appears suddenly emaciated and cadaverous: "La edad, su verdadera edad, lo había alcanzado de pronto, como si hubiera estado suspendido, mientras escribía la novela, a salvo en un limbo fuera del tiempo, y esa gracia le hubiera sido quitado cruelmente, de un solo golpe" (age, his true age, had caught up with him all at once, as if he had been suspended, while writing the novel, safe in some limbo outside of time, and that gift had been cruelly taken from him, in one fell swoop).[10] Like Faust and Dorian Gray, Jordán sacrifices moral integrity in the pursuit of pleasure and success, abusing his wife's loyalty and humiliating her in front of his latest sexual conquests. The protagonist, too, makes for an unconvincing Prometheus: he is too timid to carry through with his own robbery (of Jordán's manuscript), and his rebellion is cowardly, serving no one but himself. He follows Jordán's Faustian path, moving all too easily from youthful enthusiasm to cynicism: Jordán's complaint that his first novel lacks "el fermento humano por excelencia, la maquinación" (that human ferment *par excellence*, evil scheming)[11] is quickly remedied in the second.

The creative impasse the protagonist experiences on reading Jordán's manuscript is broken only through the power of revenge. Seeing Jordán and Cecilia at the book launch occasions a flash of inspiration: rather than writing about Prometheus, he will write about them. The solution, as is so often the case in postmodern reflexive literature, is simply to move up a level in the hierarchy of narrative and meta-narrative levels. To produce a version of Prometheus when one has already been published is discounted as an achievement of lesser value than to write *about* the production of such a version; this story is then embedded, of course, within yet another narrative frame: the novel we are reading. As a novel about the writing of a novel about the writing of a novel about a myth, *La mujer del maestro* could not be more exemplary in its use of postmodern recursion.

Artistic exhaustion and postmodern skepticism

Recursion is, of course, a form of innovation, and one taken seriously by John Barth in his influential essay "The Literature of Exhaustion." Barth extols Borges's use of reflexive techniques to overcome a widespread sense of the exhaustion of aesthetic innovation. By taking artistic constraints and philosophical impasses as his overt theme, "he confronts an intellectual dead end and employs it against itself to accomplish new human work," an act that represents an "artistic victory" over the perceived crisis in creativity.[12] In a similar manner, the protagonist of *La mujer del maestro* has found a way of engaging with literary tradition without being overwhelmed by it: the cultivation of ironic distance. However, this technique is associated in the novel with rancour and jealousy. We do not rejoice with the protagonist when he finally finds the inspiration for his novel, and we find nothing laudable in his approach: he merely shows that he has adapted perfectly to a literary environment in which books are used as tools for the promotion of oneself and the denigration of others. Martínez's representation of the creative achievements of his protagonist is thus highly ambivalent.

The epigraph to *La mujer del maestro* – "Man is half dust, half deity, / alike unfit to sink or soar"[13] – is taken from Byron's drama *Manfred* (1817), in which Faustian echoes also lend ambivalence to the portrayal of Manfred's Promethean defiance. Manfred goes on to speak of man's "mix'd essence": we breathe "The breath of degradation and of pride, / Contending with low wants and lofty will, / Till our mortality predominates."[14] Martínez never fully manages to imagine a Promethean hero for our times: the generosity and desire for freedom that motivates Prometheus's daring rebellion is replaced with a much more selfish and cynical form of ambition. If his characters are patently of "mix'd essence," they have none of Byron's tortured guilt; rather than a battle with the spirits, theirs is a much more prosaic scramble for precedence in a market-driven, mass-media society. As the protagonist comes to realize, literary success in his world is not about writing well at all but about the vagaries of critical reception, the marketability of novels, pulling off a convincing performance on the social scene, and adding some spice to one's public profile by provoking a scandal in one's private life. Critical acclaim does not reward divine inspiration but petty competitiveness, latching onto those who find an edge in an increasingly crowded market. As for Jordán's own masterpiece, which has taken him fifteen years to complete, the book launch is poorly attended and only his young rival buys a copy of the book. Jordán advises the latter, with not a little bitterness, to forget about serious literature and pursue the kind of scandal loved by the press in order to convert himself into a celebrity overnight: get someone pregnant and make her have an abortion, or sleep with another writer's wife and make sure he finds out.

For all its appeal to Romantic figures of creativity and rebellious dissent, then, *La mujer del maestro* conspicuously (and deliberately) fails to bring these to life in the contemporary world. Significantly, however, for Martínez this failure does not give credence to postmodern discourses of artistic exhaustion; on the contrary, the novel allows us to suspect that it is the dominance of such discourses, and particularly their skepticism towards rationalist epistemology, that may be responsible for the sad plight of contemporary literature. Jordán's cynicism towards artistic creativity derives at least in part from a loss of faith in the advance of human knowledge. All his life, he claims, "Confiaba en ese dibujito de la espiral, el entendimiento que se desarrolla volviéndose hacia atrás para incorporar lo anterior, y asciende al mismo tiempo en cada vuelta a nuevas alturas" (I trusted in that little diagram of the spiral, the understanding that develops by looping backwards to incorporate what has gone before, and at the same time ascends to new heights with every loop).[15] The diagram he refers to is often used to illustrate the Hegelian model of historical progress, which moves forward by sublating apparent oppositions (thesis and antithesis) into a new synthesis at a higher level. It is in this kind of progress that Jordán has lost all confidence. Although he has produced a masterpiece, Jordán no longer trusts in the increasing enlightenment of generations to come, who will appreciate the value of the work that is destined to be overlooked by his own generation. He speaks of "un quiebre en nuestra época" (a rupture in our era),[16] brought about by a realization that those who come after us may not be better, or understand more, than we do: in fact they may understand significantly less. This loss of faith in the dialectical process by which human knowledge is advanced is at the heart of Jordán's skepticism regarding innovation in literature. If artists often create for a future generation better able to understand their work, the erasure of that better future makes the work of the artist seem futile.

This connection between artistic originality and the processes of dialectical reasoning sheds significant light on the novel's otherwise rather ambiguous treatment of questions of genius and literary innovation. It prevents us from making the mistake of attributing Jordán's skepticism to Martínez's own approach to creativity in the postmodern era. In his essays, Martínez is openly critical of such defeatism, defending the power of dialectical thought in arguments that clearly associate epistemological skepticism with the discourse of artistic exhaustion. Moreover, as I will show, *La mujer del maestro* itself allows us to glimpse a different form of creativity that *does* survive in our cynical age, precisely by remaining bound to the dialectical advance of human knowledge in which Jordán cannot now believe.

In his essay "Literatura y racionalidad," Martínez argues that our era's over-hasty dismissal of rational systems of thought produces a skepticism that also undermines the possibility of innovation in the arts. That human knowledge is limited does not mean, he insists, that it is totally impotent.[17] From the perception that rationalism has been demolished stems another new rhetoric: that everything has already been said, and all that is left is repetition and parody.[18] Elsewhere, Martínez takes issue with what he identifies as a dominant notion in contemporary Argentine literature and criticism, upheld by César Aira in his essay "La nueva escritura" (1998), that the professionalization of novel-writing has led to its stagnation. Aira argues that heroic attempts to renovate the genre in a radical fashion have ended in "un callejón sin salida" (a dead end) and that the law of diminishing returns governs all attempts at literary innovation: every artist reduces more and more the space left to his successors, and it is increasingly difficult to innovate.[19] Martínez presents various objections to Aira's proposition, which he identifies as one of the most virulent "clichés" of literary discussions, circulating uncontested like a sacred truth.[20] He admits the growing difficulty of "escribir contra todo lo escrito" (writing against everything that has been written), particularly as literature has become more self-conscious.[21] But, faced with this difficulty, we should not immediately abandon hope of innovation and sink into a belief that "está todo dicho" (everything has already been said). If literature is – as Martínez sustains – a form of knowledge, then its history will be a long one of "permanente invención, variación y agotamiento de recursos y de efectos, de teorías, de retóricas y de géneros" (constant invention, variation on, and exhaustion of, resources, effects, theories, forms of rhetoric and genres). Why – he asks – should we suppose that this history has reached its end?[22]

Daedalus, the art of puzzle-solving, and Formalist literary renewal

The sheer variety of ways in which the Prometheus and Faust mythemes are employed in *La mujer del maestro* is demonstration enough of the endless potential for each period to question and reinvent its own myths. But it is the more discreet figure of Daedalus in the novel who may be seen to crystallize most effectively the reasons for Martínez's confidence in the continued potential for innovation in literature, providing an alternative model to the Promethean and Faustian ones that are more conspicuous in the novel's diegesis. Daedalus, who gives his name to a previous novel by Jordán, represents art as fine craftsmanship and was associated in the Romantic period with classical art. He is also associated with puzzle-inventing and puzzle-solving, being the creator of a mythological labyrinth so deviously intricate that he barely managed to escape from it himself. Jordán's writing desk is cluttered with games and puzzles, and at one point the analogy is explicitly drawn between writing fiction and completing a jigsaw puzzle. The comparison is surprising: we might more readily associate the deductive logic of puzzle-solving and code-deciphering with the act of literary criticism, not composition. In what sense can writing fiction be creative if it is likened to the reconstruction of a jigsaw puzzle, which involves merely discovering an order already set down by the creator of the puzzle, leaving no room for individual expression?

This picture of a writer who is not constructing a puzzle for his reader to decipher so much as engaging in an act of problem-solving himself finds echoes in Martínez's own experience of the process of composition. He describes the impression of discovering links already buried in the story, waiting to be uncovered, and the sensation of euphoria that follows "la aparición imprevista de las piezas que faltaban en el rompecabezas, con reordenamientos súbitos en los que uno alcanza a ver lo que verdaderamente había en la historia, lo que no sabía antes de empezar" (the unexpected appearance of those pieces that were missing from the jigsaw puzzle, with sudden reorderings that allow you to see what was really there in the story, what you didn't know before you began).[23] For the writer, Martínez suggests, the relationship he draws between narrative and rationality may not seem so strange: it stems from viewing each work "como un organismo con leyes íntimas que se pone en marcha y que el transcurso de la lectura (de la escritura) permite conocer" (like an organism operating according to its own secret laws, which are discoverable in the course of reading [or of writing]).[24] While this knowledge may take many different forms, it always represents a revelation, as much for the writer as for the reader.

Martínez's conception of literary composition as a form of puzzle-solving resonates strongly with the understanding of literary evolution developed by the Russian Formalists. In articles and interviews Martínez often dissociates himself from Formalist approaches: they cannot, he maintains, provide an exhaustive account of literary innovation, as a significant proportion of experimentation is dedicated not to playing with new forms and techniques but to expressing new and different modes of subjectivity. As he writes,

> No es solamente la cuestión de si sacamos o no la letra E para hacer experimentos en la literatura. La cuestión es que hay una cantidad de experimentos posibles que tienen que ver con la manera en que la gente reflexiona sobre problemas humanos que son diferentes en cada época.[25]

> Literary experimentation is not just about the issue of whether we omit the letter *E* or not. The issue is that a great number of experiments are possible that are really about how people reflect on human problems, which are different from era to era.

These human problems, he maintains, cannot be reduced to forms of textual manipulation, which seem nothing more than pyrotechnics in comparison.[26] Martínez clearly distances himself here from the work of writers such as Raymond Roussel, Georges Perec, Raymond Queneau, and others associated with the Oulipo group, who applied strict formal constraints to their literary compositions and might be thought of as precursors in some ways to Martínez's own translation of mathematical forms and concerns into literature. Perec's novel *La disparition* (1969) is composed without a single use of the letter "e," while in his *Les revenentes* (1972), "e" is the only vowel used throughout.

The rather narrow definition Martínez applies here to Formalism should not blind us, however, to some significant overlaps between his conceptions of innovation and evolution in literature and those of Formalist literary-critical approaches. For Viktor Shklovsky, as for a number of the Russian Formalist critics, the crucial quality of *ostranenie* (defamiliarization) in literature is often generated through puzzles and riddles, a play with forms and structures that estranges the reader from the content. As René Wellek explains, according to Shklovsky's approach,

> Art is putting up hurdles, it is like a game of patience or a jigsaw puzzle. Frame stories, such as *The Arabian Nights* with their constant delays and disappointments, adventure and mystery stories, detective novels with their surprises and riddles serve as examples.[27]

Martínez's suggestion that art also presents itself as a puzzle for the *writer* to solve, not just the reader, is closely aligned with Formalist views on the creative act as an act of discovery and assimilation, here articulated by Northrop Frye:

> It is hardly possible to accept a critical view which confuses the original with the aboriginal, and imagines that a "creative" poet sits down with a pencil and some blank paper and eventually produces a new poem in a special act of creation *ex nihilo*. Human beings do not create in that way. *Just as a new scientific discovery manifests something that was already latent in the order of nature, and at the same time is logically related to the total structure of the existing science,* so the new poem manifests something that was already latent in the order of words. Literature may have life, reality, experience, nature, imaginative truth, social conditions, of what you will for its *content*; but literature itself is not made out of these things. Poetry can only be made out of other poems; novels out of other novels.[28]

Of particular note here is that Frye, like Martínez, constructs an analogy between scientific and literary discovery, suggesting that both arise out of an existing structure and are related to existing forms. Martínez's understanding of literary evolution as a dialectical process means that innovation can only really take place in dialogue with the canon, not in a wildcat stroke of inspired genius. Just as the scientist must measure his new findings against those of previous studies, so the writer must carve out his original work with regard to literary tradition, which is not stultifying, but on the contrary contains an inexhaustible source of ideas and forms that have not yet been fully developed and can be redeployed for new ends. Indeed, this process is vital to ensure originality rather than mere novelty or a naïve reinvention of the wheel. Originality cannot be conceived without reference to the tradition from which it emerges and that it aims to renovate:

> *Originalidad*: entendida no como mera novedad, sino como aquello que lucha por abrirse paso entre la marea de lugares comunes, de lo ya dicho, de lo que alguna vez fue expresivo y ahora sólo es retórica. La originalidad, en este sentido, debe

> tener en cuenta necesariamente a la tradición como medida y desafío.[29]

> *Originality*: understood not as mere novelty, but as that which fights its way through the tide of commonplaces, of the already-said, of that which was once meaningful and is now mere rhetoric. Originality, in this sense, must of necessity take tradition into account as a measure and a challenge.

Martínez finds this approach to be common to literature and scientific thought, both of which require us to "luchar con lo anterior y tratar de crear nuevos paradigmas que supriman pero a la vez incluyan desde una nueva altura lo ya hecho" (battle with what has gone before and try to create new paradigms that eradicate it but also include it as part of a new, higher position).[30] This conception also reinforces Martínez's superimposition of reading or deciphering, on the one hand, and writing or creating, on the other: as writing involves writing with or against the canon, writing is also, inescapably, an act of reading.

There is also a strong correlation between Martínez's sense here of how certain forms and ideas can lose their critical edge and become exhausted, before being recombined in new ways and for new purposes, and the Formalist understanding of processes of automatization and refunctioning in literary evolution.[31] The notion of originality Martínez articulates resembles the one developed by Frye in his discussion of painting. Frye argues that originality is as much a flight *towards* convention as it is away from it:

> By breaking with the Barbizon school, Manet discovered a deeper affinity with Goya and Velasquez; by breaking with the impressionists, Cézanne discovered a deeper affinity with Chardin and Masaccio. The possession of originality cannot make an artist unconventional; it drives him further into convention, obeying the law of the art itself, which seeks constantly to reshape itself from its own depths.[32]

Equating literary evolution with dialectical rationalism also means that this dialogue with tradition is always a struggle, never a straightforward line of influence from one writer or generation to another, but one that is stimulated by contradiction and looping back to previous forms. This conception of literary evolution is very similar to the discontinuous process observed by the Formalists. As Yury Tynyanov states,

> When people talk about "literary tradition" or "succession" [...] they usually imagine a kind of straight line joining a younger representative of a given literary branch with an older one. As it happens, things are much more complex than that. It is not a matter of continuing on a straight line, but rather one of setting out and pushing off from a given point – a struggle [...]. Each instance of literary succession is first and foremost a struggle involving a destruction of the old unity and a new construction out of the old elements.[33]

La mujer del maestro illuminates the extent to which writing is always *writing against*; positing literary succession as a dialectical process and a problem-solving activity allows Martínez to demonstrate that newness does and will always emerge through antithesis and assimilation. Significantly, the much-vaunted original composition that is Jordán's novel remains a tantalizing absence in *La mujer del maestro* that cannot fully be brought into being, while it is the younger protagonist's reflexive treatment of the struggle for innovation that becomes the dominant theme of the novel we read. The contradiction that fuels creativity may be a noble battle with the Greats of literary tradition or – as here – petty feuds with fellow authors sparked by sexual jealousy and revenge. Whatever motivates the writer to join that battle (and Frye reminds us that "There is no reason why a great poet should be a wise and good man, or even a tolerable human being"[34]), it is clear that literary tradition remains, for Martínez, the fount and measure of great innovation, not a constraint upon it. His work also suggests that notions of creativity and progress borrowed from Hegelian dialecticalism and the evolution of scientific thought may shed light on the perceived crisis of artistic innovation in our era, as well as on possible ways through that apparent impasse.

NON-LINEARITY, TOPOLOGY, TURBULENCE, AND OTHER (FORMALIST) MODELS OF LITERARY RENEWAL / PIGLIA

> Only the creation of new forms of art can restore to a man sensation of the world, can resurrect things and kill pessimism.
> —Viktor Shklovsky[35]

If Martínez's *La mujer del maestro* imagines the anachronistic thrusting of Shelley's Romantic hero, Prometheus, into a contemporary world that is deeply skeptical of heroism and the possibility of genuine transformation, Piglia's *Respiración artificial* invokes Romantic figures and discourses to mark a similar series of displacements and divergences. The young writer Emilio Renzi publishes a novel based on the more sordid and scandalous episodes of his family history; this prompts a letter from his uncle, Marcelo Maggi, who has been absent for many years. The two strike up an epistolary relationship, through which Renzi learns of Maggi's efforts to reconstruct the history of the grandfather of his father-in-law, Enrique Ossorio, who was exiled from Argentina during the nineteenth-century dictatorship of Juan Manuel Rosas. The novel we read includes a number of letters, written by characters in the present about the past, and from the past about the future (which turns out to be the novel's present): this intersecting of temporalities allows Piglia to comment on the persistent presence in the late twentieth century of certain founding myths and figures in national history. More than simply establishing an allegorical relationship between the military regime in power when the novel was published (1980) and the earlier Rosas dictatorship, Piglia's novel returns to the utopian and revolutionary politics of Romanticism in Argentina, which shaped the newly independent nation, and asks what may be salvaged for the present from that turbulent period of visionary ideals and bloody political rivalry.

For both Martínez and Piglia, the anachronistic return to Romantic motifs and ideas becomes a way of posing the question of what modes of utopian thought might be possible today, in spite of our postmodern sense of endings and the ruinous collusion of language and power, or after the chillingly rational basis on which the twentieth century carried out its genocides. If Hitler's *Mein Kampf* is, as the exiled Polish philosopher Tardewski in *Respiración artificial* comes to believe, "la culminación del racionalismo europeo" (the culmination of European rationalism),[36] is it possible to resurrect philosophy as an ethical enterprise? Is social and cultural innovation destined to fail in an era in which cynicism and parody seem to have infiltrated every aspect of experience?

Against the spirit of the times, in which "está de moda ser escéptico y desconfiar de la historia" (it is fashionable to be skeptical and to mistrust history), Piglia's Marcelo Maggi, the absent correspondent of *Respiración artificial*, is – as Piglia himself describes him – "un pensador inactual, está a contramano del nihilismo deliberado que circula actualmente" (an uncontemporary thinker, swimming against the current-day tide of conscious nihilism).[37] *Respiración artificial* calls urgently for an historical approach to understanding the novel's present, Argentina under military dictatorship; Piglia's particular synthesis of Romantic themes and Formalist theories is wrought with the aim of constructing precisely such a perspective. As we will see, "history" in this sense does not refer to a single narrative of fixed meaning; neither is it a chronological exercise. Piglia's historical approach is far from linear in its understanding of causality, dealing instead with conflictive temporalities, ruptures, unresolved tensions, and unexpected congruities. Anti-institutional in its focus on marginalized figures and currents, it is often vigorously anti-historicist in its pursuit of genealogies that transcend conventional models of influence and in its championing of anachronism as a key to understanding the present. In the discussion below, I bring Piglia's approach into dialogue with Formalist thought on the evolution of literary history and also with Michel Serres's appropriation of the physics of chaotic systems in his explorations of the multitemporality of history. These approaches share a vision of the past as a storehouse of dissensions and alliances that can be endlessly revisited, renewed, and resignified to create new avenues for the present. This, as *Respiración artificial* suggests, is the key to both political and literary renewal.

The "real story" of Respiración artificial

It has become common for critics writing on *Respiración artificial* to claim that a principal function of the narrative is to hide the "real story" of Maggi's suspicious disappearance in late-1970s Argentina and simultaneously to draw attention to that covering-up. Stefanie Massman, for example, suggests that narration in the novel "es utilizada para ocultar más que para mostrar" (is used more to hide than to reveal),[38] and Mirta Antonelli is one of many critics for whom Tardewski's citation of Wittgenstein towards the end of the novel – "Sobre aquello de lo que no se puede hablar, lo mejor es callar" (on that which cannot be spoken about, it is better to remain silent)[39] – is an oblique but obvious reference to what cannot be spoken about in 1976: the violence carried out in the name of the *Proceso de Reorganización Nacional*.[40] These readings are prompted by the apparently dubious relevance of the literary and philosophical discussions in the second half of the novel to its ostensible plot, namely Renzi's correspondence with his uncle Maggi and Maggi's sudden disappearance. Rita Gnutzmann, like many other critics, observes a "clara oposición" (clear opposition) between the two parts of the novel, with history dominating the first and literature the second.[41] In his perspicacious reading of the novel, Idelber Avelar argues, against the prevailing critical consensus, that the apparently superfluous second part is not accidental to the story at all but may even be viewed as the "real" story.[42] However, in identifying the theme of this story as the limitations of narration, he ends up falling back into a position that is not so far removed from that of the dominant critical hypothesis he is at pains to challenge, that of "un relato-velo-para-despistar-censores" (story-as-smokescreen-to-confuse-the-censors):[43] he is left asserting, in a similar manner to other critics, that "*Respiración artificial* es el prólogo al texto jamás escrito. La verdadera historia no se ha narrado" (*Artificial Respiration* is the prologue to a text that is never written. The real story has not been told).[44]

The novel does, of course, lend some credence to these conclusions, perhaps most clearly when Tardewski observes to Renzi that if they have been talking all night it was to avoid speaking about Maggi because there was nothing about him that could be said. But if the characters perceive the conversation to be incidental and irrelevant to their situation, the role their discussion actually plays in Piglia's novel is neither of these. Underlying the critical accounts I have cited here is a struggle to reconcile form with content in a novel that demands to be read alongside the momentous events of Argentine politics in the late 1970s, but that seems deliberately to divert the reader's attention onto something else. In the reading of the novel that follows, I will suggest that, far from displacing or covering-up the "real" story of Maggi's disappearance, it would be more accurate to consider the discussions of literary form and evolution as the central story of *Respiración artificial*, as a novel that is primarily and reflexively concerned with its own mode of enunciation. This will lead to a rather different conclusion concerning the novel's approach to literary creativity and evolution. If, in Avelar's reading, the novel's aim is to "Narrar el fracaso, narrar la imposibilidad de escribir" (narrate failure, narrate the impossibility of writing),[45] I wish to emphasize instead its commitment to the resourcefulness and the enduring inventiveness of literature. Where Santiago Colás argues that the novel's experimentation with form expresses the "damage" that has been done by the military regime, both to the narrating subject and to representation itself,[46] I will suggest that its formal fragmentation also, and more insistently, explores the conditions of possibility for a renewed vision.

My argument takes inspiration from Russian Formalist approaches to literary criticism, which are explicitly referenced within the narrative of Piglia's novel and for which Piglia has professed an interest and admiration in several interviews. *Respiración artificial* appropriates Romantic tropes of exile, utopia, and alienation to elucidate a Formalist understanding of artistic expression and literary change; in doing so, it demonstrates that displacement and anachronism are *motors* for narrative creativity, not indicators of its impossibility. Studying the novel through the lens of Formalism not only responds to some of the difficulties raised in critical work on the novel but also, as I will show, lays the groundwork for an understanding of Piglia's use of tropes from science and technology to explore the nature of creativity in literature, placing *Respiración artificial* into a much closer relationship than has often been perceived with the concerns of Piglia's later novels and short stories.

Exile, utopia and the epistolary novel: Formalist *ostranenie* and the "mirada histórica"

Respiración artificial constructs a web of significations to link together multiple forms of temporal and spatial displacement. The first node in this network is the epistolary genre. Among the many texts cited or imagined in the novel is a sequence of letters between Marcelo Maggi and his nephew Renzi, the young writer who has just published a novel inspired by the more sordid and scandalous episodes of his family history. Maggi, a historian, is involved in a narrative project of his own: the reconstruction of the story of Enrique Ossorio, his father-in-law's grandfather, who was a key figure in the nineteenth-century regime of Juan Manuel Rosas before being exiled as a traitor. In a trunk full of papers dating from the year 1850, Maggi finds sketches for a novel Ossorio had planned to write, with the title *1979*. Although the novel is set in the past (1837–38), the protagonist receives letters from the future (1979), allowing him to imagine an Argentina that has not yet come into being.

In his diary, Ossorio reflects on the form he has chosen for his novel and its appropriateness for the theme of utopia, the second figure in Piglia's series of displacements and anachronisms:

> Entonces un relato epistolar. ¿Por qué ese género anacrónico? Porque la utopía ya de por sí es una forma literaria que pertenece al pasado. Para nosotros, hombres del siglo XIX, se trata de una especie arcaica, como es arcaica la novela epistolar.[47]

An epistolary narrative, then. Why that anachronistic genre? Because utopia is itself, already, a literary form that belongs to the past. For us nineteenth-century men, it is an archaic form, just like the epistolary novel.

Correspondence, Ossorio goes on to suggest, is itself a utopian form of conversation "porque anula el presente y hace del futuro el único lugar posible del diálogo" (because it deletes the present and makes the future the only possible locus in which dialogue can take place).[48] To utopia and the epistolary genre, Piglia adds a third term: exile. "¿Qué es el exilio sino una situación que nos obliga a sustituir con palabras escritas la relación entre los amigos más queridos, que están lejos, ausentes, diseminados cada uno en lugares y ciudades distintas?" (what is exile if not a situation in which we are obliged to substitute with written words our relationship with our dearest friends, who are far away, absent, flung far and wide in different cities and other places?).[49]

The epistolary novel was already an archaic form in the nineteenth century, looking back to a time that did not question "la pura verdad de las palabras escritas" (the pure truth of written words).[50] Equally archaic, in the context of the late twentieth century, are the utopian visions of liberty and progress that underpinned the nationalist discourses of Argentine Romanticism. And yet, their need has never been felt as much as in the present. An anonymous Argentine exile writes, in the 1970s, "A veces (no es joda) pienso que somos la generación del '37. Perdidos en la diáspora. ¿Quién de nosotros escribirá el *Facundo*?" (sometimes, I'm not kidding, I think we are the Generation of 1837. Lost in the diaspora. Which of us will write *Facundo*?).[51] *Respiración artificial* asks, in a similar way, what kind of utopian thought might be still possible, what projects of national (re)founding might be imagined, in a contemporary era characterized by violence and disillusion, and after the twentieth century's experiences of political utopianism. A significant section of the second part of *Respiración artificial* addresses fascism as the terrible culmination of European rationalism, and literature as its accomplice in forging and justifying an exclusionary politics, a relationship that would seem to destroy the ethical basis of all philosophical and literary projects. The Romantic imbrication of literary praxis and emancipatory politics in Argentina – epitomized by the Generation of 1837 – now appears to be irrevocably sundered.

However, we must read *Respiración artificial*, not simply as an articulation of this crisis, but as a path through it. In Ossorio's suicide note, with which Maggi decides to start his story, a line of direct exhortation to his readers is rendered in a bold font for particular emphasis: **"No se desapasionen porque la pasión es el único vínculo que tenemos con la verdad"** (do not lose your passion because passion is the only link we have with reality).[52] Piglia's novel, far from simply lamenting the lapse of utopianism into disillusion, or experience into parody, is full of characters in pursuit of their passions; with a persistence that matches theirs, *Respiración artificial* searches for ways to represent the *almost* unrepresentable, taking inspiration here from Kafka, who knew better than anyone that "los escritores verdaderamente grandes son aquellos que enfrentan siempre la imposibilidad *casi* absoluta de escribir" (truly great writers are those who always confront the *almost* total impossibility of writing).[53]

Piglia's crucial rhetorical operation is to take the displacements and anachronisms produced by the presence of Romantic tropes and figures in the novel, and to demonstrate – in accordance with Formalist approaches – that it is precisely these decontextualizing and recontextualizing exercises that may provide ways through a political or cultural impasse. In Piglia's conception, thinking historically makes it possible to start to understand the present, through defamiliarizing it:

> Para el Profesor estaba claro que sólo la historia hacía posible esa *ostranenie* de la que hablábamos hace un rato. ¿Cómo podríamos soportar el presente, el horror del presente, me dijo la última noche el Profesor, si no supiéramos que se trata de un presente histórico?[54]
>
> For the Professor it was clear that only history made possible that *ostranenie* we were talking about a while ago. How could we bear the present, the horror of the present, the Professor said to

me that last night, if we didn't know that we are dealing with a historical present?

Piglia borrows the Formalist term *ostranenie* (estrangement, defamiliarization) to express a distance from the present that is indispensable to a greater understanding of it, or even just to the possibility of surviving it. He reclaims the anachronisms and displacements of exile, utopia, and social/cultural marginalization as ideal preconditions for the *ostranenie* that was so central to Formalist and Brechtian approaches. There is repeated reference in the novel to a kind of "mirada histórica" (historical gaze) that is deliberately dislocated from the heat and immediacy of experience in order to better understand the broader patterns of history. This is the approach advocated by Tardewski, and it brings him into line with the Senator's search for continuities in Argentine history. As Tardewski states,

> Hay que evitar la introspección, les recomiendo a mis jóvenes alumnos, y les enseño lo que he denominado *la mirada histórica*. Somos una hoja que boya en ese río y hay que saber mirar lo que viene como si ya hubiera pasado.[55]

> You need to avoid introspection, I tell my young students, and I teach them what I've called the *historical gaze*. We are a leaf floating in that river and we need to know how to see what is coming as if it had already happened.

Understanding the present as a "historical present" in this way is only possible for those characters who take a distanced perspective. Tardewski refers to

> esa forma de mirar afuera, a distancia, en otro lugar y poder así ver la realidad más allá del velo de los hábitos, de las costumbres. Paradójicamente es al mismo tiempo la mirada del turista, pero también, en última instancia, la mirada del filósofo.[56]

that manner of looking outwards, from a distance, in another place, and in that way to be able to see reality beyond the habits and customs that veil it. Paradoxically it is at the same time the gaze of the tourist, but also, in the last instance, the gaze of the philosopher.

In Piglia's fiction more broadly, it is often the outsider, the foreigner who can barely speak the language of his host country, or the madman, who is most capable of lucid thought and clear perception.

The multiple digressions, texts-within-texts, postponements, truncations, and recommencements of *Respiración artificial* are not simply divergences from (or concealments of) the "real story": they subject the novel's events to the oblique, distanced perspective of the "mirada histórica" as defined in the narrative. For Shklovsky, art is the vision that results from "deautomatized perception," and it seeks to defamiliarize its material for the viewer/reader by impeding perception and drawing attention to unusual forms and devices.[57] What is true in our reading of literature is true in our reading of the political present: it is an attention to the *form* of narrative that enables us to see crucial continuities and ruptures that transcend the immediate clamour of content. It is also experimentation with form that permits the refreshing of vision and the creation of new experience. Anachronism and displacement are not expressions of failure in the narrative but the source of new perceptions. To read the novel's epistolary structure (as many critics have done) as evidence of the impossibility of narrating experience, as a series of monologues rather than encounters between characters,[58] is to fail to grasp the positive re-evaluation of this separation in time and space that stems from Piglia's Formalist understanding of the power of *ostranenie* to renew perception.

A Formalist reading of Argentine literature

Piglia's engagement with the approaches adopted by Shklovsky, Tynyanov, and other Formalists is made explicit in *Respiración artificial* and in a number of interviews.[59] For Piglia, Tynyanov's approaches have held – and continue to hold – supreme relevance for debates on literary criticism. "Tinianov es clave" (Tynyanov is key), he claims; his work on literary evolution is nothing less than "el *Discurso del método* de la crítica literaria" (the *Discourse and Method* of literary criticism).[60] Piglia argues that Tynyanov's attempts to understand literature as form, as the history of forms, but also to grasp the relationship between these forms and the non-verbal dimensions of the social, remain highly significant for a series of critical debates and theories, including structuralism, deconstruction, New Historicism, and contemporary discussions on the relationship between politics and literature.[61]

The discussions on Argentine literature in the second half of the novel are thoroughly underpinned by a Formalist understanding of literary evolution as *"un efecto de la lucha de poéticas"* (the product of a battle between opposing poetics):[62] not an organic, natural progression in which each generation bears the influence of the previous generation and reworks this into something new, but a much more complex and conflictual series of lateral moves, throwbacks, literary parricide and unsanctioned alliances, with continuities more likely to be evident in the work of disowned orphans and bastard offspring than of legal inheritors. It is this understanding that allows Piglia's characters to make some distinctly polemical assertions about literary influence: to claim, for example, that narratives written by the highly erudite and cosmopolitan Borges are really sequels to the nineteenth-century nationalist epic *Martín Fierro* in their use of a popular lexicon and the rhythms of oral speech,[63] or – with a brazen disrespect for literary chronology – to posit Arlt as a more modern writer than Borges.[64] Piglia/Renzi's reading of Borges is a recognizably Formalist one, focussed on the exhaustion of particular genres, signalled for the Formalists by parody, and the "refunctioning" of others.[65]

The discussions of literary history and criticism in *Respiración artificial*, devising genealogies and points of rupture between prominent figures such as Lugones, Arlt, and Borges, evidently become a way of approaching national history and the political context. Questions of how the literary establishment deals with linguistic and cultural difference, what is closed off and excluded from the national canon and what is included and given regulatory power over the rest: these cannot fail to resonate with a broader politics of the authoritarian defence of national purity against intruders of a different ideological persuasion and the exclusion of unwanted diversity of political views. Indeed, Piglia's *La ciudad ausente* makes the association abundantly clear, referring to the shared enterprise between Lugones the father (poet) and Lugones the son (chief of police under the Uriburu regime and widely supposed to have been the first to introduce the cattleprod as a method of torture):

> El comisario Lugones dirigió la inteligencia del Estado y realizó y llevó a su culminación la obra de su padre y fue su albacea y el encargado de prologar todas las composiciones poéticas y literarias del poeta, avanzó y profundizó en el espíritu nacional y del mismo modo que su padre escribió la *Oda a los ganados y las mieses*, él usó un instrumento de nuestra ganadería para mejorar el control del Estado sobre los rebeldes y los extranjeros.[66]
>
> Superintendent Lugones headed up state intelligence and he put into practice his father's work and brought it to fulfillment, and he was his executor and the one in charge of writing prefaces to all the poet's literary compositions, he progressed and went deeper into the national spirit and, in the same way that his father wrote *Ode to the Cattle and the Grain*, he used an instrument from cattle-ranching to heighten state control over rebels and foreigners.

Piglia reverses here the conventional relationship of priority established between literature and history by sociological criticism, according to which shifts in literary form may be explained according to "external" social changes. He suggests instead that it is literary form (the purity to which Lugones the father aspired) that shaped social change (the intolerance of political difference that motivated Lugones the son).

A Formalist emphasis on the evolution of literary style as an effect of an *internal* dialectic within Argentine literature allows Piglia to avoid producing a simplistic social reading of these texts, according to which writers might be understood as reflecting or reacting against dominant ideas in society on nationhood, immigration, or modernization. Renzi's analysis does not centre principally on how writers have engaged with the "external" events of Argentine politics but how their texts can be understood as a series of readings of other texts, often revealing surprising alliances or divergences that militate against established narratives of Argentine literary history. This focus alone should warn us against the folly of reading *Respiración artificial* as a "dictatorship novel" with a primarily external referent in the form of military violence and persecution. Instead, I would contend, the text is much more accurately understood as a conscious intervention in another battleground – Argentine literature – and a reflexive exploration of the nature of literary evolution.

It is the Formalist understanding of literary evolution as a series of truncations and oblique connections that links the discussions of the second half of the novel to the ostensible plot concerning the relationship between Renzi and Maggi and the literary-historical pursuits of both. Roberto Echavarren is among a number of critics who have signalled the significance of the disruption to father-son relationships in *Respiración artificial*. These are replaced by relationships such as those of uncle/nephew (Maggi-Renzi), grandfather/grandson (Enrique Ossorio-Luciano Ossorio) and father-in-law/son-in-law (Luciano Ossorio-Maggi), relationships that – as Echavarren observes – follow an oblique family line, skip a generation or are founded on association rather than bloodlines.[67] For Echavarren, the two halves of the novel contrast with each other: the first recounts an investigation, the second abandons it; the first is structured around letters, the second, dialogue; the first tells a fictitious story, the second explores real history;[68] the first is concerned with "literariedad" (literariness) and the second with "no literariedad" (non-literariness).[69] Although he notes a shared interest in both halves in "una preocupación con la tradición literaria y su capacidad de iluminar un proceso histórico" (a concern with literary tradition and its capacity to illuminate a historical process),[70] this vital link remains undeveloped in his reading of the text. This may be because he does not relate the lateral and dislocated family lines he observes to a statement made within the text of *Respiración artificial* itself on this oblique form of lineage as one that best demonstrates the workings of literary influence: "Alguien, un crítico ruso, el crítico ruso Iuri Tinianov, afirma que la literatura evoluciona de tío a sobrino (y no de padres a hijos)" (someone, a Russian critic, the Russian critic Jury Tynyanov, asserts that literature evolves from uncle to nephew, and not from parents to children).[71] It was Shklovsky, in fact – although similar phrases are to be found in a number of Formalist essays – who in an oft-quoted formulation declared that in the liquidation of one literary school by another, the inheritance is passed down, not from father to son, but from uncle to nephew.[72]

The dramatic reversals in familial rifts and allegiances that Renzi writes about in his novel (the story of his uncle and his cabaret-dancer lover) mirror a similar story on the national level of collusion, betrayal, exploitation, and exile (Rosas and Ossorio). Both Maggi's family drama and Ossorio's political career are marked by radical change and reversals of fortune: the sudden ascendancy to power and the equally swift exile or imprisonment of those falling out of favour, and momentary or unexpected allegiances and betrayals. That these themes – family resemblances, the truncation of certain lines of influence and the reappropriation of alternative ones, disinheritance, literary-critical disputes – are also the central motifs of the novel's discussions of Argentine literature allows us to reverse the usual approach taken in analyzing the novel. It is not the "real" story that is postponed or concealed by *Respiración artificial*'s experiments with narrative form; it is those experiments with form that open up possible readings of the novel within its precise social context. Many of the novel's characters are forced to forge relationships with uncles or grandfathers because their biological fathers came to an early violent end or were exiled. The profound sense of orphanhood, fractured communities, and a crisis of succession that were the intellectual legacy of the Argentine dictatorship becomes an extreme case of the need for the kind of literary renovation theorized by the Formalists. The oblique passage of literary inheritance from uncle to son therefore becomes the key to the survival of a whole generation of intellectuals and artists persecuted by the military regime. Formalist theory maintains that where one artistic line is exhausted or truncated, another will emerge, moving in from the margins, forging new alliances or revitalizing forms from the past: a message of hope and survival in the context of the decimation of Argentina's literary and intellectual community through imprisonment, death, and exile.

The conscious reworking of filiations and genealogies to construct new (and often surprising) lines of descent or dissent has been a dominant theme in contemporary Argentine literature and literary criticism. Indeed, Edgardo Berg observes that "el motivo de linaje ocupa un lugar central" (the lineage motif occupies a central place) throughout the history of Argentine literature, in which "La búsqueda y construcción de genealogías o filiaciones de procedencia arman cierta cadena de textos" (whole series of texts are assembled from the search for, and construction of, genealogies and lines of descent).[73] Marta Morello-Frosch finds this tendency to be much heightened in the work of contemporary writers, who have revisited and revised the literary history of the nation as part of their own textual projects, giving rise to "a radically original reading of the dialectics of a national culture." As she argues, with clear relevance for the argument I am pursuing in relation to *Respiración artificial*,

> This confrontation and rapprochement of seemingly estranged literary programs form the basis of a recent literary consciousness in Argentina. Through these strategies of reappraisal, the continuity of national literary heritage is assured especially at a time when cultural process is threatened by state intervention or historical stagnation.[74]

The pursuit of anachronism in *Respiración artificial*, as well as providing a distanced historical perspective, therefore also acts in the manner described by the Formalists to renew literature by looping back to find alternative influences, to mix lineages and create complex literary genealogies. In his anachronistic choice of an epistolary form, Ossorio deliberately chooses not to read the writers of his own time but searches for inspiration "en libros pasados de moda" (in old-fashioned books).[75] His reading list contains a mixture of Enlightenment satirists and Romantic non-conformists; many of the works mentioned are epistolary works and/or utopian novels. Recycling material and forms from the past leads not to empty parody but to renewal through the creative interplay between similarity and dissimilarity. Tardewski experiences this power when, quite by chance, he comes across a footnote in a critical edition of *Mein Kampf* that allows him to postulate a vision-changing encounter between Kafka and Hitler:

> Al leer esa pequeña nota al pie se produjo una instantánea conexión, lo único parecido a eso que los científicos y los filósofos suelen experimentar, o al menos describir con alguna frecuencia y que llaman un *descubrimiento*: la inesperada asociación de dos hechos aislados, de dos ideas que, al unirse, producen algo nuevo.[76]

> Reading that little footnote sparked off an instant connection, similar to that usually experienced by scientists and philosophers, or at least that which they often describe and that they call a *discovery*: the unexpected association of two isolated events, of two ideas that, in coming together, produce something new.

The sense of both history and literature as archives full of intriguing footnotes and marginalia simply waiting to be (re)discovered, the sense of the infinite and meaningful trajectories that just one individual might construct as he moves from one dusty edition to another, or of the impact such chance connections might have on our whole understanding of the events of history: this is the potential Piglia sees in the oblique uses of the past that underpin Formalist notions of literary creativity and evolution.

A Formalist reading of Argentine history

In his first letter to Renzi, Maggi tells him that "La historia es el único lugar donde consigo aliviarme de esta pesadilla de la que trato de despertar" (history is the only place where I am able to escape from that nightmare from which I am trying to awake).[77] The citation is often referenced by critics of the novel to support a reading of the novel as a staged covering-up of the real story. In Joyce's *Ulysses*, Stephen Dedalus states that *history* is a nightmare from which he is trying to awake; Maggi's suggestion that history provides the only *refuge* therefore places the nightmare firmly in the present. The novel as a whole, then, in focussing on the historical person of Ossorio, might be read as taking refuge in history in order to escape from the nightmare of present Argentine reality, as that which exceeds the possibility of narration. Piglia himself concurs in part with this interpretation but suggests a very different conclusion:

> la pesadilla, sin duda, está en el presente, en 1976. Y la historia es el lugar en el que se ve que las cosas pueden cambiar y transformarse. En momentos en que parece que nada cambia, que todo está clausurado y la pesadilla del presente parece eterna, la historia, dice Maggi, prueba que hubo otras situaciones iguales, clausuradas, en las que se terminó por encontrar una salida.[78]

> the nightmare, of course, is in the present, in 1976. And history is the place where we can see that things can change and transform themselves. At moments when it seems that nothing changes, that everything is closed off and the nightmare of the present stretches out into eternity, history, says Maggi, proves that there were other situations the same, closed off, in which a way out was eventually found.

This is a crucial articulation of the visionary (textual) politics of *Respiración artificial*. History is not a "refuge" in the sense that it allows us respite or an escape from the present. It is a source of hope in the form of alternative visions that would revitalize the present and open up the possibility of thinking about the future at a time when utopian projects have ground to a halt and even simple survival is far from guaranteed. The Rosas regime is not primarily brought into *Respiración artificial* as an allegory for a more recent dictatorship, in order to circumvent censorship by speaking more obliquely about the experience of oppression and exile; rather, the novel enacts a conscious return in time to another crisis in history that shares some characteristics with the present one, in order to mine it for alternative directions and to rescue the present from stagnation. There is more than an echo here of the Formalist notion of regeneration through a return to "submerged" lines.[79] Oddly enough, perhaps, it is in history that we can see the possibility of change and transformation, in contrast to the impasse in which the present finds itself. As Piglia states, "la historia es la proliferación retrospectiva de los mundos posibles" (history is the retrospective proliferation of possible worlds).[80] Art has a unique role to play in reviving those possible worlds and creating new experiences. As Shklovsky claims, "Only the creation of new forms of art can restore to a man sensation of the world, can resurrect things and kill pessimism."[81]

What are the effects of using the tools of (Formalist) literary criticism to analyze the events of history, as the novel seems to exhort us to do? Firstly, it encourages a focus on the *forms* that underlie political discourse – unexpected continuities that connect utopian nationalist projects to the dystopian police state, for example – rather than the immediate content. Political power, Piglia insists, is exercised through the act of narration;[82] he calls us not to focus solely on the content of the state's fictions but their form. To uncover this, it is perhaps literature that provides us with "los instrumentos y los modos de captar la forma en que se construyen y actúan las narraciones que vienen del poder" (tools and modes of capturing the form in which narratives of power are constructed and operate).[83]

Secondly, the vision of history constructed becomes an essentially anti-Romantic one in its relative disregard for the agency of individual human actors. Piglia's characters are engaged instead in a sustained quest to discover the immanent laws that transcend history and link together a diversity of events (and texts). The Senator feels near to discovering

> una línea de continuidad, una especie de voz que viene desde la Colonia y el que la escuche, ése, el que la escuche y la descifre, podrá convertir este caos en un cristal traslúcido. Por otro lado hay algo que he comprendido: *eso*, digamos: la línea de continuidad, la razón que explica este desorden que tiene más de cien años [...].[84]

a line of continuity, a kind of voice that comes from colonial times and whoever listens to it, yes, he who listens to it and deciphers it, may transform this chaos into a translucent crystal. On the other hand there is something I have understood: *that*, shall we say: the line of continuity, the reason that explains this disorder that has lasted more than a hundred years [...].

To apply Formalist logic to history in this way is to remove the individual motivation from particular episodes and to search for immanent patterns that might account for the ascendancy of particular forms and functions in the dialectical struggle that underlies history as well as literature. In the Senator's vision, history becomes a "gran máquina poliédrica" (great polyhedral machine) and a "fábrica de sentido" (factory of meaning);[85] only those able to remove themselves from the swings of fortune and the immediacy of personal experience may even glimpse something of its workings. Piglia constructs a vision of history that is not the cumulative sum of the works of great men, heroes or villains, but the turning of a vast machine that transcends the individual and that governs the repetition of forms within a series of cycles. This idea, as we will see in chapters to come, becomes central to the formal experiments of *Prisión perpetua* and *La ciudad ausente*.

History and the science of chaos and turbulence

Piglia's Formalist approach to history in *Respiración artificial* bears some resemblance to Michel Serres's topological approach to time and history. Time, for Serres, is a crumpled handkerchief, pulling into proximity points that had seemed distant;[86] it does not flow in a linear fashion, but through "stopping points, ruptures, deep wells, chimneys of thunderous acceleration, rendings, gaps."[87] Serres replaces "naïve," linear conceptions of history – too simplistic to account for "a formidable complexity, for the strongest multiplicities, for what we rightly call history"[88] – with a polytemporal model borrowed from the physics of chaotic systems, principally turbulence. The complex interaction in turbulent flows of multiple eddies at various scales eludes simple, deterministic analysis. In a similar way, Serres insists that what we refer to as history combines different times, including "the irreversible, that of entropy, the fall towards disorder; that, on the other hand, which goes against the current, that of negentropy; the reversible, that of clocks, of the solar system, of our dating, that we have so long taken for that of history."[89] It is this approach to history that allows Serres to place the Roman poet and philosopher Lucretius "in the same neighborhood" as modern theories of turbulence, despite the distance that appears to separate them in time.[90] This non-linear understanding of historical relationships also, as we have seen, enables Piglia to construct unexpected genealogies that show little respect for chronological succession.

As we have seen, the Senator in *Respiración artificial* searches for "una línea de continuidad" (a line of continuity) that might convert the chaos and disorder of more than one hundred years of Argentine history into something more legible.[91] Serres claims to have glimpsed something similar beneath the apparent disorder of history, a "quasi-invariant of very great duration."[92] There is a striking resemblance in the language of fluidity and crystallization used by both Piglia and Serres to express something of the complexity of historical time, which "passes and doesn't pass;"[93] both writers have recourse to geological metaphors to describe this slower-moving constant. Serres imagines a tectonic plate that advances imperceptibly but causes drastic changes in the "tormented, complicated" visible landscape above.[94] The Senator pictures ice floes to express a very similar idea. As if he were a bird flying high, he sees:

> abajo, en las planicies heladas, a la izquierda, casi sobre las últimas estribaciones montañosas, lejos del mundo, de su tumulto, lejos de su lúgubre claridad, hay grandes masas, grandes masas que parecen petrificadas pero que *sin embargo* se deslizan, se mueven, a pesar del reflujo, avanzan, crujen al deslizarse, como los grandes témpanos de hielo.[95]

> below, in the frozen plains, to the left, towards the last foothills of the mountains, far from the world, from its tumult, far from

its lugubrious light, there are great masses, great masses that seem petrified but *nevertheless* glide, move, in spite of the ebbing tides, advance, creaking as they glide, like great ice floes.

The higher he flies, the more clearly visible those movements become, but they cannot be grasped from a single perspective. He hopes – knowing in advance that he will fail – somehow to express in words "la cualidad múltiple de esa Idea, de esa concepción que viene desde el fondo mismo de la historia, de esa voz [...] múltiple que viene del pasado y que es tan difícil de captar para un hombre que está solo" (the multiple nature of that Idea, of that conception that comes from the very depths of history, of that multiple voice that comes from the past and is so difficult for one man alone to capture).[96]

If history, in Serres's vision, is "aleatory and stochastic," arising from "background noise," this does not mean that it is disordered, but that the relationship between cause and effect is not linear, and that confluences, systems, and orders emerge in the complex ways that have been described in theories of chaos and emergence. The task of history is "The recognition and description of these emergences."[97] Crucially, history is not the imposition of order on a chaotic world but the emergence of order from within the chaos. The Senator knows how urgent it is that we learn how to perceive this kind of order, to understand what emerges from Argentine history as "a la vez único y múltiple" (at the same time unique and multiple) and to decipher those deeper movements that will shape the future.[98] As Steven Connor suggests, Serres's preference for topological to linear time may be attributed to the fact that the latter is "founded on and sustained by violence [...] formed out of the monotonous rhythm of argument, contradiction and murder."[99] This linear world of "endless conflicts, upheavals and usurpations" – Hegelian, as Connor notes – is very much the world bequeathed to the present by the nineteenth century in *Respiración artificial*, in which Piglia also observes that "los gentleman argentinos eran, sin saberlo, hegelianos" (the Argentine nobles were Hegelian without knowing it) in their eagerness to kill each other in the name of honour and power.[100] The illusion of breaking with the past leads only to stasis for Serres; instead, a topological approach to history leads to greater peace and the potential for creativity. In Connor's words,

> Innovation springs, not from attempting to separate oneself from history, but from maintaining the possibility of rereading historical continuities, of revisiting the uncompleted past and being revisited by it, with new mutations of understanding emerging as the result.[101]

If the (Hegelian) line that Piglia sees extending from history into the future is one of "Asesinatos, masacres, guerras fratricidas" (assassinations, massacres, fratricidal wars),[102] then revisiting the past, perceiving its continual foldings into the present and the future, may also allow new perspectives and alternative ideas to emerge.

Formalism, testimonialism, and the utopian function of literature

At the risk of passing with too much haste over the abyss that divides chaos theory from Russian Formalism, the vision of history developed in Piglia's *Respiración artificial* does, I think, permit the cautious suggestion of one or two points of conceptual affinity. Both methods look for the emergence of order and discernible change at a level far higher that of the individual and aim to theorize the complex interactions between different systems. Eichenbaum, Shklovsky, and Tynyanov were among the Formalists who made the most serious attempt to understand the relationship between systemic change in literature and in other social or economic systems. If they rejected the sociological or biographical modes of literary criticism inherited from the nineteenth century, this was not because they considered social, political, or economic spheres to have no relevance for the evolution of literature but because they approached such relationships as complex and non-linear rather than ones of simple causality. It is in this spirit that Tynyanov denounced as "particularly fruitless" the "direct study of the author's psychology and the construction of a causal 'bridge' from the author's environment, daily life, and class to his works."[103]

Piglia's choice of a Formalist framework, with its emphasis on the internal evolution of literary form, might seem extraordinary during the 1970s in Argentina, when the impact of political events on literary and artistic culture, and on the individual lives of writers and intellectuals, was so clearly in evidence. Piglia's interest in Formalism is filtered, as he himself explains, through Brecht's considerable influence on left-wing aesthetic production in Latin America during the 1960s. In the experience of the Soviet avant-garde, in Russian Formalism – and especially Tynyanov's critical oeuvre – and in Eisenstein's cinema, a generation of Latin American writers and artists found the potential for a relationship between left-wing ideology and artistic production that was not fettered to realism.[104] Tracing Piglia's acknowledged debt to Formalist approaches allows us to perceive more clearly the critique of testimonialism implicit in his work. In the prominence given to politics in Argentina of the 1970s and early 1980s, literature risks being reduced to the status of a historical document, a political manifesto or a vehicle for personal testimony; in this context, we might view Piglia as returning to the terms of another battle, waged by the Russian Formalists in the 1920s, to "rescue" literature from a similar fate of psychologism and to assert its autonomy from other spheres.

It would be difficult to overstate the radical difference between the distanced, external, historicizing perspective advocated by Piglia, on the one hand, and, on the other, the emphasis on the immediate, the experiential, and the personal in the testimonial narratives that gained prominence in the 1970s and 1980s. For Piglia, it is clearly the position of exile rather than direct experience that allows for a greater understanding of the present. In his writing on Ossorio, Maggi explains to Renzi that he tries to remain faithful to the facts but at the same time he wants to "hacer ver el carácter ejemplar de la vida de esa especie de Rimbaud que se alejó de las avenidas de la historia para mejor testimoniarla" (reveal the exemplary nature of the life of that Rimbaud-like figure who withdrew from the avenues of history, all the better to bear witness to it).[105] Renzi admires Maggi's own commitment to such rigorous thought, mistrusting the clichés and conditioned reflexes of immediate responses. As he insists, "Hay que pensar en contra de sí mismo y vivir en tercera persona" (one has to think against oneself and live in the third person).[106] Indeed, *Respiración artificial* could be read as an exercise in thinking in the third person, with each narrative voice mediated through others in chains of dizzying length. Throughout the narrative, repeated phrases such as "dice Tardewski" (Tardewski says) and "me dijo la mujer" (the woman told me) build into extraordinarily precise formations such as "me dijo la mujer, cuenta Tardewski que le dijo Marconi" (the woman told me, Tardewski says that Marconi had told him).[107] The reductions, recyclings and redirections that result have nothing to do with the "truth" of immediacy and direct, first-person experience that govern the textuality of testimonialism.

In this sense, Piglia's novel may be read as an intervention into an ongoing discussion with Rodolfo Walsh on the possible forms of political literature in a post-Auschwitz era. Both before and after Walsh's death at the hands of the military in 1977, Piglia has paid sincere homage to his work, which represents for him "uno de los grandes momentos de la literatura argentina contemporánea" (one of the great moments in contemporary Argentine literature).[108] Piglia's own literary project, however, in many ways presents a counterpoint to that of Walsh. In a famous interview published for the first time in 1970, Walsh outlines to Piglia his decision to reject fiction in favour of journalistic modes of investigation and denunciation, as "la denuncia traducida al arte de la novela se vuelve inofensiva, no molesta para nada, es decir, se sacraliza como arte" (denunciation translated into the art of the novel becomes inoffensive, it doesn't upset anyone, that is to say, it takes on the sacred nature of art).[109] If the novel once played an important subversive role, it is now no longer operating in this way, although Walsh clearly leaves open the possibility that it might recover such a role: "tienen que existir muchas maneras de que vuelva a desempeñarlo" (there have to be many ways in which it could take it on again).[110]

Piglia takes up the challenge of finding just such a way. As Laura Demaría observes, if Walsh (according to Piglia's analysis) takes up a line of Argentine literature that began with Sarmiento's *Facundo* – in which fiction and politics appear antagonistic – then Piglia's response is to take forward an alternative line, to continue the work of another literary forebear, Macedonio Fernández.[111] In Macedonio's vision, fiction enters into a new relationship with politics. As "la antítesis de Sarmiento" (the antithesis of Sarmiento),

Macedonio overturns all his assumptions: as Piglia asserts, "Une política y ficción, no las enfrenta como dos prácticas irreductibles. La novela mantiene relaciones cifradas con las maquinaciones del poder, las reproduce, usa sus formas, construye su contrafigura utópica" (he unites politics and fiction, he doesn't oppose them as if they were two irreducible practices. The novel maintains encoded links with the machinations of power, it reproduces them, uses their forms, constructs a utopian counterfigure to them).[112] In Piglia's hands, we see something of the potential in fiction to mimic, distort, and reveal the *forms* of political power in this manner. In a characteristically reflexive move, the novel becomes, firstly, an exercise in Formalist-style critique in its attempt to uncover the forms and the broader dynamics that govern politics and history in Argentina, transcending individual events and articulations; and, secondly, a means of intervening in those spheres by constructing a "utopian counterfigure" to them.

Anachronism, displacement, defamiliarization, refunctioning: these may be the techniques by which literature continually renews itself according to Formalist analysis, but they are also, for Piglia, literature's most effective tools of political intervention:

> la literatura está siempre fuera de contexto y siempre es inactual; dice lo que no es, lo que ha sido borrado; trabaja con lo que está por venir. Funciona como el reverso puro de la lógica de la *Realpolitik*. La intervención política de un escritor se define antes que nada en la confrontación con estos usos oficiales del lenguaje.[113]

> literature is always out of context and anachronistic; it says what is not, what has been erased; it works with what is yet to come. It functions as the complete opposite of *Realpolitik* logic. A writer's political intervention is based more than anything on a conflict with those official uses of language.

Piglia's thinking is very much aligned here with Ernst Bloch's understanding of the utopian function of literature and art: its anticipatory illumination of unfulfilled desires. For Piglia, as for Bloch, literature takes place in the "not yet" and cannot therefore be dismissed in a traditional Marxist manner as engendering the false consciousness of ideology. As Douglas Kellner explains, Bloch understood ideology to contain "errors, mystifications, and techniques of manipulation and domination," but also "a utopian residue or surplus that can be used for social critique and to advance progressive politics."[114] In Bloch's words, "the blossoms of art, science, philosophy, always denote something more than the false consciousness which each society, bound to its position, had of itself and used for its own embellishment."[115] Piglia follows Bloch in finding in history a repository of potential alternatives for the future, and in literature a wealth of "imaginative ideas" that do not merely describe the world around "but extend, in an anticipating way, existing material into the future possibilities of being different and better."[116] Literature works with those potential, latent possibilities, and the past is its source of creativity.

Stephen Eric Bronner summarizes the importance of the past in Bloch's work in ways that reveal a shared conception of the non-linear operations of artistic renewal that – as we have seen – form the central tenet of Piglia's theory and literary praxis:

> Realizing the utopian *Novum* in the future depends upon tapping the potential from the past. And this, in turn, is dependent upon the degree of consciousness generated in the present. The future is thus no mechanical elaboration of the present; nor does it emerge from a series of "steps" or "stages" deriving in linear fashion from the past. The future is open; determining the "horizon" of the present is possible only through unearthing the "anticipatory consciousness" embodied in the cultural achievements of the past.[117]

The multiple, overlapping time-frames of *Respiración artificial* allow us to glimpse a similar vision of history in which the utopian potential of literature can be released, in the perception and construction of proximities and rifts that defy linear organization. The novel's partial setting in other times is not primarily an attempt to evade censorship or to conceal, through allegory, its "real" story: it is instead a performative act, constructing new (non-linear) genealogies in the pursuit of literary and cultural renewal. The understanding forged in Piglia's first novel of history and literature as non-linear, operating in multiple temporalities, together with the utopian dimension of literature, become constants in his fiction and critical essays. Chapter 2 will discuss in more depth Piglia's experimentation with concepts of chance and complexity, together with his construction of literature as a laboratory of the future, with primary reference to the narratives published in the *Prisión perpetua* collection. It is in *La ciudad ausente* (the focus of Chapter 4, together with *Nocturno blanco*) that Piglia gives fullest development to the depersonalized, displaced and distanced perspective advocated in *Respiración artificial*, exploring a series of associations between the text and the machine to emphasize the importance of artificial, anonymized experience in the survival and regeneration of literature.

2 | Allegories of Reading in an Age of Immanence and Uncertainty

The insistent presence of detectives in fiction by Martínez, Cohen, and Piglia serves, as in much postmodern literature, to highlight epistemological uncertainty. The provisional, mistaken, or derailed conclusions of criminal investigations become analogies for a broader failure to read and interpret a tumult of signs in the cultural, social, and material world around us. These authors part company with many postmodern theorists and writers, however, as the failed operations of human logic and the unattainability of transcendent forms of knowledge do not give rise here to epistemological skepticism. Instead, they clear the way for the development of new ways of understanding how patterns may emerge from seeming chaos and how texts may generate meaning and meaningful experience.

In this chapter, I focus on the use of mathematical and scientific theories and models to construct allegories of reading in Martínez's *Crímenes imperceptibles* (2003), Cohen's *El testamento de O'Jaral* (1995), and a series of short stories and essays by Piglia, mostly drawn from the *Prisión perpetua* collection (1988). References to chance, chaos theory, Gödel's incompleteness theorems, and Heisenberg's uncertainty principle abound in these texts, employed in part to express a suspicion of metanarratives and to point to the limits of human reasoning. However, in Piglia and Cohen these theories are not primarily placed at the service of postmodern skepticism but of more utopian visions of the unending self-renewal of literary forms. The failed quest for metalanguages here does not signal the end of epistemology but the potential for new (less transcendent) approaches to knowledge and for new theories of becoming rather than being. If, for Martínez, we are led away from the truth by a simplistic and over-hasty logic that constantly invents meaning when we read, for Cohen no such transcendent truth exists: the act of interpretation blinds us to the immanent nature of the world. It is in Piglia's work that we find a fully developed theory of reading, not just as an exercise that constructs meaning for past experience, but as a form of (future) experience. This theory gives rise to a resignification of science-fiction topoi (virtual reality, psychic transference, memory implantation, and the multiverse) as tropes for the act of reading. If narrating is the art of implanting memories in the reader that can be more vivid than direct experience itself, then the implantation of artificial memories may take on a positive connotation, associated here with the creative work of literature.

SERIAL POLYSEMIA: CRIMES OF LOGIC / MARTÍNEZ

> Truth is a kind of error without which a certain species of life could not live.—Friedrich Nietzsche[1]

While Piglia and Cohen – as we will see – point away from notions of transcendence in questions of truth and literary interpretation, Martínez leaves the principles of scientific rationalism intact: objective truth does exist, although (following Nietzsche) he demonstrates again and again in his fiction our choice to make decisions based on emotion rather than logic. It is not science that has failed us, but we who have failed science, on two counts: by applying its insights with insufficient rigour, or in the wrong context. The tragedies of Martínez's novels are often tied to his characters' deficient grasp of the mathematical basis of chance and probability: their misinterpretations of events lead to fatal mistakes of judgment.

Martínez chose to set his detective thriller *Crímenes imperceptibles* in Oxford rather than Buenos Aires to bolster the sense of enigma: in Argentina, he explains, if a crime remains unsolved, everyone would immediately guess it was the police officer.[2] The city becomes the scene of a sequence of deaths, each accompanied by the release of a mathematical symbol, which together appear to form a series. A world-famous British professor of logic and an Argentine mathematics postdoc join forces to solve the series and by that means to discover the identity of the killer.

The novel traces similarities between the methods and "aesthetics" of mathematics and those of criminology in order to question the human capacity for logical thought and the limits of logic itself. It testifies to our propensity to search for patterns, analogies, and metaphors and to use them, inaccurately and even dangerously, to shape our understanding of the world. This tendency is also what allows the writer – like the criminal or the magician – to distract the reader with a false story and to surprise him with a final revelation of the real one, which has been developed, undetected, alongside it. Martínez proposes a reworking of the detective genre – in part following lines established by Borges and Piglia – that neither rests on the irrefutable logic of the detective's reasoning (as in the traditional version) nor abandons intellectual resolutions to insist on the intractability of social problems (as in the hard-boiled variant). Instead, it returns to questions of logic, but with the aim of demonstrating the gap between truth and proof, in crime just as in mathematics, and to suggest that our use of logic is guided more by aesthetic principles than by scientific rigour. And yet, as *Crímenes imperceptibles* makes clear, it is our imperfect reasoning that provides the necessary condition for the storyteller's artistry: Martínez turns an account of the flawed logic of the reader into a celebration of the creative intelligence of the writer.

Gödel's incompleteness theorems: the gap between truth and proof

The novel's protagonist is a fictional mathematician, Arthur Seldom, made famous for his work on the philosophical ramifications of Gödel's theorems of the 1930s. Martínez draws on Gödel's incompleteness theorems to suggest that the distinction between what is true and what can be proved in mathematics is analogous to that which governs criminal investigations. The distinction between the true and the demonstrable, Seldom explains, is a common phenomenon in justice: there *is* a truth – someone committed the murder – but it cannot always be ascertained beyond doubt by studying the evidence and drawing logical conclusions. Just as it is not within the scope of axiomatic methods to demonstrate the validity of all mathematical truths, the truth of a crime may also be "undecidable" in this sense of remaining beyond proof.[3]

From an early stage, then, we are warned – in a divergence from the conventions of the traditional detective genre – that there may not be a coincidence between truth and logical proof. The mathematicians of *Crímenes imperceptibles* send themselves and the police on an elaborate wild-goose chase to solve the puzzle of a series of symbols sent to them each time the serial killer appears to strike again. As in Borges's "La muerte y la brújula" – of which Martínez's novel is a conscious reworking – the mysterious symbols are eventually discovered to be a clever smokescreen, veiling the real crime by stringing it together with other murders that are really simulated or the product of chance. Again as in "La muerte y la brújula," the solution to the enigma – here, the series of symbols is linked to an ancient Pythagorean cult – does not provide the solution to the crime: it does not reveal the identity of the murderer and has nothing to say about the human emotions of love and revenge that motivate the crime or its concealment. Caught up in mathematical speculation, the characters seem momentarily to forget that the symbols are "solamente dibujos, líneas sobre el papel" (only drawings, lines on paper)[4] and are blinded to the rather less tidy human context of the crimes.

The abstract symbols and logical sequences of *Crímenes imperceptibles* fail to account for the unpredictability of chance encounters and the irrational allegiances that might compel one man to kill in order to protect his daughter and another to cover up a murder for exactly the same reason. In an inversion of the Platonic worldview, according to which the everyday world is an imperfect approximation of an unchanging reality, we are led to understand that the logical consistency of axiomatic reasoning can only imperfectly approximate the messy reality of everyday experience. This disjuncture is heightened by Martínez's ironic choice of the series of symbols, given the Pythagorean belief that the cosmos is structured by numbers and that the contemplation of these is the route to understanding the universe. The *tetraktys*, the last symbol in the series, held a special significance as it combines the first four numbers to produce the number ten: it was therefore synonymous with divine wisdom and associated with the oracle. In Martínez's novel, however, symbols and numbers manifestly fail to reveal much of any importance about reality or the future acts of the supposed serial killer.

Nietzsche on logic, and the "aesthetics" of reason

The creator of the series relies on the fact that, like Borges's Lönnrot, the narrator, the police and the press will be seduced by the possibility of an intellectually coherent solution rather than one in which chance and unruly passions play a large part. *Crímenes imperceptibles* becomes a reflection on how the "aesthetics" of reason affects our formulation of ideas. Martínez makes repeated reference in his fiction to our propensity to believe simple, neat theories, even if they are preposterous from a rational or empirical perspective. We prefer, Seldom claims, "una estética de simplicidad y elegancia que guía también la formulación de conjeturas" (a simple and elegant aesthetic that also shapes how we formulate conjectures).[5] Martínez's first novel, *Acerca de Roderer* (1992), had drawn on Nietzsche's description in *The Gay Science* of the development of human logic as the consequence of a long series of simplifications, necessary for survival but essentially illogical. These rest, according to Nietzsche, on a powerful inclination "to deal with the similar as the equal," in order to be able quickly to categorize different animals as food sources or dangerous. Over a long period,

> the beings not seeing correctly had an advantage over those who saw everything "in flux." In itself every high degree of circumspection in conclusions, every sceptical inclination, is a great danger to life. No living being might have been preserved unless the contrary inclination – to affirm rather than suspend judgment, to mistake and fabricate rather than wait, to assent rather than deny, to decide rather than be in the right – had been cultivated with extraordinary assiduity.[6]

Like Nietzsche, Martínez's protagonist suspects that logic, given its inclination to "tratar las cosas parecidas como si fueran iguales, a desestimar lo cambiante y lo transitorio, a suprimir las fluctuaciones" (treat similar things as if they were the same, to underestimate the changing and the transitory, to suppress fluctuations) is nothing more than "un antiguo malentendido que el sopor de la costumbre no nos deja ver" (an age-old misunderstanding that the torpor of habit does not allow us to see).[7]

Martínez's fiction often reveals the extent to which our apparently coherent beliefs and actions are not grounded in rationalism at all but in superstition and self-protection. We are unable to apply a properly scientific approach to understanding events that affect us. In a more recent novel, *La muerte lenta de Luciana B.* (2007), the narrator is chastised for thinking that a series of apparently connected deaths must be linked, as they present too great a set of coincidences. Kloster, his literary nemesis, ridicules him for having written a book entirely dedicated to chance (with the title *Los aleatorios*) but never having taken the trouble to toss a coin and to discover that "el azar también tiene sus formas y sus rachas" (chance also has its forms and phases).[8] Later, in a bar, he tosses a coin and is alarmed to discover the length of many of the strings of repeated heads or tails: "Aún la ciega moneda parecía tener nostalgia de repetición, de forma, de figura" (even the blind coin seemed to feel a nostalgia for repetition, form, shape).[9] Chance is not the same as disorder: it sometimes produces, at random, surprising moments of apparent order or symmetry. A misunderstanding of chance as synonymous with an absence of order or patternings affects the characters' ability to read events correctly and leads in the novel to further tragedy.

Likewise, in *Crímenes imperceptibles*, it is a misuse of mathematical logic to account for the world of human behaviour that directly leads in the novel to suffering and death that might otherwise have been avoided. Seldom explains that his love for mathematics in part stems from the comfort of knowing that a conjecture made in the abstract world of numbers and symbols has no lasting consequences: it can simply be erased. In contrast,

> cuando usted plantea hipótesis sobre el mundo real introduce, sin poder evitarlo, un elemento de actividad irreversible que nunca deja de tener consecuencias. Cuando mira en una dirección deja de mirar en las demás, cuando persigue un camino posible, lo persigue en un tiempo real y luego puede ser tarde para intentar cualquier otro.[10]

> when you create a hypothesis about the real world you introduce, without being able to prevent it, an element of irreversible action that will always have consequences. When you look in one direction you stop looking in the others; when you pursue one possible path, you pursue it in real time and then it can be too late to try another.

In practice, even mathematical conjectures may produce irreversible consequences in the "real" world. When Seldom publishes in a newspaper his hypothesis about the logical series of symbols, this act of conjecture gives the perpetrator of the final murders an alibi, resulting in the death of ten schoolchildren. Left to remain within the bounds of its own discipline, mathematics may be a harmless and abstract intellectual exercise; wrenched out of context in order to explain a world of flesh and blood, it may lead to catastrophic consequences.

The bloody penetration of theory into reality: Martínez readily acknowledges yet another echo here of "La muerte y la brújula."[11] Indeed, it is this idea, more than any other, that embeds his work most convincingly within the broader Argentine cultural context. He himself suggests that his work is shaped by a conviction stemming from a particular national experience of persecution and militancy: "la convicción de que las ideas no son enunciados abstractos o figuritas intercambiables, sino que tienen su áspera terrenalidad y piden cuentas" (the conviction that ideas are not abstract enunciations or collectible toy figures, but have their own rugged earthiness and call us to account).[12] For Martínez as for Borges, the latter writing in 1942, our philosophies may be arcane or abstract but they may also be highly dangerous.

Towards a new iteration of the detective novel

Thus far, *Crímenes imperceptibles* may seem to offer little more than a rehash of "La muerte y la brújula," with the unexpected twist that we assume Seldom to be a dispassionate analyst of the sequence of symbols, and at risk (like Borges's Lönnrot) of being the murderer's next victim, when actually he is the author of the series. But Martínez may be credited with adding some original elements to Borges's reworking of the conventions of the detective story. One of these lies in his use of Wittgenstein's rule-following paradox as a structuring device for the novel. In his *Philosophical Investigations*, Wittgenstein posits that a sequence of numbers can be continued in multiple different ways, each of which can be argued to conform to a rule.[13] Many commentators agree that this paradox is summarized most effectively in an axiom given further on in the text, stating that "no course of action could be determined by a rule, because any course of action can be made out to accord with the rule."[14] The final twists of the plot of *Crímenes imperceptibles* acquire a peculiar force by revealing the extent to which our thinking naturally converges on a single solution, holding it to be the only possible one and discounting other hypotheses, when logically there is more than one possible resolution of the plot, just as a series of symbols, as Wittgenstein proved, may be continued in many different ways. The last paragraph of the novel even casts doubt on the solution to which we are eventually led, leaving the ending open and ambiguous: is Seldom's final confession to be trusted? In a further twist, both murderer and accomplice accuse the narrator-protagonist of having inspired the crime in the first place and supplied the method of covering it up.

The uncertainty of its ending, together with its consistent undermining of the operations of logic, locate the novel within what Claudio Cid has identified as a third derivation of the detective story in Argentina. Following on from the classic model established by Poe and others, and a period of experimentation in the 1980s with the hard-boiled version, or *novela negra*, Cid argues that there has been a more recent return to the mystery-enigma novel in the work of writers such as Juan José Saer (*La pesquisa*, 1994), Juan Pablo Feinmann (*El cadáver imposible*, 1992), and Pablo de Santis (*Filosofía y Letras*, 1998).[15] This new manifestation takes us back to the scenario of the classic "novela de enigma" but with a different emphasis, this time not so much on the final revelation of truth, Cid suggests, but on the mechanisms of its discovery or construction. The indeterminacy that hovers over the dénouement of *Crímenes imperceptibles* does not lend credence to notions that the truth is either fundamentally unknowable or irrelevant; its effect is to shift the focus from the *revelation* of truth to the *construction* of narrative and meaning.

The figure in the frieze: allegories of reading and writing

Openly acknowledged as one of the major influences on his writing, Henry James is an ever-present figure in Martínez's novels. *La mujer del maestro* is in many ways a reworking of James's *The Lesson of the Master* (1892), tracing similar relationships between literature, marriage, and mercenariness. The protagonist's desperation to get his hands on Jordán's manuscript also echoes the obsessive compulsion to uncover literature's secrets that dictates the destinies of James's characters in *The Figure in the Carpet* (1896). And yet the allegories of reading and writing developed in *Crímenes imperceptibles* mark a point of significant divergence between James and Martínez. *The Figure in the Carpet* oscillates with radical indeterminacy between two incompatible propositions: that there exists a hidden scheme that binds Vereker's novels together, "something like a complex figure in a Persian carpet,"[16] or that there is absolutely nothing to Vereker's claims at all; that the critic's task is to unlock the secrets of a text, to plumb its hidden mysteries, or that no such secrets exist and any suggestion of an occult patterning is merely "a bait on a hook, a piece of cheese in a mouse-trap" to catch the unwary critic.[17] As well as a figure in a carpet, the scheme that may (or may not) link together all of Vereker's works attracts other metaphorical descriptions, as a bird in a cage, or the string on which the writer's pearls are strung.

In Martínez's own choice of metaphor in *Crímenes imperceptibles* for what lies undiscovered in a text, we see the basis of a very different allegory of reading. From the figure in the carpet to the figure in the frieze: in his confession to the narrator, Seldom tells him a story about an artist who hides a sketch of the king severing his daughter's head in an enormous frieze dedicated to the theme of the king as warrior, with such skill that

> Nissam, y después de él generaciones y generaciones de hombres, sólo vieron lo que el artista quería que se viera: una sucesión abrumadora de imágenes de las que el ojo pronto se despega porque cree advertir la repetición, cree capturar la regla, cree que cada parte representa al todo.[18]

> Nissam, and generations and generations of men after him, only saw what the artist wanted them to see: an overwhelming succession of images from which the eye quickly peels away because it believes it has discovered repetition, captured the rule, it believes that every part represents the whole.

The story lays bare Seldom's own technique in hiding a crime by constructing patterns around it that distract the eye. The truth is there, but we cannot see it because our minds are trained to find patterns and repetition, not the crucial variation that holds the secret to the artist's design. Unlike James in *The Figure of the Carpet*, who is far more ambivalent about the matter, for Martínez there *is* a single, hidden truth, but our powers of deduction are insufficient to prove it, and indeed lead us merrily into error.

It is the tendency of our minds to simplify and to look for patterns that allows the artist, as well as the criminal, to create illusions and smokescreens.

Martínez holds that the best detective stories are those in which the truth is everywhere present in the text but nevertheless eludes the reader's notice. Martínez's essay "El cuento como sistema lógico" explicitly acknowledges a debt to Piglia's "Tesis sobre el cuento," which in turn closely conforms to theorizations of the structure of detective fiction by Shklovsky and other Formalist critics. Following Piglia, Martínez argues that every short story contains two stories, one overt and the other hidden; the task of the writer is to bring the secret story gradually to the surface, only revealing it in its entirety at the end. This idea, he observes, coincides with the most frequent image he entertains of the storywriter, as an illusionist who distracts the audience's attention with one hand while performing an act of magic with the other.[19] Both Martínez and Piglia clearly echo Shklovsky here, in his perception that "the false or misleading solution is a very common element of either a tale or a mystery novel. The manipulation of false and true solutions is what constitutes the method of organizing the mystery. The dénouement consists in shifting from one to the other."[20] The particular merit of this kind of approach to narratives, as Martínez points out (very much in a Formalist vein), is that "permite mirar al cuento no como un objeto terminado, listo para los desarmaderos de los críticos, sino como un proceso vivo, desde su formación" (it allows us to see the story not as a finished object, ready for critics to dismantle, but as a living process, from the perspective of its construction).[21]

Both Piglia and Martínez cite Borges as a master of the technique of shifting from the initial, "false" plot to the other, more "authentic" one that the writer develops in parallel but is not evident to the reader until the end.[22] For both writers, "La muerte y la brújula" is a paradigmatic example of this technique. Martínez points out, as an example, that Borges uses the euphemism "hechos de sangre" (bloody events) instead of "crímenes" (crimes) in the first paragraph of the story; effectively, not all the deaths turn out to be murders. Martínez uses this device in his own novel, for the same reason carefully referring to "muertes" (deaths) rather than "crímenes" in the first paragraph.[23] There are also plenty of warnings to the reader that the series of symbols is nothing more than a smokescreen: Seldom himself points out that crimes committed for intellectual reasons occur in books but not in real life,[24] and warns the narrator of the error of ignoring explanations that are "más inmediatas" (more immediate).[25] Another idea to which the narrative returns more than once, foreshadowing the final revelations, is the sacrifice and danger a parent might be prepared to embrace for the sake of a child.

We only later realize that Martínez has done precisely what he was telling us all along that he would do: he has performed a magic trick "con todas las cartas sobre la mesa" (with all the cards on the table).[26] If the novel's characters misread clues and form erroneous ideas that act to conceal the real truth, we cheerfully engage in precisely the same mistakes, ignoring all details that do not fit our neat theories about the truth behind the crimes, even though we are fully aware that the conventions of the detective genre dictate that we will be deceived in this manner. Interestingly, the reason Borges gives for the need for a story to have two plots is that "el lector de nuestro tiempo es también un crítico, un hombre que conoce, y prevé, los artificios literarios" (the reader of our time is also a critic, a man who is familiar with, and anticipates, literary devices).[27] For this reason, too, Martínez's magician in *Crímenes imperceptibles* is named as René Lavand, who is one-handed: only a grand master of illusions could hoodwink the reader who already knows all the tricks.

The criminal, the magician, the writer: all have a secret that may be uncovered, but our preference for aesthetic elegance and coherence, even in the application of logic and scientific method, often obscures the truth from us. This commitment to the existence of truth, however much it may elude our grasp, is what distances Martínez's understanding of reading and literary criticism – and interpretation in general – from that of both Piglia and Cohen, even while he shares their interest in taking hermeneutical failure as a starting-point for a reflexive exploration of the processes of reading and writing, and an experimentation with different modes of textual construction. While it is true, as Matías Eduardo Moscati states, that in *Crímenes imperceptibles* "la aplicación del método matemático se encuentra condenada a la frustración y al naufragio intelectual" (the application of mathematical method is doomed to frustration and intellectual failure),[28] it is also true that the *metamathematical* exercise of reflecting on the use of mathematical ideas *does* produce knowledge, revealing a great deal about our propensity to search for patterns, analogies, and metaphors and to use them, often inaccurately, to shape our understanding of the world.

Unlike the great majority of novelists and theorists who have cited Gödel's theorem as proof of the inadequacy of our tools of logical analysis, Martínez points the finger of blame not at those tools but at our inability to use them effectively or to apply them in the right contexts. If – as in *La mujer del maestro* – Martínez often draws on the dialectical model of scientific advance in thinking about the processes of literary innovation, in *Crímenes imperceptibles* the relationship is reversed: it is our love of aesthetic elegance that may account for the development (and the impairment) of our mathematical understanding. Although – unlike Cohen and Piglia, as we will see – Martínez retains a belief in the existence of an objective truth, the (Formalist) emphasis in his fictional and critical work on questions of construction rather than interpretation often brings his writing to resonate with theirs, as does a sense that epistemological "failure" is not the end, but the beginning of new kinds of knowledge. Like the painter of the king's frieze, whose life depends on his ability to embed the truth within a successful illusion, the writer – pursued by his critics as a criminal is hunted down by detectives – finds, in their very eagerness to rationalize and perceive patterns, an opportunity to innovate and outwit them. As in the dialectical model, error and the failure of a particular method simply become opportunities for greater understanding and innovation.

INTERPRETATION AND INTERPRETOSIS IN AN IMMANENT WORLD / COHEN

> Behind the hieroglyphic streets there would either be a transcendent meaning, or only the earth.—Thomas Pynchon[29]

Marcelo Cohen is an incisive reader of Thomas Pynchon, and the central place given to the question of transcendence and certain scientific ideas in

Cohen's texts – chaos and entropy in particular – owes much to Pynchon's own exploration of these themes. Indeed, Cohen explicitly grounds his theory of "realismo inseguro" (unstable realism) in the kind of non-linear, diffusive structures that abound in Pynchon's fiction.[30] It is precisely in this reflexive use of thermodynamic theories to probe the creative processes of writing, however, that we may perceive a key difference between the two authors. If the complex nature of causality in non-linear systems often becomes for Pynchon a metaphor of the difficulty of reading and interpreting the world around us, for Cohen it becomes much more emphatically a model for the endless creative potential of writing and a source of new forms of meaning that derive from a vision of immanence rather than transcendence, a vision less positively embraced in Pynchon's work.

Paranoia and interpretosis in Pynchon and Cohen

Cohen contests the common description of Pynchon's writing as "paranoid," claiming that the paranoiac's madness is "cohesivo, inclusivo, causal, lógico, jerarquizado, polarizador" (cohesive, inclusive, causal, logical, hierarchical, polarizing), pertaining to a rigid sense of destiny and fatalism, whereas the same cannot be said of Pynchon's novels themselves. These, by contrast, are "hechas de disrupciones e interferencias, clímax múltiples, dispersión, analogías, inverosimilitud" (made of disruptions and interferences, multiple climaxes, dispersion, analogies, improbability).[31] Pynchon's characters – one thinks of Oedipa Maas in *The Crying of Lot 49* (1966), for example – oscillate between a paranoid sense that everything is connected and has a hidden meaning and the even more terrifying possibility that everything is meaningless. Cohen cites Slothrop's musings on the subject from *Gravity's Rainbow* (1973):

> If there is something comforting – religious, if you want – about paranoia, there is still also anti-paranoia, where nothing is connected to anything, a condition not many of us can bear for long. [...] Either They have put him here for a reason, or he's

just here. He isn't sure that he wouldn't, actually, rather have that *reason* …[32]

Cohen's characters waver in a similar fashion between a paranoid apprehension that everything is significant and an equally uncomfortable, paralyzing suspicion that everything is meaningless.

This anxiety over interpretation is all-pervasive in *El testamento de O'Jaral*. Cohen's protagonist moves through a world governed by shadowy alliances between politics and huge commercial consortiums. He seeks some form of transcendence in an ultra-neoliberal society of proliferating images and messages and tries to find a path of resistance to the logic of the same on which the market's overwhelming power is based. He continually comes up against the painful prospect that neither is possible, and sinks further and further into penury and social isolation, becoming a drug-dependent vagrant. It is only in this position of wretchedness and humility that he is able to access what appears to be a vision of the immanent nature of the world, but as he is unable to communicate it to others, it remains nothing more than a personal glimmer of enlightenment or consolation before a swift and bathetic end.

The confusion produced in O'Jaral by the complex codes and messages with which he is constantly bombarded is mirrored in the challenges the novel presents to its readers. A sense prevails in the novel in which nothing is a coincidence, and no meeting is a chance encounter, but that everything may be predestined according to some grand scheme of which we and the characters have little understanding. Nothing is natural, everything seems constructed: O'Jaral wonders, for example, whether his meeting with Yola is really the outcome of chance or whether someone had put her into the story so that he had somewhere to hide for a while. He hesitates between believing that he is caught up in a conspiracy, that "bajo la grasosa acumulación de fenómenos había una fluidez clandestina hacia donde distintos agentes lo estaban guiando con guiños, con señuelos" (beneath the greasy accumulation of phenomena there was a clandestine fluidity that different agents were guiding him towards, with winks, with baits),[33] and thinking on the other hand that everything is meaningless, that "no hay nada que adivinar" (there is nothing to guess).[34]

This paranoia, we are led to understand, is rooted in a hermeneutical error: the mistaken assumption that signs can be "interpreted" to yield a hidden meaning that lies somewhere beyond them. Deleuze and Guattari identify the belief that meaning or truth exists independently and merely awaits our discovery as one of the chief expressions of "humankind's fundamental neurosis," a "disease" to which they give the name "interpretosis."[35] In their work, this observation forms part of a critique of certain Freudian strands of psychoanalysis, which assume that affects and desires always refer back to an originary trauma or loss. Deleuze and Guattari expose the use of language to interpret language as a serious category mistake: signs lead only to more signs, as "interpretation is carried to infinity and never encounters anything to interpret that is not already itself an interpretation."[36]

El testamento de O'Jaral produces this same vertigo of endless recursion. Cohen's characters live in a hypermediatized and narcoticized society in which they often find it difficult to distinguish between reality and projections. The matter is not usually cleared up for the reader either: we cannot simply attribute the text's slidings between reality and fantasy to the influence of a drug-induced delirium or the incursion of simulacra into a realm of reality that lies beyond these. No frames or boundaries appear to mark the separation between reality and representation on the city streets, and characters cannot always tell whether what is happening around them is really happening then and there or is a projection from another time or space:

> A O'Jaral le pareció que un robot fumigador se detenía en la esquina para meter la manguera en una alcantarilla. Una interferencia arrugó la escena, que era parte de una operación filmada en otro barrio.[37]

> To O'Jaral it looked as if a fumigator robot had stopped on the street corner to insert its hose into a drain. Interference wrinkled the scene, which was part of an operation being filmed in another neighbourhood.

In this example, the illusion is exposed for what it is; at other points, it becomes impossible to decide whether what is being narrated is taking place in a material, a virtual, or a metaphorical realm. As O'Jaral's drug addiction deepens, he is described as projecting images of his own onto the images shown on the screens erected around the city. Onto an advertisement for margarine he projects suitcases slowly advancing along the baggage belt of an airport, and onto the features of the president he superimposes a grey-haired cannibal who eats a human arm before running to meet a short woman. What status are we to accord these images, which are described as projections but appear to interfere with other images that seem to exist independently of O'Jaral's imagination? Like O'Jaral, as readers we learn to mistrust our ability to read signs, which may refer to material phenomena or just to more signs, and thus the mental image we build of the novel's world is a multiple and fractured one in which the reality status of events and objects is often undecidable.

Causality in non-linear systems: reworking the paradigms of detective fiction

As in the famous "butterfly effect," which demonstrates the complexity of causality in non-linear – or "chaotic" – systems, Cohen's world is one in which phenomena are intimately linked in ways that are not always visible, and in which tiny changes at the microscopic level produce disproportionate effects at the macroscopic. The impossibility of predicting such effects, and of tracing the chain of events that produces them, becomes the cause of a particular kind of epistemological anxiety in the novel. Such processes are not random but determined, but it is beyond our ability to predict their outcomes. "En un mundo holístico y no lineal, todo acontecimiento tenía que ser significativo" (in a holistic and non-linear world, every event had to be significant):[38] or, at least, that is the theory O'Jaral assumes to be guiding the actions of Ravinkel, the half-brother he has been contracted to hunt down, and the best way to find him seems therefore to embrace his logic.

If everything is connected to everything else, this has a profound effect on the structure of the detective story, which is thoroughly reworked here.

The traditional methods of the detective, chasing clues and using his powers of interpretation to hypothesize about their meaning, are useless here. O'Jaral rarely goes in pursuit of clues or suspicious people but instead waits for them to come to him, as they invariably do. When Badaraco chastises him for wasting time and forgetting that he is contracted to find Ravinkel, O'Jaral gives as an explanation a description of a Peano curve, a self-intersecting curve that passes through every point of a two-dimensional plane, or as O'Jaral puts it, "una línea que es un plano" (a line that is a plane).[39] He does not have to pass through all those points: they will make their way to him. The conventional approach of the detective, reading signs as clues to a hidden reality, is as radically undermined here as it is in a Paul Auster novel. Just as in Auster's *New York Trilogy* (1985–86), for example, surfaces in *El testamento* do not yield to penetration but merely reflect the image of the protagonist back to himself. In the following description of a shop window, what is behind the glass becomes confused with what the glass reflects, defying attempts to separate the two and instead uniting them in a single plane of vision:

> estas cosas, que parecen estar detrás del vidrio, se confunden con la suciedad del vidrio y con lo que el vidrio refleja, una pera mordida en la acera, un hombre con un perro en brazos, la charla de dos vendedoras en la zapatería de enfrente, y el brillo de la vidriera de la zapatería y el parpadeo de las cotizaciones en una pantalla y el desfile del tráfico con sus tules de humo, y todo junto, más la cara sorprendida de O'Jaral, forma un mundito completo, inaprensible en su plenitud […].[40]

> these things, which seem to be behind the window, become confused with the dirtiness of the glass and what the glass reflects, a half-eaten pear on the sidewalk, a man carrying a dog in his arms, the chatting of two shop assistants in the shoe shop opposite, and the shine of the shoe shop's window and the blinking of share prices on a screen and the procession of traffic with its veils of smoke, and everything together, plus O'Jaral's

surprised face, forms a complete little world, enigmatic in its plenitude [...].

Objects and images, perceptions and reflections, observed and observer fold together to create a world that cannot be seen and analyzed from any external perspective; there is no vantage point from which tested hermeneutical principles can be brought to bear on the subject in question.

The problem of the new in a non-transcendent world: metaphors from Gödel and thermodynamics

This, indeed, is the understanding that derives from the many references to Gödel's theorems in the novel. O'Jaral studies a book on the consequences of those theorems, which "discuten si es cierto que ningún sistema formal puede justificar desde adentro todas las verdades que propone" (question whether it is true that no formal system can justify from within all the truths it proposes).[41] Muzzone asks him, "¿Cómo sabe uno que la lógica que aplica es especial, distinta, si para entenderse no tiene más que esa lógica?" (how does one know that the logic one applies is special, different, if one only has that same logic to understand with?).[42] As Gödel proved, no formal system can prove its own coherence using only the terms contained within it. His theorem is appropriated in Cohen's novel to articulate both the logical impossibility of transcendent knowledge and the equally impossible prospect of political change. In both cases, the crucial question with which O'Jaral battles is: where will new ideas and inspiration come from, if we are trapped in an immanent world and cannot gain any kind of external perspective on it?

The question of political change is an urgent one in the hyper-neoliberal world of *El testamento de O'Jaral*, in which big business has consolidated its control over every aspect of political, social, and personal life, including spirituality and art. There is little to differentiate the governments that come and go, forming cabinets that are "planos como dibujos animados" (flat, like cartoon animations) and that simply give the institutions of the weakened state a quick makeover rather than introducing real change.[43] Both these and the powerful consortiums are managed by a murky, sinister force referred to as "Los de Arriba de Todo" (Those Above Everything), who cleverly manage to exploit all criticism and conflict for their own purposes. Badaraco explains to O'Jaral that his consortium accepts dissenters and opposers with enthusiasm: "son un fermento necesario: de las nociones equivocadas que propaga ese gente nacen inquietudes, de las inquietudes nuevos deseos en el ciudadano [...]. Alentamos la crítica y a veces la financiamos" (they are a necessary catalyst: from the mistaken notions these people spread, anxieties are born, and from anxieties, new desires in the citizen [...]. We encourage criticism and sometimes finance it).[44] Conflict and rebellion serve only to stimulate the market, as business knows exactly how to translate these into higher levels of consumption.

If the system swallows up all criticism into itself, how and from where is resistance to be mounted? The only thing the consortiums fear is indifference and non-participation in consumption and citizenship (like business and the state, the two have become synonymous). Badaraco's consortium is alarmed to note a decline in social and political participation, and "un rechazo deliberado a la información" (a deliberate rejection of information) that borders on "una indiferencia casi vegetal" (a vegetable-like indifference).[45] Ravinkel's people, who do perform certain acts of resistance, become of concern, not because they oppose the status quo or propose an alternative to it, but because they appear to have no objectives at all. They do not want to gain anything, not to gather numbers, nor to attack the consortiums, nor to create a new political agenda: in short, they desire nothing that the system could turn into the kind of aspiration that foments consumerism. Ravinkel's principal method is to introduce uncertainty and chaos by duplicating and fabricating the myriad images produced by the state and the consortiums. The people working with him – "Superficiales" is an apt name for an immanent world – infiltrate the media with a series of falsifications and perfect duplicates, including doubles of well-known actors and fake advertisements for non-existent products. These falsifying operations cannot be assimilated and neutralized by the System, because they appear to have no particular end in sight.

However, Ravinkel's methods become the object of O'Jaral's scathing criticism. In effect, O'Jaral accuses him of an insufficient grasp of the scientific principles behind thermodynamics, chaos, and complexity, marshalled here as analogies for the workings of a social system. If the consortiums have managed to create a total system and maintain it close to equilibrium, O'Jaral rightly presumes that Ravinkel's aim is to introduce greater turbulence in order to move the system away from a state of equilibrium. A system close to equilibrium is subject to entropy, a gradual decrease in available energy, heading towards a stasis described as a kind of "muerte colectiva" (collective death).[46] Beyond a certain level of complexity, on the other hand, a system far from equilibrium is subject to unpredictable alterations and that disorder can create new structures: O'Jaral cites Bénard cells as an example, which spontaneously organize themselves into hexagonal patterns as a consequence of the random microscopic movements caused by convection. Similar processes can be seen, he reminds Ravinkel, in desert sands or snowflakes after a storm.

O'Jaral attacks Ravinkel's logic with two – not entirely compatible – arguments. On one hand, he chastises him for performing acts whose consequences are irreversible and unpredictable: of not taking into account the "arrow of time," which means that one cannot, in non-linear processes, posit a return to initial conditions. In other words, Ravinkel is unleashing changes over which he has no control. In the first place, then, O'Jaral's objection is that the new structures that will be produced by Ravinkel's actions to introduce greater chaos into the system are dangerously unpredictable. On the other hand, he criticizes Ravinkel for believing that shaking up the old could ever produce the new. Chaotic processes can lead to creativity, says O'Jaral, but in this case they will lead simply to more of the same, in a slightly different guise: "Vino viejo con odres restaurados. El mismo perro con otro collar" (old wine in patched-up wineskins. The same dog with a different collar).[47] Given the impossibility of stepping outside of the system they are in, in searching for new systems they can only draw on the past, which provides "un repertorio de sociedades muy pobre" (a very poor repertoire of societies).[48]

The incompatibility between these two critiques is significant because it points to a bigger question that O'Jaral is not able to resolve: whether the system under discussion – the world in which he lives – is analogous to an open or a closed system in thermodynamic terms. Closed systems are subject to entropy, while open systems, maintaining traffic across their borders, have a greater capacity to change and evolve, becoming more complex and assuming new structures. Is the world subject to entropy or can new elements from beyond its borders allow it to generate new forms? O'Jaral understands that, imprisoned as he is within this system, he is unable to formulate a genuinely new idea. Believing, however, that he is destined to discover something of great significance, he frequently returns to the same anxiety:

> Se preguntaba, y sabía que era preciso decidirlo, si el mundo era *del todo* inmanente. Porque si no había más que lo que parecía haber, si todo era tal cual era, sin ajenos soplos de animación, y cualquier esperanza debía estar en el Aquí, ¿de dónde iba a caerle a él la claridad [...]?[49]

> He wondered, and knew that it was essential to decide, whether the world was *completely* immanent. Because if there was nothing more than what there appeared to be, if everything was exactly what it was, without any animating breath from beyond, and any hope had to reside in the Here-And-Now, from where was clarity going to descend upon him [...]?

The inspiration that would permit innovation has to come from outside: "debe caer como un aerolito" (it must fall like a meteorite), he thinks.[50] But where can new ideas and innovation come from if we are trapped in an immanent world, and there is nothing beyond what is visible, no greater meaning or force, no higher being or alternative plane of existence? If there is no transcendence, O'Jaral believes – conflating thermodynamics, chaos, emergence, Gödel, theology, and political theory with giddy aplomb – there can be no possibility of genuine newness in the governance of his world.

Romanticism, transcendence and immanence

Both Eberhard Alsen and Joel Black concur in finding Romantic roots for Pynchon's sense – articulated most strongly in *Gravity's Rainbow* – of "an animate Earth in which all matter participates in an ongoing process of gestation."[51] For Black, however, the novel is "post-Romantic" because it is "unable to posit a transcendent source of value beyond itself,"[52] while Alsen, who *does* find a belief in transcendence articulated in its pages, prefers the term "neo-romantic."[53] The difference is less absolute than it might appear: what Alsen offers as evidence of a "belief in transcendence" is the realization that "God [...] is a force that dwells in all things" and "immanent in nature,"[54] or as Bland says in *Gravity's Rainbow*, "the wonder of finding that Earth is a living critter, after all these years of thinking about a big dumb rock."[55] It seems a little perverse to claim that a realization of immanence is proof of the operation of transcendent knowledge: the conclusions Pynchon's characters reach do not therefore, in my view, fully sustain a belief in a spiritual world that transcends the physical, lending meaning to its transience.

Both "neo-Romantic" and "post-Romantic" are terms that could justifiably be used in respect of Cohen's *El testamento de O'Jaral*. Although the primary frame of reference for Cohen's holistic worldview may be a Buddhist one, the novel's exploration of immanence and of the world as a living, animate entity, in which we participate, also leads us back to certain Romantic conventions. It is left unclear whether O'Jaral achieves any part of the enlightenment for which he has been searching. But he certainly experiences small epiphanies that afford him a glimpse of the interconnectedness of all things, the dissolution of the self within the surrounding world, and the irreducible materiality of objects, which acquire a kind of meaning through a process of intense and unhurried visual observation. Amidst the many reflective surfaces and the superimposed images of the world of *El testamento*, O'Jaral finds a dusty bottle that reflects precisely nothing, "rudimentario y suficiente como un Morandi" (as rudimentary and sufficient as a Morandi), that seems to erase all other images and to announce the possibility of bringing together all the world's fragments to form a constellation.[56] Like a Morandi still life, O'Jaral's bottle is an unremarkable, simple, everyday object that seems to acquire freshness through patient and intense contemplation, and through its opacity and resistance to abstract interpretation.

Another moment of epiphany comes when O'Jaral is suddenly possessed of the idea that "no hay nada que adivinar" (there is nothing to be guessed) and intuits instead that he simply *is* everything he sees around him, including the lentils at the bottom of the pot, the rust of the pipework, voters from opposing camps, and the barking of a dog.[57] There is no attempt to distinguish here between divine and human creations, the natural world and the products of man-made mechanics: O'Jaral is at one with the urban detritus everywhere around him as well as with what the Romantics would have elevated as Nature. Similar to this vision – this time unambiguously Romantic in its appeal to the fragment – is one in which he understands every part to contain within it the whole, that what had appeared to be a miscellany of meaningless fragments is imbued with the infinite universe:

> cada cosa, guinche, pescante, neumático, amapola, pantalla, pierna o nube, guardaba las relaciones que en un momento eran el todo. En su momento, una astilla de vidrio era una familia universal.[58]

> every thing, winch, hoist, tyre, poppy, screen, leg or cloud, contained within it the relations that were in that moment the whole. In that moment, a splinter of glass was a universal family.

It is typical of Cohen that this vision is immediately deflated: "Después venía otro momento" (then came another moment). O'Jaral's epiphanies do not provide the certainties that a transcendent perspective on the world might afford but are simply the transitory impressions, intuitions, and modes of being and becoming that are proper to immanence.

The persistence of another Romantic convention can also be seen in the significance accorded in the novel to solitude and withdrawal from society as a necessary condition for receiving inspiration. In O'Jaral's thoroughly post-theistic philosophy, however, that inspiration can come only from oneself, and may well remain elusive. If, as he is only too aware, language is the measure of our thought, then the only path to renew that thought is by discovering a new language, having previously purged himself of all learned thought-patterns. Inspiration would only come

> Porque previamente uno se ha retirado, se ha limpiado hasta el extremo de rasparse la osamenta, ha elegido cada uno de sus pensamientos. Ha estado solo, cercenado del circuito, borrado, disuelto. Uno crea un sistema autónomo de realimentación positiva. Llegado el momento, aflorará, germinará o caerá sobre uno el lenguaje diferente, y el pensamiento posible gracias a ese lenguaje. […] Quizá. No hay ninguna seguridad.[59]

> Because one had previously withdrawn, cleansed oneself deeply to the point of scraping one's bones, chosen each thought. Had been alone, severed from the circuit, erased, dissolved. One creates an autonomous, self-renewing system. Come the moment, a different language will flower, germinate or descend upon one, and with it the thought that language will make possible. […] Perhaps. There is no certainty.

The events of the plot play out this Romantic model of inspiration-from-reclusion with bitter irony. Penniless, utterly ravaged by wasting illness and drug addiction, O'Jaral – like an absurdly hyperbolic version of a Romantic poet – descends to the very depths of misery but does not find the answers he is looking for and would certainly be unable to impart them to anyone else.

O'Jaral himself abhors Romanticism, deploring "la neurasténica exaltación de Shelley pidiéndole a un viento que lo hiciera volar como una hoja, ese mequetrefe de Novalis adjudicándole ingenio a la naturaleza, tanto joder todos con las ruinas y los fantasmas" (the neurasthenic agitation of Shelley begging the wind to make him fly like a leaf, that good-for-nothing Novalis attributing inventiveness to nature, all that screwing around with ruins and ghosts).[60] He also thoroughly demolishes Romantic notions of heroism and revolution, accusing them of drawing too closely on the battles of Classical myths that depose one giant only to replace him with another.

In the end, the only effective means of contesting the system has nothing to do with Romantic individualism but precisely its reverse. O'Jaral understands that the only defence is indifference, to aspire to nothing, and to become "un ciudadano difuso" (a diffused citizen).[61] He receives comfort and stimulation from a book he keeps constantly at his side, with the title *Donde yo no estaba* (the title given to a future novel by Cohen). The book contains in diary form the meticulous and often mundane observations of the owner of a lingerie store. O'Jaral finds the writer both refreshingly rational and utterly bewitching: "Era un ciudadano completo pero aspiraba a no ser nada" (he was a full citizen but he aspired to become nothing).[62] Embracing Romantic immanence but eschewing its belief in divine inspiration and the individual genius, O'Jaral finds a way of being in the world that is more authentic and compassionate and that involves patient observation rather than over-reaching interpretation. He learns that "las alianzas que las cosas pasajeras entablan entre sí son más amplias cuanto menos él las interpreta" (the alliances that transient things strike up between themselves are fuller, the less he interprets them).[63] Meaning does not vanish in an immanent world but is enriched for those who learn to see it in the multiple and continually transforming relations between living and non-living things. Unlike Pynchon's characters, who – like Oedipa Maas in *The Crying of Lot 49* – are condemned to search for a transcendence that eludes them, many of Cohen's learn to live in an immanent world and to participate in the multiple and meaningful encounters with difference that it affords.

LITERATURE: THE LABORATORY OF THE FUTURE / PIGLIA

> Writing has nothing to do with signifying.
> It has to do with mapping, surveying, even realms that are yet to come.
> —Gilles Deleuze and Félix Guattari[64]

Like Cohen, Piglia seeks to undermine the quest for meaning and metanarratives and to initiate us in new ways of reading (texts, others, our environment) that do not remove us from the unceasing flux of the material for which we are attempting to account. In constructing the various models and allegories of reading that circulate in his fiction, he frequently draws on mathematical and scientific notions of chance and uncertainty. Gödel's theorems of incompleteness provide a way of exposing the self-referentiality involved in using language to interpret linguistic phenomena. The futility of this exercise is clearly demonstrated in the short story "La isla" (*La ciudad ausente*, 1992). The questions of determinism, probability, and prediction that are central to the mathematics of chaotic systems are enmeshed in Piglia's writing with his understanding of literature – drawing on Bloch – as "una fiesta y un laboratorio de lo posible" (a celebration and a laboratory of the possible).[65] For Piglia, literature does not ultimately derive from (record or comment on) the past experience of the author but creates future experiences for the reader, becoming not so much an archive of the past as a laboratory of the future. It is in this vein that we may best approach Piglia's experiments with science-fiction topoi such as virtual reality, psychic transference, memory implantation, and the multiverse, which are resignified in his work as tropes for the act of reading and its construction of (artificial) experience. In Piglia's texts the implantation of artificial memories represents, not (only) the powerful incursion of the technological state into individual consciousness, but also the work of literature in expanding consciousness and producing a kind of trans-subjective experience. This work is theorized in "El último cuento de Borges" (*Formas breves*, 1999) and *El último lector* (2005); it becomes a keystone of Piglia's fictional praxis in *Prisión perpetua* (1988).

Uncertainty and metalanguage in "La isla"

The island of Piglia's eponymous story is populated by political exiles and refugees of so many different nations that their native tongues have joined to form a single language, which undergoes a frequent and unpredictable metamorphosis. At the start of each new cycle – which may last weeks or a single day – all the inhabitants have an instant and complete grasp of the new language and immediately forget the old one. On the island, no one is a foreigner; indeed, no fixed notion of identity can be constructed as the erratic, rapid cycling through languages renders cultural transmission impossible and erases all personal and collective memory.

The extent and speed of linguistic transformation on the island refer hyperbolically to the constant evolution of language and meaning in our own world. In the complete absence of a stable, durable linguistic system, the transmission of cultural knowledge – always subject to the vagaries of contemporary interpretation – becomes unthinkable. The status and interpretation of the island's few written texts shift continually, and there exists no possible hermeneutical method to establish the veracity of any one view. A fragment found written in the island's original language is for some inhabitants a religious text, taken from Genesis; for others, it is a kind of prayer or divination game; for the island's historians it is a paragraph from a suicide note left by an exiled political militant.

The island's peculiar language system is the subject of intense study by linguisticians, but their attempt to produce a descriptive linguistics is destined for frustration. Their most valiant efforts have not given rise to a system that can fully account for the uncertainty of language-change. The unpredictability of change has made it impossible, we are told, to construct any kind of external, artificial system of signs that does not itself become subject to constant mutation: "Si *a* + *b es igual a c*, esa certidumbre sólo sirve un tiempo, porque en el espacio irregular de dos segundos ya *a* es $-a$ y la ecuación es otra" (if $a + b$ equals c, that certainty only lasts for a time, because in the irregular space of two seconds a has already become $-a$ and the equation is a completely different one).[66] There is no stable point of reference upon which to construct a signifying system that is not subject to the very same changes for which it is attempting to account: truth lasts only as long as the words with which it is articulated.

Published as one of the narratives of the storytelling machine in *La ciudad ausente*, "La isla" takes its place among a series of explorations of uncertainty and virtual realities inspired by Gödel's theorems of incompleteness. These demonstrate that "Ningún sistema formal puede afirmar su propia coherencia" (no formal system can prove its own consistency).[67] Gödel's theorem shattered the formalist project in mathematics to construct an axiomatic system for mathematics, which had rested on the possibility of separating out the language in which theory is inscribed from theory itself; instead, it demonstrated that the tools of analysis are logically inseparable from the object of that analysis.

For this reason, in their study of the island's language, Trinity College's best linguisticians only manage to invent "un lenguaje que muestra cómo es el mundo, pero que no permite nombrarlo" (a language that shows what the world is like but doesn't allow it to be named).[68] This language manifests, in its constant shifts and mutations, principles of uncertainty but cannot with any certainty account for them. It does not enjoy the status of a metalanguage but is simply another system for the expression of uncertainty. In the language, we are told, "Existen tiempos lentos y tiempos rápidos, como en el cauce del Liffey" (there are slow times and fast times, like in the course of the [River] Liffey).[69] Language is not outside of time but subject to it, and time does not proceed in a linear fashion but according to the uneven flows of a stream tumbling over rocks, whirling in eddies, or stagnating in pools. Language cannot effectively describe or fix the world because it is part of it, governed by the same uncertainty and experience of time that it attempts to explain or to overcome.

It is unsurprising that the island's sacred text should be Joyce's *Finnegans Wake*, a novel so heterolingual that it can be understood whatever the current state of the island's language. *Finnegans Wake* becomes "un modelo en miniatura del mundo" (a model in miniature of the world)[70] that reproduces the transformations and the uncertainties of life on the island itself. No one knows the true origin of the book, but readings of it abound, infinitely: "Las interpretaciones se multiplican y el *Finnegans* cambia como cambia el mundo" (interpretations multiply and *Finnegans* changes as the world changes).[71] This resistance to unitary, stable interpretation is what allows the book to be read as a sacred text on the island: readable by all, usable by all, whatever language they are in and whatever their ideological or religious persuasion. The island and *Finnegans Wake* (re)produce each other; in the same way, it is implied, all literature and critical commentaries are not representations of the world but part of the flux of experience, simultaneously effecting change and being subject to it.

Yet in the impossibility of transcendence lies literature's peculiar capacity to construct and define everyday experience. If the meaning of a text cannot be anchored in the context of its production, it may be endlessly and creatively transformed: *Finnegans Wake* becomes, not an account of past events and journeys but a map for future ones, multiple and shifting, each yielding a new story, and no one on the island can conceive of an end to its proliferations and transformations. By embracing every alternative, the novel survives them all. This lends it the authority of a myth of origin and the miraculous quality of "un texto mágico que encierra las claves del universo" (a magical text that contains the keys to the universe).[72]

The relativist perspective on textual meaning expounded in "La isla" may initially appear to be of fairly standard (post-)structuralist stock. However, the emphasis is not placed here on the failure of hermeneutics to fix the meaning of a particular text, but on the endless creativity that results from the continually changing relationships between the islanders and their modern "Bible": as their own use of language changes, different parts of the text acquire legibility or sink into obscurity, and different maps of meaning emerge to challenge or complement previous ones. At every shift, the text is recreated, and so is the experience of the island's inhabitants. This is what renders the island a utopian space of multiple possible futures. As we will see, other narratives by Piglia radicalize this notion of literature as a map of the future rather than a record of the past.

Piglia's photographer: reading, between the real and the virtual

The prologue to *El último lector* relates the story of a photographer who keeps a wood-and-plaster replica of the city of Buenos Aires in the attic of his house in Flores. When the narrator sees the replica with his own eyes, he perceives that "lo que vi era más real que la realidad, menos indefinido y más puro" (what I saw was more real than reality, less vague and purer).[73] He acknowledges that the "objective" viewpoint he is afforded creates the illusion of a coherent whole, transcending temporality. The illusion of divine control is such that the photographer believes that the real city depends on his model for its existence and that what happens in the model city is duplicated in the real. For this reason, the narrator concludes, he is insane.

Thus far, Piglia's narrative would seem to concur with the thrust of Susan Stewart's argument in *On Longing: Narratives of the Miniature, the Gigantic, the Souvenir, the Collection*, in which the creation of the model or the miniature "presents the desiring subject with an illusion of mastery, of time into space and heterogeneity into order."[74] For Stewart, the creation of the miniature is bound up with the desire for a kind of transcendent time "which negates change and the flux of lived reality."[75] It is a perspective that grants a distance, a transcendence and an objectivity that are incommensurate with lived experience and existence within the city. Stewart points to the nostalgia that informs such representations and the reifications they imply. She perceives "the many narratives that dream of the inanimate-made-animate as symptomatic of all narrative's desire to invent a realizable world, a world which 'works'."[76]

In contrast, however, the many models and microcosms of Piglia's narratives represent no such desire to tame the messiness of reality. His models are not ideal, perfected abstractions of the real world, but crucially intertwined with it in a complex relationship of mutual unmaking and redefinition. The suggestion that the photographer is insane is followed immediately by another alternative: that this is no mere photographer at all, and that he has indeed managed to alter the conventional relationship between reality and representation, such that the real city is the one hidden away in the attic of his house, and the one outside is nothing but a mirage or a memory. The narrator does not pronounce a final verdict: we are not told whether he is ultimately convinced, as the photographer is, that damage or modifications to the model are reproduced in the real city in the form of passing catastrophes and unexplained accidents. In any case, our sense of logic might prevent us from understanding this as a serious proposition about the real world. But there is an important way in which the model does point to the transcendence of distinctions between the real and the replica: in its evocation of the act of reading.

The narrator grasps the reason behind the photographer's decision to allow just one visitor to see the model at any one time: "reproduce, en la contemplación de la ciudad, el acto de leer. El que la contempla es un lector y por lo tanto debe estar solo" (he reproduces, in the contemplation of the city, the act of reading. The one who contemplates is a reader and for that reason he must be alone).[77] What the "reader" perceives in the model will be carried with him back to the city outside, existing as a kind of virtual, parallel city alongside the real one. The model, like the act of reading, "trata sobre el modo de hacer visible lo invisible y fijar las imágenes nítidas que ya no vemos pero que insisten todavía como fantasmas y viven entre nosotros" (is about ways of making the invisible visible, and focussing on those vivid images that we no longer see but which assert themselves like ghosts and live among us).[78] The miniscule city is the actualization of the photographer's memory of the real city; through the act of contemplation/reading, this memory takes root in the mind of the visitor and accompanies him in his trajectories through the city itself. Travelling back after seeing the model himself, the narrator sees an image of the model take shape in the darkness of the subway tunnel, "con la fijeza y la intensidad de un recuerdo inolvidable" (with the persistence and the intensity of an unforgettable memory).[79]

The photographer's model maintains a secret connection, we are told, to certain *rioplatense* literary traditions, namely that "como para Onetti o para Felisberto Hernández, la tensión entre objeto real y objeto imaginario no existe, todo es real, todo está ahí y uno se mueve entre los parques y las calles, deslumbrado por una presencia siempre distante" (in the same way as for Onetti or Felisberto Hernández, the tension between real and imagined objects does not exist: everything is real, everything is here and one moves through parks and streets, dazzled by an always distant presence).[80] To these names we would of course add that of Borges, whose "El Aleph" is the strongest of these presences: the narrator's description of the model clearly reproduces the language of Borges's story as well as the moment of vertiginous epiphany produced by the sight of the Aleph within the Aleph.

In the marked difference between the two narrators' reactions, however, lies the decisive resignifying operation of Piglia's text, in which the contemplation of "el inconcebible universo" (the inconceivable universe)[81] in the attic of Borges's story becomes an allegory of the act of reading. Borges's narrator, who also travels back on the subway after his revelation, fears that what he has seen will haunt him forever and rob him of the experience of surprise and newness. Fortunately, the fear is shortlived, and the cost appears to be only a few sleepless nights. Piglia's narrator, by contrast, welcomes the intrusion of the virtual into the real and suddenly grasps "lo que ya sabía: lo que podemos imaginar siempre existe, en otra escala, en otro tiempo, nítido y lejano, igual que en un sueño" (what I already knew: what we can imagine always exists, on another scale, in another time, vivid and distant, just as in a dream).[82] The dizzying vision of the city's replica does not provoke fear or horror but an understanding of the way in which real experience is continually inflected by and infused with the ghostly presence of the imagined, the dreamed, and the remembered. Reading is our portal into this multiverse, which does not always distinguish between the real and the imagined, the visible and the invisible, and in which art is not a picture of a world to be contained and mastered but structures our very experience of that world.

"Encuentro en Saint-Nazaire": literature as oracle

This role of literature in constructing future experience for the reader – rather than registering the past experience of the writer – is given fuller and more radical treatment in Piglia's "Encuentro en Saint-Nazaire," a novella published in the *Prisión perpetua* collection. The narrator, a writer, arrives to take up a three-month residency at the *Maison des écrivains étrangers et des traducteurs*. He is keen to meet the previous resident, Stephen Stevensen, who plans to stay on in Saint-Nazaire in a nearby hotel. The narrator initially assumes that the miscellany of personal objects and documents he finds at the *Maison* has been carelessly left behind by Stevensen. The lengthy enumeration of these dissimilar items reinforces for the reader a sense of the random nature of chance that has brought together a map of Copenhagen, a photograph of John Berger, and a report in *Le Monde* on a counter-attack against the IRA, among other notes and items. Only later does the narrator realize that these objects were deliberately placed and that these remnants and traces do not aid the narrator's attempt to reconstruct something of Stevensen's past life so much as Stevensen's attempt to construct the narrator's future.

He discovers that Stevensen has developed a method of predicting the course of seemingly random events by analyzing his own diary. Stevensen wants to understand what had led him the previous year into a deep depression and to the edge of suicide; he thinks that his diary must contain the answer, "un enigma que tenía que descifrar y que le iba a permitir entender todo" (an enigma that he had to solve and that would allow him to understand everything), and starts searching initially at random to find "una pista que me orientara en la selva oscura de mi vida" (a clue to guide him through the dark forest of his life).[83] He becomes more methodical, constructing long sequences of events and following a single event through "una cantidad casi infinita de variantes y ramificaciones" (an almost infinite number of variations and ramifications).[84] As the network of overlapping sequences grows, he discovers a crucial set of repetitions and a common trait underlying apparently disparate events. He struggles until he realizes that his approach is wrong: instead of returning to the past, he needs to move from the present towards the future, as "El Diario debía ser leído como un oráculo" (the Diary had to be read like an oracle).[85] In those details and events that happen only once and are not subject to repetition, he finds "el jeroglífico donde se cifra el porvenir" (the hieroglyph in which the future is encoded).[86] Eventually Stevensen is able to write a diary entry that predicts a "chance" re-encounter with a blonde fellow traveller, with staggering chronometrical precision. As he grows more adept in analyzing his diary, he is able to predict future events with greater accuracy, including those of the narrator's first days in Saint-Nazaire.

Stevensen attributes to his sister, a mathematician working in air traffic control, the inspiration for the method he develops. She teaches him to understand the future differently: not as the consequence of any "moral decision" whose effects unroll in a linear fashion into the distance, but as a series of complex but calculable events, whose predictability is based on "el grado de exactitud con el que se puedan prever las alternativas cifradas en el presente" (the degree of precision with which it is possible to predict the alternatives encoded in the present).[87] As an example, she points to the power of Kasparov's version of the Scheveningen Variation of the Sicilian Defence in chess, which in a famous match with Karpov "era tan sutil [...] que uno podía asimilarla a la magia y a la divinación" (was so subtle that it could be compared to magic and divination).[88] It did not merely predict how the game would unfold but produced each and every one of his opponent's moves, "como si le construyera un oráculo" (as if it were constructing an oracle for him).[89] In a similar manner, Stevensen's sister shows him the intricate web of lights on a computer screen that represent the trajectories of future flights crossing the airspace overhead. All the unexpected variations are predictable according to the logic of Heisenberg's uncertainty principle, she claims: "Llamamos azar [...] a una función elíptica de la temporalidad" (what we call chance is an elliptical function of time).[90]

The suggestion that Heisenberg's uncertainty principle might be harnessed to predict the trajectories of aeroplane flights is scientifically perverse in more ways than one. This principle, which states that the position and momentum of an electron cannot be simultaneously measured, explicitly points to the *unpredictability* of such values. Further, it describes the behaviour of subatomic particles, not jumbo jets, whose trajectories respond quite obligingly to Newtonian laws of gravity and motion, within a small margin of error for less predictable weather conditions. Equally, there is, of course, no mystery to such prowess in constructing defences in chess: they are based on an exact grasp of the alternative moves available at any point in the game.

Piglia's impressionistic (or deliberately capricious) use of science in "Encuentro en Saint-Nazaire" has the effect of bringing sharply into focus the question of which trajectories – of objects through space, games, or human destinies – might or might not yield their secrets to analysis, acquiring a degree of predictability. Neither chess moves nor flight paths pose a serious challenge to prediction, given the right computing capacity; however, we naturally baulk at the idea that human lives might respond so meekly. Stevensen's computer-assisted analysis of the repeated motifs and patterns of his diary entries suggests that what may appear to be the workings of chance in the insignificant events of our daily lives may turn out to be intricately determined, if only we could discover the laws that govern an apparently random sequence of events. By presenting as unpredictable phenomena that can be fully explained by existing laws, and conversely discovering laws governing phenomena that are apparently unpredictable and the product of chance, Piglia plunges us into the complex world of post-Newtonian physics, in which the deterministic eludes measurement, and the apparently chaotic may produce unexpected patterns. This world, as Prigogine reminds us, locates itself "somewhere between the two alienating images of a deterministic world and an arbitrary world of pure chance."[91] If the first "leaves no place for novelty" and, in the second, "everything is absurd, acausal, and incomprehensible,"[92] Piglia's texts shuttle between the two, dramatizing the uncertainties of interpretation in a probabilistic universe.

The fragments contained in a kind of postscript to the main narrative of "Encuentro en Saint-Nazaire" are presented as what remains of Stevensen's diaries. Grouped under the title "Diario de un loco" (Diary of a Madman), the sections are ordered alphabetically and frequently switch between the first and third persons. This collage of short meditations and micronarratives includes an account of the linguistic research conducted by Stevensen's sister, the capture and killing of a young female IRA terrorist known to her, and episodes that appear to indicate future events in the lives of Stevensen, his sister, and "el argentino" (the Argentine), as Stevensen refers to the narrator. These sections are interspersed with others that make frequent reference to unusual scientific phenomena, mathematical conjectures, paradoxes, and unresolved theorems, such as Lombroso's theories of criminology, Fermat's last theorem, Gödel's incompleteness theorems, Russell's type theory, diffraction in optical physics, and Pavlov's experiments. Many of the sections are linked by common themes and narrative patterns: forms of repetition and/or exceptionality, on the one hand, and, on the other, the untimely or premature termination of a creative work.

In other words, Piglia's narrative is constructed out of series, plus interruptions to those series. The theme of the unfinished work is perhaps most poignantly developed with reference to "Kubla Khan," the poem Coleridge claimed to have dreamt in its entirety but of which he could write down only forty-five lines before an interruption erased the rest from his memory. It is also pursued in the list of mathematicians, poets, and composers who contribute works of genius at a precocious age, before destroying themselves or sinking into obscurity. The positioning of these fragments at the end of "Encuentro en Saint-Nazaire," following the revelation of the nature of Stevensen's project and his sudden disappearance, encourages us to read them proleptically as narrative prefigurings of Stevensen's own death, foretold in his diaries, according to the method he has developed. This ending is never made explicit in the text, but his failure to reappear after the narrator unplugs the computer in his hotel room strongly suggests that he is no longer alive, as does the last message left on the screen before the flickering green text fades into nothing: "Estoy aquí, en Saint-Nazaire, porque quiero conocer el final de mi vida" (I am here, in Saint-Nazaire, because I want to know the end of my life).[93] Indeed, in one of the diary fragments, Stevensen predicts that the Argentine writer will be the one who truncates his life's work: "Primero irrumpió en la Maison, luego irrumpió en mi laboratorio del Hotel de la République y por fin irrumpió en la vida de mi hermana" (first he burst into the Maison, then he burst into my laboratory in the Hotel de la République and finally he burst into my sister's life).[94]

What the narrative "reveals" is not insight into inner motives, or mental acts that precede and explain external actions, but a set of narrative forms and patterns that seem to transcend the individual and all idea of intentionality. The existence of these patterns becomes the reflexive theme of those fragments that focus on the research carried out by Stevensen's sister into proverbs and aphorisms. Erika treats these sayings as microscopic forms that encode the events and stories of previous eras: "las ruinas de un relato perdido; en el proverbio persiste una historia contada y vuelta a contar durante siglos" (the ruins of a lost story; in the proverb endures a story that has been told and retold for centuries).[95]

The ghost in the machine

At a simplistic level, "Encuentro en Saint-Nazaire" articulates the Heideggerian "language speaks us" that underpins much post-structuralist thought. We do not simply write our lives in our diaries: our perceptions are shaped by the language we speak, and, if so, then why not also the direction of our lives? But Piglia takes this further to construct a thoroughly anti-psychological theory of reading and writing. One of the segments of Stevensen's diary refers to the concept of mind developed by Gilbert Ryle:

> Había soñado anoche con "El fantasma de la máquina" del doctor Ryle, el distinguido profesor de la Universidad de Oxford. "Todos (decía Ryle) vivimos dos vidas. Una vida real, donde rigen las leyes del destino, y otra que es inconfesable y secreta. Podemos imaginar una máquina lógica que nos ayude a fijar, en una tela invisible, esa experiencia privada."[96]

> He had dreamt last night about "The ghost in the machine" by Dr. Ryle, the distinguished professor from the University of Oxford. "We all (said Ryle) lead two lives. A real life, governed by the laws of destiny, and another that is secret and unspeakable. We could imagine a logical machine that would help us to fix, on an invisible cloth, that private experience."

Stevensen distorts Ryle's argument, which is in fact a critique of the "double-life theory,"[97] or the assumption underlying Cartesian dualism that the mental world can be distinguished from the physical one.[98] Ryle exposes the myth of "the Ghost in the Machine"[99] by challenging the idea that a person participates in two parallel histories, the first of which is comprised of what happens in and to his body, taking place in the public, physical world, and the second of which consists of what happens in and to his mind, taking place in the private, mental world.[100]

Stevensen's misquotation notwithstanding, Piglia's narrative supports Ryle's theory of mind at several points. Ryle maintains that another person's mental acts are not hidden or mysterious to us; motives do not reside in the mind before becoming expressed in behaviour as mental processes are not separable from physical existence. We discover the motives of others through "an inductive process, an induction to law-like propositions from observed actions and reactions."[101] We work with "dispositions," laws that govern tendencies to think and behave in certain ways. As Ryle states, "I find out most of what I want to know about your capacities, interests, likes, dislikes, methods and convictions by observing how you conduct your overt doings, of which by far the most important are your sayings and writings."[102] This procedure is very similar to the one adopted by Stevensen, who studies the text of his own diary to understand the events of his past, to discern laws governing them and thereby to predict future behaviour. He does not need to subject the narrator to psychoanalysis to discover hidden motives and desires, or what Ryle refers to as the "occult causes"[103] that might shape his destiny: he simply needs to observe patterns in his actions.

Piglia uses these insights to critique psychoanalytical modes of reading-as-interpretation and to suggest alternative ways of approaching a text. The text is not a series of external symptoms pointing to a hidden set of motives or states of mind: the understanding a text may yield resides in how its operations are conducted. The diary does not reveal hidden meanings that might explain characters' actions, but patterns of events and actions; in the same way, the "meaning" of a text is to be found by studying the laws that govern its development. As Susan Sontag argues, "it is the habit of approaching works of art in order to *interpret* them that sustains the fancy that there really is such a thing as the content of a work of art," a fallacy we have inherited from the Greek theory of art as mimesis, and that in due course allowed Freudian and Marxist approaches to posit a latent, "true" content beneath the manifest content of the text.[104] Instead, Sontag advocates a different mode of reading the text: "The function of criticism should be to show *how it is what it is*, even *that it is what it is*, rather than to show *what it means.*"[105] Similarly, for Piglia, the text does not yield the "secrets" of psychological causality; instead, it points to its own construction, and to the narrative patternings that seem to inhere in human experience across time. This idea becomes, as we will see, the primary narrative device of *Prisión perpetua*.

Prisión perpetua: reading, experience, and memory implantation

Many of the characters of Piglia's *Prisión perpetua* try to interpret potential signs around them with the same paranoia as Cohen's protagonist in *El testamento de O'Jaral*. Like Cohen's, Piglia's rejection of transcendence does not bring an end to meaning but reorients it along an immanent plane of potentially infinite connections and resonances. In *Prisión perpetua*, Piglia affords us a clearer sense of how these repetitions and recursions become, not signs yielding a meaning somewhere beyond them, but the principles and materials from which literary texts are constructed.

The ex-prisoner of "En otro país" feels that "Todo se cargaba de un sentido múltiple; las relaciones entre acontecimientos dispersos eran excesivas" (everything seemed charged with multiple meanings; disparate events were linked to a disproportionate degree).[106] Despite his attempts to allow randomness to intervene in his erratic journey to New York, hopping from one mode of transport to another and inventing a different past for himself every time he is asked, "Sabe que lo vigilan, no cree en las coincidencias ni en el azar. Todos los acontecimientos están entrelazados; siempre hay una causa" (he knows that they are watching him, he doesn't believe in coincidences or chance. All events are interlinked; there is always a cause).[107] His paranoid neurosis produces, and is produced by, the compulsive reading and over-interpretation of signs. This fanatical search for a hidden order or pattern is shared by several characters in *Prisión perpetua*, including the ex-preacher who mans a suicide assistance phoneline and listens again and again to the conversations he has recorded, in an attempt to "captar el centro de la obsesión secreta de Nueva York" (capture the heart of the secret obsession of New York).[108]

In the same way that the second part of "Encuentro en Saint-Nazaire" presents fragments that we are led to believe come from the diaries referred to in the first part, the second part of "En otro país" comprises a series of narrative sketches that we presume to represent sections of the unfinished novel mentioned in the first. One of them – the story of the suicide assistance phoneline – appears to have the status of a paratext, although it is not marked as such: we suspect that the other vignettes are stories told by the phoneline's anonymous callers. This is made most explicit at the end of the ex-convict's story, when we are told that he occasionally makes calls to a suicide assistance phoneline. The form of "En otro país" therefore reinforces for the reader a sense of the interconnectedness of everything, suggesting the existence of subterranean relationships that link together apparently disconnected events and experiences and allowing us to believe that everyone has a secret and that hidden patterns and meanings are simply waiting to be discovered.

The persistent use of coincidence and repetition in Piglia's narratives allows him to explore to the full this sense of hesitation between accident and design, the laws of chance and operations of a hidden order or system. Motifs, names, and plots recur frequently in the separate stories that make up *Prisión perpetua* and between that collection and the stories embedded in *La ciudad ausente*. Lucía Nietzsche (whose biography corresponds to that of Joyce's daughter Lucia) appears in "Encuentro en Saint-Nazaire" and "El fluir de la vida," as well as "En otro país"; she reappears as Lucía Joyce in *La ciudad ausente*. The stories are linked by a whole host of repeated locations, objects, and narrative events, including hotel rooms, trains, psychiatric clinics, photographers, exiled European scientists, rings, recording devices, suicides, and casino games. A substantial section of "Encuentro en Saint-Nazaire" is incorporated into the text of *La ciudad ausente*.[109] This teasing sense of repetition has us searching the texts as if they could be decoded in some way to reveal a central organizing idea. As we become implicated as readers in the same activity of deciphering and decrypting as the characters, we may think we begin to glimpse an originary, masked narrative lying behind or beneath these variations, which remains tantalizingly out of reach. But the signs simply circulate, undergoing transformations and displacements, colliding kaleidoscopically and transiently with other signs before separating again.

Reading becomes, not an exercise in finding a hidden narrative to link the apparently coincidental encounters of the text, but the space, or the act, in which those encounters take place. To use a biological metaphor, the repeated elements of *Prisión perpetua* act like viruses, multiplying themselves and moving through a population by inhabiting a series of hosts. It is narratives that are in movement, while characters often seem to be mere places of transit. For example, the historian in "En otro país" who obsessively collects proverbs and maxims, considering them to be "ruinas de grandes relatos perdidos" (ruins of great stories that have been lost),[110] reappears metamorphosed into Erika Turner in "Encuentro en Saint-Nazaire," the linguistician who is writing a book on proverbs, which she also treats as "ruinas de relatos perdidos."[111] Rather than a metamorphosis undergone by a particular character, however, it would be more accurate to suggest that the gist or kernel of the narrative leaps from one character to another, as if from one host organism to the next.

Everywhere in *Prisión perpetua*, texts are engaged in the process of generating other texts. Steve Ratliff's unfinished novel, a subject of fascination for the narrator of "En otro país," ostensibly provides the inspiration for the text that follows, "El fluir de la vida." So great is its influence on him that the narrator confesses, "Cuando escribo tengo siempre la impresión de estar contando su historia, como si todos los relatos fueran versiones de ese relato interminable" (when I write I always have the impression that I am telling his story, as if my stories were versions of that unending story).[112] Indeed, the similarities are immediately obvious to the reader: "El fluir de la vida" repeats a number of ideas and anecdotes that had been attributed to Steve in "En otro país." When, for example, Lucía tells el Pájaro that "El matrimonio es una institución criminal" (marriage is a criminal institution),[113] she echoes the exact words of Steve in a story he had told the narrator.[114]

Neither plagiarism nor intertextuality can adequately account for the transmission of narrative ideas from Steve to the narrator (called Piglia). "En otro país" attests to the power of storytelling to create mental pictures so vivid that they become indistinguishable from real experience in memory.

The narrator recalls a scene described by his author-friend Steve as if he had witnessed it himself, and, to this extent, he states: "La novela de Steve ha terminado por formar parte de mi propio pasado" (Steve's novel had ended up forming part of my own past).[115] From this confusion between reading and lived experience arises a definition of reading that underpins many of Piglia's texts. To remember with the memory of another is "una metáfora perfecta de la experiencia literaria" (a perfect metaphor for literary experience), as "La lectura es el arte de construir una memoria personal a partir de experiencias y recuerdos ajenos" (reading is the art of constructing a personal memory from the memories and experiences of others): scenes from books we have read remain with us as if they were part of our own past.[116]

"To write is not to recount one's memories and voyages, one's loves and griefs, one's dreams and phantasms," Deleuze maintains: if we believe that novels can be created "with our perceptions and affections, our memories and archives, our travels and fantasies, our children and parents, with the interesting characters we have met," we misunderstand the nature of the novel, "which goes beyond the perceptual states and affective transitions of the lived."[117] In the same way, for Piglia, we should not read literature for what it transmits to us about an author's past experience, but for what it reveals to us of literature's capacity to create new experiences and perceptions in the reader.

This ability of literature to embed itself into the memory of the reader, together with the continual transembodiment of narratives in Piglia's fiction, leads to a resignification of one of the most sinister tropes of science fiction: memory implantation. Piglia references the common dystopian version of this trope in his account of the clinic in "Los nudos blancos" (*La ciudad ausente*), where dissident citizens are reprogrammed with false memories as a method of control. These operations are carried out against the wishes of patients by doctors whose actions recall those of the military officers whose torture of prisoners during the Argentine dictatorship frequently produced forms of amnesia. More broadly, as Piglia observes in an essay, in the dystopian visions of writers such as Burroughs, Pynchon, Gibson, and Philip Dick, we often witness "la destrucción del recuerdo personal" (the destruction of personal memory), or – more accurately – "la sustitución de la memoria propia por una cadena de secuencias y de recuerdos extraños" (the substitution of individual memory with a chain of sequences and foreign memories).[118] Personal identity and individual memories are replaced in these paranoid, postmodern narratives with uncertainty about the past and a dissolution of identity and memory into the impersonal or the artificial.

For Piglia, many of the most well-known of Borges's narratives also revolve around "la incertidumbre del recuerdo personal, sobre la vida perdida y la experiencia artificial" (the uncertainty of personal memory, the loss of life and artificial experience).[119] The function of the surveillance state in stories such as "La lotería en Babilonia," for example, is to "inventar y construir una memoria incierta y una experiencia impersonal" (invent and construct a false memory and an impersonal form of experience).[120] Artificial memories are also, Piglia suggests, inculcated by mass culture; here again he aligns his insights with those of Borges, for whom mass culture becomes "una máquina de producir recuerdos falsos y experiencias impersonales. Todos sienten lo mismo y recuerdan lo mismo y lo que sienten y recuerdan no es lo que han vivido" (a machine for producing false memories and impersonal experiences. Everyone feels the same and remembers the same and what they feel and remember is not what they have lived).[121] The same idea is considered by Junior in *La ciudad ausente*, who muses that to watch television is to read the minds of millions of people.[122]

However, the implantation of artificial memories is also associated in Piglia's work with the creative and life-giving work of literature. To write is to implant a false memory into another, to "Incorporar a la vida de un desconocido una experiencia inexistente que tiene una realidad mayor que cualquier cosa vivida" (incorporate into the life of an unknown person a non-existent experience that is more real than anything lived).[123] The power of the storytelling-machine in *La ciudad ausente* – discussed in detail in Chapter 4 – lies entirely in her ability to insert artificial memories into her listeners/readers, "relatos convertidos en recuerdos invisibles que todos piensan que son propios" (narratives that become invisible memories that everyone thinks are their own).[124]

It is to invoke this creative function of reading that texts are often used as divination systems in Piglia's narratives, and literature is read as an oracle, a source of private messages to the reader that predict and construct future experience. In an essay in *El último lector*, for example, Robinson Crusoe does not read the Bible to discover a hidden meaning to his existence; he believes in its prophetic power and searches it for guidance, and therefore "la lectura se realiza en su vida" (what he reads becomes fulfilled in his life).[125] A woman in "En otro país" imagines life to be a roulette wheel and that all bets – as in Borges's "La lotería en Babilonia" – change the real-life destiny for their players. Like the protagonists of Philip K. Dick's *The Man in the High Castle* (1962), she starts to consult the *I-Ching*, the ancient Chinese *Book of Changes*, using it as a divination system to help her structure her empty days spent alone. The difficulty of choosing paths through "la maraña microscópica de posibilidades" (the microscopic tangle of possibilities) is alleviated when she realizes that, rather than decision-making, all she needs to do is decipher directions embedded in the text.[126] She becomes so dependent on it for every aspect of life that "A veces consultaba el *I-Ching* para saber si debía consultar el *I-Ching*" (sometimes she consulted the *I-Ching* to know whether she should consult the *I-Ching*).[127]

Perhaps it is partly our propensity towards what Deleuze and Guattari call "interpretosis" (see the discussion of *El testamento de O'Jaral* above) that accords literature its peculiar power to intervene performatively in our lives. Piglia's perception of the encoding in fiction of "lo que está por venir" (what is yet to come)[128] engages with Bloch's understanding of the utopian, anticipatory function of literature (see Chapter 1); it also resonates with Deleuze's declaration that literature creates the future, in the sense of producing new perceptions and affects. Piglia's affirmation that "lectura se mezcla con la experiencia, busca emociones, sentimientos, formas corporales" (reading mixes with experience, in search of emotions, feelings, bodily forms)[129] establishes literature and the act of reading as a process of (virtual) embodiment rather than something done by an embodied self. For this reason, metempsychosis, transmigration and reincarnation – among other cherished tropes of fantasy, SF, and cyberfiction – are often chosen in Piglia's essays and fiction as metaphors for the effects of reading. For Piglia, as for Deleuze, texts are not maps for the discovery of existing worlds but for the projection of future ones: "the expression and creation of what is not yet, not present or other than actual."[130] Reading creates connections that traverse time and space, bridging the real and the virtual, forging experiences that we have not lived in an embodied sense but that cannot be dismissed as false or artificial. For that reason, literature should not be read as an archive of the past or a record of the present, but as a map of the future.

3 | Mathematics and Creativity

The mathematical dilemmas and discoveries narrated in Martínez's *Acerca de Roderer* (1992) and Cohen's *Un hombre amable* (1998) set the stage for a broader reflection on the persistence of certain elements of Romantic thought in postmodernism. In *Acerca de Roderer*, Martínez's repeated use of Romantic narrative topoi – the solitary creative genius, self-destruction with the aid of opiates, the Faustian pact – acquires a particular irony in a novel that mounts an impassioned defence of rationalism. Romantic perspectives on creativity are held in tension here with approaches that can be identified closely with Formalist ideas, and it is the latter that point most convincingly towards an alternative to what Martínez refers to as the "dead ends" of postmodern parody and cynicism.

The mathematical-philosophical questions explored in Cohen's *Un hombre amable* (1998) – chief among them, Platonism versus constructivism, or whether mathematical entities are created or discovered – provide a point of entry into debates within literary theory concerning the ethics of narrative reflexivity and irony. Cohen's novel reworks the legacies of Romantic irony and the Romantic understanding of chaos and order that remain evident in postmodern literature and theory. In so doing, it counters one of the most prevalent postmodern fictions: that self-awareness and reflexivity leads only to narcissistic detachment and not to the expression of an ethical commitment to the world beyond the text. Cohen draws on the more contemporary conception of the relationship between chaos and order suggested by theories of complexity and emergence, much less polarized than that proposed in Romantic literature and theory. This newer understanding allows us to situate literary innovation as part of the broader, unceasing, creative flux of the universe at large. In turn, this conception leads to a more nuanced appreciation of the contradictions within Romantic thought, and the theorizations of Friedrich Schlegel in particular.

Both novels explore the possibility of non-binaristic modes of thought, but only in Cohen's does this become a principle of textual construction. Martínez's faith in the dialectical progress of Reason is mirrored in his Formalist understanding of literary evolution, in which opposing forms can give rise to new syntheses, and familiar or forgotten ideas can provide fresh insights if they are put to new uses. His sense of literary (and scientific) history as a discontinuous process that stems from negation, rupture, and refunctioning differs from Cohen's vision, in many ways more akin to that of Schlegel, who wrote of ancient poetry that "Everything interpenetrates everything else, and everywhere there is one and the same spirit, only expressed differently."[1] Cohen's epistemology is not built on a dialectical process but a commitment to nondualism, which positions the writer within the flux of the creative universe, not above it: it is therefore of little consequence whether our theories about it are accurate or not, and their much-vaunted demise may in fact permit us to construct a more honest, intimate, concrete, and yet still self-aware, approach to being in the world and to narrating it, two activities that often become synonymous in Cohen's work.

CREATIVE CONTRADICTIONS AND THE MATHEMATICS OF POSTMODERN THOUGHT / MARTÍNEZ

> Always doth he destroy who hath to be a creator.—Friedrich Nietzsche[2]

> One must always assume from the start that an idea is not totally new. [...] But here, in this case, in this connection and under this light, it may indeed turn out that what has existed before

is new after all, new to life so to speak, original and unique.—
Thomas Mann[3]

An erstwhile mathematician turned novelist, Guillermo Martínez is particularly well placed to appreciate the creative potential in appropriating mathematical and scientific ideas for literary use, if also to observe the distortion of such ideas as they cross disciplinary boundaries. Martínez has often criticized the misuse in postmodern thought of certain theories – most fashionably, those of uncertainty, incompleteness, and chaos – that are often cited in triumphant pronouncements concerning the demise of scientific rationalism as an epistemological project. As he claims, for example, "las extrapolaciones apresuradas y las analogías demasiado ligeras" (the hasty extrapolations and frivolous analogies) that mark the appropriation of Gödel's incompleteness theorem by other disciplines "han llevado a conclusiones tremendistas, erróneas, a veces incluso risibles" (have led to conclusions that are alarmist, erroneous, or even laughable).[4] Our world may contain chaotic phenomena and natural catastrophes, but it is also governed, he reminds us, by immutable laws and regularity.[5]

A section of Martínez's book *Gödel para todos* (2009) outlines ways in which he considers Gödel's theories to have been used too loosely by thinkers such as Kristeva, Deleuze, and Lyotard. As I suggested in the Introduction, Martínez closely follows the line of critique established by Alan Sokal, Jean Bricmont, Jacques Bouveresse, and others of the use of mathematical and scientific ideas in French philosophy. Like them, Martínez objects to a version of the history of science that rapidly gained currency in the latter part of the twentieth century, according to which absolute empiricism reigned until the sudden irruption of certain theories (Gödel, Heisenberg, etc.) completely destroyed the premises of rational enquiry.[6] For Martínez, the idea that human reason is utterly incapable of accounting for reality – widely accepted and repeated as a commonplace among recent thinkers and writers – represents "un pase de manos demasiado rápido" (too quick a sleight-of-hand), leaping rashly from an affirmation of the limitations of reason to its total incompetence.[7] Seldom in Martínez's *Crímenes imperceptibles* reminds us that mathematics as a discipline did not come to a full stop with the publication of Gödel's theorem.[8] In a similar vein, Sokal and Bricmont point out that, far from confronting scientists with a dead end, chaos theory has opened up "a vast area for future research."[9]

If Martínez's *Crímenes imperceptibles* reveals our tragic propensity to misapply half-understood mathematical reasoning to the messiness of real life (see Chapter 2), *Acerca de Roderer* (1992) mounts an impassioned defence of rationalism and dialectical thought in the pursuit of creativity and new forms of knowledge. In many postmodernist caricatures, science is depicted either as hopelessly clinging to fixed laws that cannot explain the complexity of the universe or alternatively (or additionally) as nothing more than a set of myths and social constructions. Both perspectives may be considered hangovers from Romanticism, in its anti-Enlightenment approach to science and its development of irony as a self-conscious destruction of the illusions of fiction. Martínez's appropriation of Romantic narrative topoi in a novel about a discovery of paramount importance for mathematics and the philosophy of logic therefore acquires a particular irony of its own and works in specific ways to unsettle the dichotomy between Reason and Romanticism that still dominates much contemporary thought.

The contradictory combination of Romantic and Formalist ideas in *Acerca de Roderer* engages with and effectively reconfigures, I will argue, broader tensions between these inherited frameworks within postmodernism. That postmodern thought may be defined by the conflictive co-presence of these two currents is the provocative argument advanced by the Serbian mathematician Vladimir Tasić in his *Mathematics and the Roots of Postmodern Thought*, translated into Spanish in 2001 by Martínez himself.[10] I will explore Tasić's argument in some detail as the parallels he draws between the development of mathematics and postmodern thought suggest a more productive attempt to bring science and philosophy/literature into dialogue than the simplistic and often erroneous appropriation in postmodern texts of theories of uncertainty and chaos, whether as metafictional flourishes, as dubious analogies for social systems, or as evidence of the downfall of scientific rationalism.

Rationalism and Romantic creativity

Acerca de Roderer relates the encounters – as boys and as men – between the narrator and an unusual school companion, Roderer. Roderer is Martínez's most gifted and iconoclastic thinker, a self-taught genius who sets himself the task of overturning the law of excluded middle. This law, described in the novel as the most precarious in logic, rests on *reductio* reasoning[11] and refers to the premise that between being and non-being there cannot exist a third alternative. Roderer's project is to dismantle the apparatus of thought that invented logic in the first place and to find a new system of thought that transcends this binary structure. His body wracked with pain and enfeebled with morphine, he claims to have discovered just such a system, but dies – conveniently for Martínez – mere hours before he can commit it to paper.

The novel frequently repairs to conventional Romantic representations of the creative genius, including the association of creativity with insanity or illness. Roderer, like the archetypical Romantic artist, is dishevelled, unpredictable, totally focussed on his creative work, addicted to opium, and oblivious to social mores. He is afflicted with a heavily Romantic conviction of finitude, battling against the passing of time and the increasing frailty of his body. His inspiration is supernatural and his rebellion against institutions is total. At school – for which Roderer has little time – his genius remains wholly untapped, but he becomes a figure of awe for his fellow classmate, the novel's narrator. The boys' mathematics teacher differentiates between two kinds of intelligence: the first is primarily "assimilative," quick to analyze and synthesize different ideas, and associated with success in our world; the second, much rarer, rejects all previous assumptions and often brings madness or alienation, but may, through startling revelations, teach us to "mirar de nuevo" (see in a new way).[12] The narrator recognizes instantly that his own intelligence falls into the first category and that Roderer's belongs firmly in the second.

The second approach is clearly associated in the novel with Romantic notions of creativity: it is the work of the inspired individual genius and involves the violent overthrow of the structures of previous knowledge. In the first approach, the individual plays a part in a more collective and cyclical process of stagnation and revitalization, appropriating and reworking forms and structures from the past. This concept of how newness emerges is related in Martínez's work both to the dialectical tradition of scientific advance and to Formalist theories of literary evolution. If Roderer's creativity is more often imagined in terms of the second kind of innovation, Martínez imagines and executes his own revitalizing project very much in terms of the first. The complexity of *Acerca de Roderer* stems, however, from his refusal to treat Romantic and Formalist ideas of creativity as antagonistic but to seek instead to hold them in tension as a way of challenging old dichotomies and creating new syntheses of thought.

For all the likeness he bears to a Keats or a Byron, Roderer is not a Romantic poet but a self-taught mathematician and philosopher, and his work is carried out within the rigours and constraints of systematic, logical thought. If he is to succeed in overturning previous knowledge and replacing it with an entirely new system, he first needs to teach himself the language of mathematics and logic. His new understanding of the universe is achieved through the scrupulous exercise of reason, not against it, even if it requires him to reinvent the logic on which reason is founded. He expresses an adherence to the dialectical method and a belief in the potential of human reason, stating "toda nueva oposición es sólo en apariencia oposición: en realidad señala la próxima altura a conquistar y la razón la recoge en sí al pasar, se alimenta de ella" (every new opposition is only an apparent opposition: in reality it points to the next height to be conquered and reason absorbs that opposition within itself as it moves along, feeding off it).[13] Roderer's return to the past to mine it for new possibilities, desperately trying to recuperate "todos los estados intermedios del pensamiento, los razonamientos precarios, los nexos perdidos u olvidados" (all the intermediary states in thought, shaky points of reasoning, links that were lost or forgotten),[14] is carried out in accordance with dialectical methods of thought, but also recalls the Formalist idea that literary innovation often involves a step backwards to find paths truncated or left unexplored by previous generations, recollecting what Jurij Striedter calls "collateral lines."[15]

Thus the novel gives rein to Romantic notions of genius and creativity while extolling the virtues of methodical, dialectical thought and taking as its subject an enterprise of vast potential import for rationalist epistemology: to refound on a more accurate set of axioms the logic that underpins much mathematics and philosophy. By giving such overtly Romantic expression to this rationalist project, Martínez effectively subverts the dichotomy between Romanticism and Reason that has persisted in different guises in postmodern thought. Postmodernism's penchant for "lo incompleto, lo azaroso, lo indeterminado, lo fragmentado, lo imposible de conocer" (the incomplete, the risky, the indeterminate, the fragmented, the impossible to know) has, as Martínez comments, Romantic roots; likewise its portrayal of Reason as "prosaica, árida, mezquina, de patitas cortas" (prosaic, arid, small-minded, short-lived).[16] Martínez refuses to respect such divisions in the presentation of his protagonist: the highly intellectual Roderer enters battle with the zeal and desperation of any Romantic hero, ready to sacrifice everything – even his soul – to advance mathematical knowledge.

More importantly, however, Martínez recuperates the antagonism between Romantic inexpressibility and Reason as a battle that takes place within mathematics itself. Challenges to the law of excluded middle have been mounted by a number of mathematicians and logicians, chief among them L.E.J. Brouwer, Arend Heyting, and others associated with intuitionist approaches in the early twentieth century, and later in that century, by the philosopher Michael Dummett in his work on realism and anti-realism. For Martínez, these challenges – although yet to be incorporated into "mainstream" mathematics – play an essential role in the dialectical tradition that constitutes the foundation of scientific rationalism. He insists that we should not confuse rationalism with binary logic: rationalism is a historical process in which many more subtle forms of logic have been developed than that which rests on the distinction between true and false, incorporating "valores intermedios, valores probables, valores difusos" (intermediary values, probable values, diffuse values) into contemporary mathematics.[17] In a similar vein, *Acerca de Roderer* articulates a commitment to the pursuit of knowledge through reason, but a reason that is elastic and provisional as well as rigorously dialectical.

Creative contradiction in Nietzsche

The significant presence of Nietzsche within *Acerca de Roderer* also points to a synthesizing intent: Nietzsche's understanding of contradiction as the source of creativity speaks both to Romantic ideas and to the processes of dialectical thinking. Roderer's refusal to accept the law of excluded middle responds to Nietzsche's call to start precisely with this axiom in a much-needed overhaul of thought. Nietzsche exhorts us to question the presuppositions of the law of contradiction, a particularly important task if it is (as Aristotle claimed) the "most certain of all principles […] upon which every demonstrative proof rests."[18] The axioms of our formal logic, Nietzsche suspects, are "not adequate to reality," as logic is a human construct, an attempt to comprehend the world by making it "formulatable and calculable."[19] Roderer joins Nietzsche in questioning the adequacy of the axioms on which logic and mathematics have been founded since Classical times; this does not necessarily suppose an eschewal of all axiomatic thinking but certainly fits with what Nietzsche calls the "Attempt at a Revaluation of All Values."[20]

Nietzsche's understanding of creativity is also directly referenced in *Acerca de Roderer* at several points. Martínez's narrator is stupefied by Roderer's decision to get rid of his extensive library of books and does not understand his elliptical explanation: "ya fui el camello en el desierto y el león; sólo me queda la transformación en niño" (I have already been the camel in the desert and the lion; now all that is left is the transformation into a child).[21] The phrase recalls Nietzsche's "three metamorphoses of the spirit," which describe "how the spirit became a camel, the camel a lion, and the lion at last a child."[22] In its context in *Thus Spake Zarathustra*, this transformation evokes not (or not simply) the end of history but the possibility of a new creativity. After the "reverent spirit" of the beast of burden and the rebellion of the lion fighting for freedom, "Innocence is the child, and forgetfulness, a new beginning" and a "holy Yea," which is needed for the "game of creating."[23] This expression of hope seems antithetical to Nietzsche's account of nihilism as a state of utter disillusion in which "all that happens is meaningless and in vain."[24] Identifying this as an ambivalence in Nietzsche's work, Alessandro Tomasi suggests that "Nietzsche seems to be offering two versions of nihilism, for which he offers no conceptual discrimination: a type of nihilism favorable, or even necessary, to creativity, and one that prevents any creative effort."[25] For Justin Clemens, this ambivalence is more accurately understood as a paradox inherent within nihilism, which is at once "the terminus of history *and* a transitional moment, [...] poised on the brink of the unprecedented" and offering "the desirable-necessary chance for a new beginning."[26]

In Nietzsche, the critique of the law of excluded middle forms part of a broader exhortation to create afresh by tearing down existing structures, and in this respect his thought resonates clearly, not only with the Romantic conception of creativity from destruction, but also of contradiction as a source of that creativity. The contradictions in Nietzsche's work, as Phyllis Berdt Kenevan attests, stem from a resistance to the need to simplify; they produce "not simply chaos but a fertile sort of disorder," opening up "creative potentialities."[27] However, that Nietzsche did not, or did not simply, advocate the overthrow of human reason is evident, not least in his admiring portrait of Goethe as a man who "strove against the separation of reason, sensuality, feeling, will."[28] The quest of *Acerca de Roderer* to bring together Romantic notions of creativity and a commitment to dialectical reasoning is pursued with something of this spirit.

Postmodern parody vs. montage

This synthesizing approach is very much evident in the novel's engagement with literary tradition. The particularly close relationship it develops with Thomas Mann's *Doctor Faustus* (1947),[29] itself a novel about artistic renovation, suggests that another form of renewal is stake: of literature, rather than philosophy or mathematics. Martínez's recourse to intertextuality must be distinguished from the openly parodic or self-referential use of such techniques in some postmodern literature, which he targets with an astringent critique:

> cinismo, frialdad, parodia, intertextualidad, literatura en segundo grado, autorreferencia, aburrimiento, ¿qué es lo que hay

de común en estos elementos? Un único terror por no dejarse sorprender, por no quedar nunca más al descubierto. Al que no cree, por lo menos, nadie lo tratará de ingenuo, al que nada afirma nada se le podrá refutar. Del mismo modo, la parodia no puede ser parodiada ni la intertextualidad vuelta a mezclar. Nuestro fin de siglo, con un reflejo de mano escaldada, busca refugio en los estados terminales del escepticismo. [...] Pero el escepticismo, como posición, es tan inatacable como estéril, y en el dominio de la literatura – está a la vista – conduce rápidamente a caminos cerrados.[30]

cynicism, coldness, parody, intertextuality, second-degree literature, self-reference, boredom: what do these elements have in common? One fear, of allowing oneself to be surprised, or left vulnerable. If you do not believe, you cannot be treated as naïve; if you do not assert anything then nothing you say can be refuted. In the same way, parody cannot be parodied; nor can intertextuality be mixed up again. Our *fin de siècle*, like the reflex of a burned hand, looks for refuge in the deadly realms of skepticism. [...] But skepticism, as a position, is as sterile as it is unassailable, and in the field of literature – as is evident – it leads quickly to dead ends.

Acerca de Roderer articulates this sense of the exhaustion of artistic forms that is widespread in postmodern thought but also gestures towards a possible way through the impasse. It is interesting, given Martínez's comments above, that this is largely achieved through techniques of intertextuality and reflexivity; as I will show, however, these are given a serious, historicizing function in the novel that distances them from the more cynical, defensive or whimsical modes of postmodern parody criticized above.

Martínez engages closely with the themes of artistic exhaustion and reinvention developed in Mann's *Doctor Faustus*. Roderer, like Mann's Adrian Leverkühn, is a Faustian figure who destroys himself as he gives himself wholly to his new creations. Even Nietzsche's importance in *Acerca de Roderer* is prefigured in the earlier novel, as Mann drew heavily on Nietzsche's life to construct his text, including his experience at the Cologne bordello and the precise symptoms of the disease he contracts. If he does not mention Nietzsche by name, this is – as Mann acknowledges – "because the euphoric musician has been made so much Nietzsche's substitute that the original is no longer permitted a separate existence."[31] Although the plots of both *Doctor Faustus* and *Acerca de Roderer* are of good Romantic pedigree, focussing on the deeds and misdeeds of the genius whose individual creative powers may transform art and knowledge, their authors can be seen to experiment with a rather different kind of creativity in the form of their novels. Newness in both cases involves the careful return to a range of sources and voices from the past, to place these in surprising and productive relationships with the present. Like Mann before him, Martínez appears to be interested in revitalizing a tradition of montage, rescuing it from a collapse into mere pastiche or cynical parody.

Mann used the term "montage" to describe his technique in *Doctor Faustus*, which had its genesis in a "wild medley" of "notes from many fields – linguistic, geographic, politico-social, theological, medical, biological, historical and musical."[32] He openly admitted to the flagrant and unattributed reproduction or glossing of whole sections of Adorno's as-yet-unpublished *The Philosophy of New Music* and expressed relief that Adorno, who collaborated closely with Mann, was "gracious" in his response to such plagiarism,[33] unlike Schoenberg, who unleashed a bitter campaign against him for appropriating his ideas without acknowledgment, most notably the invention of twelve-tone serialism. In its extensive citations and paraphrases of an eclectic range of texts, *Doctor Faustus* performs a literary version of the techniques of montage often associated with the music of Mahler, resignifying familiar or simple motifs and styles by inserting them into new contexts.[34] In a similar manner, *Acerca de Roderer* is Martínez's most sustained attempt to bring together a heterogeneous range of ideas and discussions, drawing from the fields of biology, mathematics, philosophy, theology, and literature and weaving together citations from multiple texts as an example of the kind of imaginative repositionings and recontextualizations that may result in newness.

Mann writes of his attempts to draw the musical innovations of Schoenberg and others into the form of his novel, acknowledging that "my book itself would have to become the thing it dealt with: namely a musical composition."[35] Arguably, Mann's novel is nothing of the kind, or at least it reflects very little of the mathematical rigour shaping the musical compositions he discusses: it does not participate in any consistent manner in the avant-garde search, exemplified in the music of Berg, Webern, and the later Schoenberg, for new formal constraints to give meaning to old ideas. We see here nothing of the precise mathematical forms of constructivism in music but often a loosely connected series of digressions. Mann himself attests to his struggle to impose a form on the manuscript, once it had been written, to give it greater coherence; he experimented with and then abandoned a plan to split the chapters into six sections in a bid for greater clarity of form.[36]

Likewise, the narrative of *Acerca de Roderer* is not constrained by prominent formal devices, but its use of motifs and montage is similarly extensive. While both Mann and Martínez express an interest in the generative potential of serial music or logical series, their own aesthetic relies less on strict sequences or formal patterning and much more on the combinatory, montage practices associated with earlier music on the cusp of modernity, such as that of Mahler or the early Schoenberg. As one of Mann's critics acknowledges, there is nothing essentially new about the introduction of leitmotifs and montage to the novel; what is remarkable in this case is the extent and the tenacity of their use.[37] Martínez, like Mann, is interested in exploring the revitalizing potential in the tradition of montage, bringing texts and events from the past into a dialectical relationship with the present, breathing new life into old configurations, and rescuing potential clichés through the imposition of new forms. As the musican protagonist states in *Doctor Faustus*: "One must always assume from the start that an idea is not totally new. When it comes to notes, what is ever absolutely new! But here, in this case, in this connection and under this light, it may indeed turn out that what has existed before is new after all, new to life so to speak, original and unique."[38] This sense of giving new meaning to old clichés by embedding them within an innovative construction is what underpins both serialism and montage, even if one compositional technique is really the inverse of the other: the first generates, through "chance" (the application of strict mathematical iterations), patterns that occasionally throw up forms belonging to older patterns, such as tonality, while the second consciously ransacks forms from the past, producing a sense of newness by placing old forms in new or unexpected contexts.

Martínez's choice of intertext – *Doctor Faustus* is already, in James Schmidt's words, "a phantasmagoria of correspondences, imitations, resemblances"[39] – lays bare a giddying vision of an endless textual mise-en-abyme. The effect, however, is not to empty out signification or to produce blank parody: it is to undertake a critical exploration of the present and the past in search of correspondences and differences, and to resituate older practices within new contexts in such a way that they acquire new meanings. Precisely how such textual citation differs from the kind of skeptical postmodern parody and recycling Martínez denigrates may be appreciated in the following example. In the article cited above, Martínez criticizes postmodern skepticism for its assumption that everything has already been said, which condemns artistic creativity to "dos vías muertas: la parodia y la repetición" (two dead ends: parody and repetition).[40] Almost exactly the same words are used in the text of *Acerca de Roderer*, but this time they are used to summarize the theme of Heinrich Holdein's *La visitación*, a fictional novel by a fictional writer. Roderer claims that Holdein's text confronts the central problem facing art in his time:

> la gran apuesta de la novela es afrontar el problema crucial del arte en esta época: el agotamiento progresivo de las formas, la inspección mortal de la razón, el canon cada vez más extenso de lo que ya no puede hacerse, la transformación terminal del arte en crítica, o la derivación a las otras vías muertas: al parodia, la recapitulación.[41]

> the novel's great undertaking is to confront the crucial problem of art in this era: the progressive exhaustion of forms, the deadly examination of reason, the ever more extensive canon of what can no longer be done, the fatal transformation of art

into criticism or its rerouting towards other dead ends: parody, recapitulation.

It becomes clear that Holdein's novel, like Martínez's own, is a version of Mann's *Doctor Faustus*, which – and this will hardly be a surprise – also contains a critique of art's "unvital" refuge in parody as a response to a sense of staleness in artistic form.[42] These repetitions and mirrorings do not, however, serve to parody previous discourses. To perceive connections between the contemporary sense of art's exhaustion and that which characterized an earlier period – in Mann's novel, the shift from late Romanticism to early Modernism in music – is not to conflate them or to repeat an earlier gesture, but to uncover the cycles of exhaustion, parody, and renewal that structure the history of art and human knowledge: there is nothing unique about the postmodern moment that should necessarily lead us to assume that exhaustion will not be followed by renewal as it has at other junctures in history.

Although the sincerity of Martínez's citations from Mann's novel might lead us to consider that categorizing his approach as "parodic" would be a mistake, it would nevertheless sit comfortably within Linda Hutcheon's much broader definition of parody. For Hutcheon, parody may operate in modes that range "from scornful ridicule to reverential homage" and is perhaps best defined as "ironic trans-contextualization" or "imitation with critical ironic distance."[43] A critical distance is certainly marked by the appropriation of Romantic motifs in a story about the axiomatic grounding of mathematical logic: Martínez is deliberately playing on our (Romantic-inherited) sense that emotion and reason are opposed. Furthermore, within the novel's diegesis Roderer criticizes Holdein – in terms that could easily be applied to Mann – for lacking courage in the characterization of his protagonist. Holdein cannot stay true to his original casting of a cold, inhuman figure but instead inserts an unconvincing affair with a prostitute, as (Romantic) literary tradition dictated that any passion (love, hate, jealousy) could be taken to extremes except intellectual passion, identified with frigidity. At this thought, Roderer exclaims, with incredulity: "¡Como si la inteligencia no pudiera arder y exigir las hazañas más altas, la vida misma!" (as if intelligence were not able to burn and demand the greatest exploits, life itself!).[44] Martínez does not commit Holdein's/Mann's "error" of this unwarranted deference to Romantic archetypes: his protagonist is enslaved only to the passions of the mind, oblivious to all carnal desires or human emotions. Martínez's appropriation of Mann's text is not parodic in the sense of holding a previous text or genre up for ridicule, and neither does it simply quote or pay homage: it demonstrates the intent to transform it through critical distance to form a new synthesis, in the way that Hutcheon describes.[45]

Mathematics and postmodern thought

Postmodern discourse frequently pits an "old" science against a "new" one: reductionism and the adherence to fixed laws in the "old" science contrasts with postmodernism's (Romantic) penchant for the undecidable and the inexpressible, while the "new" science is often depicted in terms that render it, as Jacques Bouveresse argues, as "poco diferente de la filosofía y la literatura" (little different from philosophy and literature): if both are simply forms of discourse or narrative, there can be little distinction between them.[46] Martínez challenges the "bad old science, good new science" premise that informs much postmodernist literature by making it clear that the more diffuse mathematics favoured by poststructuralists has emerged *within* the scientific tradition of reason and dialectical thinking, not against or in spite of it. The interplay in Martínez's fiction between a commitment to rationality and logic on the one hand and a Romantic sense of the inexpressible on the other can be read as internal conflicts within mathematics itself. This makes all the difference: instead of Reason overthrown by chaos, the inexplicable simply stimulates the next step in a dialectical process.

If the over-simplistic opposition between Romanticism and Reason is unsettled in this way, the path is open to consider different ways that we might choose to understand the relationship between mathematics and postmodern thought. The suggestive hypothesis explored by Tasić in his *Mathematics and the Roots of Postmodern Thought* is that both mathematics and postmodernism have been shaped by a series of exchanges taking place between these disciplines throughout the twentieth century. In his aim to recover historical connections between mathematics and continental philosophy that might "go deeper than today's tedious incantations of chaos, fractals, and fuzziness,"[47] Tasić goes as far as to propose that some of postmodernism's contradictions may be located in debates initially conducted within the field of mathematics. His contention is that postmodern theory may be viewed as "a curious 'product' of the irreconcilable differences between intuitionism and formalism" in mathematics.[48]

Tasić argues firstly that certain Romantic ideas, including the inexpressibility of a reality that resists capture in language, resurface in the preoccupations of early twentieth-century intuitionist mathematicians – the key referent here is Brouwer – and then filter through the work of other continental philosophers, such as Poincaré, to influence thinkers like Derrida and Deleuze. Against Russell and Frege, Poincaré insisted that mathematical understanding is not reducible to logical inference: "there is always an unidentifiable subjective contribution, a creative-intuitive act of some kind" involved in the process.[49] An emphasis on that which resists formalization, and on the subjectivity of interpretation, is of course all-pervasive in postmodernist thought. Tasić finds Deleuze and Guattari's ideas fairly incomprehensible from a mathematical perspective. Nevertheless, he observes that their "strange" work *Anti-Oedipus*, positing the possibility of a liberated, non-binary form of thought that will not apply the law of excluded middle, resonates with the lineage of Romantic-intuitionist thought he is tracing: there are key similarities, for example, between "all those fluctuations and flows of desire" and the intuitionist continuum.[50]

Tasić then argues in a similar fashion for the continuity of certain formalist ideas in postmodern thought, which are sometimes – in the cases of Wittgenstein and Derrida – combined in rather complex ways with Romantic-intuitionist ones. Here he focusses on the work of Jean Cavaillès, the philosopher of science who "can be viewed as bridging the great divide between Hilbert's formalism and certain parts of postmodern theory."[51] Cavaillès, to expand a little on Tasić's argument, attempts to shift the focus of the theory of science from conscious acts of creativity to a kind of "conceptual becoming which cannot be stopped" that transcends the consciousness of individual scientists and ultimately generates, and responds to, "the necessity of a dialectic."[52] Tasić suggests that these ideas could be seen to lay the groundwork for Foucault's approach to knowledge and truth as discursive practices.[53] He cites Foucault's premise that "it is not man who constitutes [the human sciences] and provides them with a specific domain; it is the general arrangement of the *episteme* that provides them with a site, summons them, and establishes them – thus enabling them to constitute man as their object."[54] This de-anthropologizing perspective is in clear conflict with Romantic/intuitionist notions of *a priori* knowledge and Brouwer's treatment of the "creating subject" of mathematical activity.

Postmodern theory then, according to Tasić, is most accurately understood as a "deeply divided edifice," riven with contradictory modes of thought that may be traced back to competing philosophies of mathematics. It may be viewed

> first, as a revival, or a re-invention in somewhat different terms, of a challenge that mathematicians who were influenced by romanticism once issued to logical reductionism; and second, as an extraordinary radical dismissal of romantic humanism, a dismissal whose roots can in part be traced to mathematics, and which in its postmodern edition becomes a rather extreme form of formalism.[55]

When Tasić alludes to formalism, he is of course referring to mathematical formalism, not the kind practised by Russian literary critics. However, the two approaches do share some defining characteristics, particularly in their desubjectivizing approaches. Cavaillès's understanding of scientific advance as a "conceptual becoming that cannot be halted" relegates the individual scientist to a secondary place in a way that recalls the Formalist account of literary evolution, in which the individual creator (as Shklovsky insisted) is "simply the geometrical point of intersection of forces operative outside of him"[56] in the battle between genres and forms through which art continually renews itself.

Tasić's argument is ambitious enough to provoke contention in many quarters. Indeed, his introduction to the book makes clear that his aim is "to demonstrate that mathematics *could* have been a formative factor in the rise of postmodern theory," and he suggests that "it is probably best to think of this book as a story – a speculative reconstruction of a story – and an invitation to a polemic."[57] In broad terms, however, it seems at least plausible to see in postmodern notions of creativity the persistence of two paradoxical lineages of thought: on one hand, the Romantic rejection of the mechanistic Enlightenment understanding of human creativity and, on the other, a privileging of text and discourse over authorial intention or the creative act of an individual in accounts of artistic evolution or the advance of scientific knowledge, which can be associated with mathematical and literary formalisms (and in their reworking in structuralism and post-structuralism). And of course Tasić's major contribution here – like that of Martínez – is to complicate any monolithic conception of logic and mathematics as antithetical to postmodernism, and to situate those areas of affinity postmodernism has recently discovered with the "new" science of uncertainty within a much longer series of exchanges between science, art, and philosophy. His arguments bring us to suspect that what appear to be battles between disciplines may more properly be understood as internal conflicts within them.

While Martínez would certainly echo Sokal and Bricmont's insistence that "Science is not a 'text'"[58] or merely a mine of tropes for the description of broader cultural phenomena, he is more willing than they are to perceive the creative potential for mathematical and scientific ideas in literature and philosophy. In *Acerca de Roderer*, such ideas form a vital part of Martínez's metafictional critique of postmodern declarations of the end of art and philosophy (as well as science) and allow him to imagine a way through the impasse of postmodern parody. What postmodern theorists stand to learn from mathematics is that even the most fundamental axioms of logic can be questioned without destroying the whole bedrock of rational and scientific enquiry: there is space for anti-rationalistic modes of thought within the dialectical process of rationalism. Certain schools of mathematics, Martínez shows us, have shown as much interest in undermining binaristic logic as the most ardent postmodernist. To tear down the entire edifice of rationalist enterprise at the first sight of limitations in our logic or problems with our epistemologies is not only mathematically inaccurate but also leads in

Martínez's eyes to a loss of faith in aesthetic renovation as well as scientific progress. As he suggests,

> El escepticismo, en tiempo de derrumbes, puede hacerse pasar fácilmente por inteligencia. Pero la verdadera pregunta de la inteligencia es cómo volver a crear.[59]

> Skepticism, in times of destruction, can easily pass for intelligence. But the real question intelligence poses is how to create once again.

Martínez's own recyclings of past texts bears little resemblance to postmodern parody, often criticized as conservative in its intent to mock other artistic forms without offering any serious aesthetic alternatives. They adhere much more to the version of parody elevated by the Russian Formalists, for whom – as Hutcheon states – parody is also "capable of transformative power in creating new syntheses."[60]

POST-ROMANTIC PRINCIPLES OF CREATIVITY IN A SELF-ORGANIZING UNIVERSE / COHEN

> Suppose these houses are composed of ourselves,
> So that they become an impalpable town, full of
> Impalpable bells, transparencies of sound,
> [...]
> Confused illuminations and sonorities,
> So much ourselves, we cannot tell apart
> The idea and the bearer-being of the idea.
> —Wallace Stevens[61]

From his revolving stool, Dainez lifts his hand and brings a world into being: where his palm meets the air, lines spring forth and meet others to form surfaces and volumes. As it passes in front of him, his hand sketches out the smoke released from the chimney of a plastic container factory, an ATM booth with pensioners inside, pondering over brochures, and vans resting under the canopy of the Kum Chee Wa supermarket. In its wake, the hand reveals a muddle of squat dwellings, some of them just basic frames covered in canvas, interspersed with little shops with broken windows.

This is the "zone" of Cohen's *Un hombre amable* (1998), which hovers enigmatically between mental construct and material reality, seeming at times to depend on the imagination of a single man but at others to exist autonomously in its own right. When he is not attending to the zone, Dainez, its primary creator and the protagonist of Cohen's novel, is employed to discover prime numbers to crack security codes for electronic messages. Although the internet is not mentioned directly in this parallel world, prime numbers appear to play the same role in guaranteeing the security of electronic messaging there as they have done in public key cryptography in our own world since the 1970s: the unpredictable distribution of primes makes it impractical to factorize huge numbers at current computing speeds.

The nature of Dainez's work on prime numbers allows Cohen to frame the uncertain ontological status of the zone within the broader constructivist debate over whether mathematical entities are created or discovered, or, as Dainez puts it, the difficulty of deciding "si los entes matemáticos existen de veras y por su cuenta" (whether mathematical entities exist in reality and on their own account).[62] In turn, as I will show, these mathematical-philosophical questions provide the starting-point for an intervention into debates within literature concerning the relationship between the creating subject and the object of representation. This is also the concern that informs the novella's exploration of the dynamics of complexity and self-organization as paradigms of literary composition. Denied a transcendent position of distanced observation, literature is confirmed as wholly immanent to the flows of energy and matter that shape and renew life in the biological and physical worlds. This approach allows Cohen to recover some of the more fecund perspectives of Romanticism that have been sidelined or abandoned in postmodern thought, and to challenge other Romantic legacies that persist within it, among them the transcendent perspective of the Romantic ironist. In doing so, he counters a number of the most prevalent postmodern fictions: that self-awareness and reflexivity lead only to narcissistic detachment, that the end of ideology means the end of ethics, and that, by mediating between us and the world, language and literature hinder any genuine encounter with otherness.

Creativity between the imaginary and the material: mathematical constructivism and non-dualist thought

Prime numbers are often considered to be the "building blocks" of mathematics, as all other numbers can be generated by multiplying primes together; for this reason, they have been described as the mathematical equivalent of the periodic table,[63] and their existence is regularly submitted as proof of the universality of mathematics. G. H. Hardy demonstrates his adherence to a Platonist view when he claims in *A Mathematician's Apology* that "317 is a prime not because we think so, or because our minds are shaped in one way or another, but *because it is so*, because mathematical reality is built that way."[64] Prime numbers, understood to exist independently of subjective (and therefore potentially culture-influenced) observation, are commonly imagined to be one of the first means of communication with an alien species.[65] The famous case of the Indian mathematician Ramanujan is also frequently cited to support claims of the universality of mathematical objects. Isolated from the mathematical community in Europe and with no formal training, Ramanujan astounded Hardy and other mathematicians with his work on primes and his rediscoveries of some of Riemann's theories, albeit notated in an extremely unorthodox language.[66]

Both the unique qualities of prime numbers and the story of Ramanujan are woven into the narrative of *Un hombre amable* to express the Platonist view of the objective existence of mathematical objects. However, through his depiction of the zone, Cohen also presents the opposing – constructivist – position, which contests the claim that mathematical objects exist independently of our perceptions and that the task of the mathematician is simply to discover them. At points, the zone seems to owe its existence to Dainez's consciousness: if he were to faint, he thinks, the zone would disperse and die, and indeed at one stage the zone is described as fading out to black as Dainez becomes distracted. But curiously, it is not – or not always – simply rooted in the perception of a single individual, as "El que la ve puede ponerle lo que se le antoje" (whoever sees it can put whatever they wish into it).[67] Dainez himself fluctuates between a belief that the zone is autonomous and separate from his own perception and a suspicion of that very belief. On one hand, "Dainez sabe que en cierto modo se ha establecido sola" (Dainez knows that, in a way, it built itself),[68] and he certainly does not have any supernatural ability to foresee or intervene in what takes place in the zone: he is described at one point as passing through it "en busca de lo imprevisto" (in search of the unforeseen).[69] Against the accusation that the zone is merely a product of his imagination, he insists that "El barrio existe por su cuenta" (the neighbourhood exists on its own account).[70] On the other hand, he recognizes that "es como la matemática: lo que tiene coherencia parece un mundo real" (it's like mathematics: what is coherent appears to be a real world).[71] Here he aligns himself with constructivist views voiced not just by mathematicians but also, for example, by the neuroscientist Jean-Pierre Changeux, for whom the fact that mathematical objects can take written form seems to suggest that they are independent of our brains: their true nature as cultural representations is belied as they acquire in this way a "special coherence [...] which gives them the *appearance* of autonomy."[72] Echoing these views, Dainez says of mathematical theorems that "si uno cree que existen fuera del cerebro es porque se pueden escribir en un papel" (if one believes that they exist outside of one's head it is because they can be written down on paper),[73] and reflects that "Bastaba un poco de cohesión para que una persona convenciera a otra de la entidad de fantasma que había visto o imaginado" (a little cohesion was all that was needed for one person to convince another of the object of fantasy he had seen or imagined).[74]

The contradictory presentation of the zone – does it originate in Dainez's thoughts or exist independently of them? can both statements be true? – becomes part of a broader exploration of the creative act in *Un hombre amable*. The novel erodes distinctions between creator and created through techniques of mise-en-abyme, inversion, and the construction of tangled hierarchies. Dainez and the zone are engaged in a process of mutual creation and definition, not a unique act of bringing-into-being carried out by a single individual at an identifiable point in time, but an ongoing exchange with the result that "con cada aparición la zona se volvía más compacta y él más ágil, no nuevo pero al menos recreado" (at every appearance the zone became more compact and he became more agile, not new but recreated at least).[75] The inventor is created by his invention; both bring each other into being:

> De una apariencia de calvo barrigudo con camisa a cuadros la zona había inventado al Dainez que él era ahora, y de un tul de gases envolviendo semiedificios él había inventado la zona. Se pertenecían: habían surgido al mismo tiempo, lo mismo que una pirámide y su ingeniero, que Pitágoras y su teorema [...].[76]
>
> From the appearance of a paunchy bald man with a checked shirt, the zone had invented the Dainez he now was, and from a tulle of gases enveloping half-buildings, he had invented the zone. They belonged to each other: they had emerged at the same time, like a pyramid and its engineer, like Pythagoras and his theorem [...].

As Dainez makes the zone appear, day after day, he reflects that this act is not merely one of charity: he learns from it, and it has a diffusive effect on his identity that he welcomes: "ese Dainez que resurgía con las cosas iba perdiendo tirantez mientras ganaba transparencia de ánimo" (the Dainez who re-emerged along with the things began to lose his tautness and to gain a transparency of spirit).[77]

Further confusion between creator and created is brought about in the sections narrated by Dainez's daughter, which produce a folding-together of narrative hierarchies: she relates the story of Dainez's life but is at the same time a product of his imagination. Dainez's created world is itself full of inventors and creators, from the kiosk owner who invents a new snack in the form of "borlangos" – fried balls of dough that somehow turn out soft on the outside and crunchy on the inside – to Roxana, who is pregnant with the child of a man she has stitched together from body parts she discovers in icecream tubs and which almost add up to a full set. The sole characteristic shared by the motley inhabitants of the zone is a resourceful creativity that transforms their lives and those of others; like Dainez's own construction of the zone, these creations and transformations often slide imperceptibly between the imaginary and the material. For his own part, Dainez considers that abstract mathematics and chicken livers really share the same plane of reality, as the exercise of one is transformed into money to pay for the other. Cohen thrusts us into a world of quantum realities in which, as he reminds us, "Partículas u ondas (los, se supone, constituyentes últimos de la materia) son formas de abstracción, dice David Bohm" (particles or waves [believed to be the most basic constituents of all material] are forms of abstraction, says David Bohm).[78] The radical undecidability governing any distinction between the imaginary/abstract and the material pervades the language and style of the narrative. When LaMente is described by Dainez as "fundiéndose" (merging) with the people of the zone or with its scraps of waste,[79] the ontological uncertainty reigning in the narrative is such that the reader is not sure whether to understand this literally or metaphorically.

Arguments for the indivisibility of mind and matter, subject and object, have of course a long history in both Western and Eastern thought: with reference to Cohen's work, one could cite the influence – with ample justification – of both Spinozan immanence and Buddhist nondualism. In much postmodern literature, the most immediate references for such thinking are often to be found in a combination of Eastern philosophy and quantum theory, a fusion of mysticism and science that the physicist Erwin Schrödinger found entirely natural:

> The world is given to me only once, not one existing and one perceived. Subject and object are only one. The barrier between them cannot be said to have broken down as a result of recent experience in the physical sciences, for this barrier does not exist.[80]

Cohen's writing draws to a significant extent on both of these traditions: his vision of the universe as a dynamic web of energy flows underlines the alliance between the holistic worldview and contemporary particle physics that has been noted by many theorists.[81] Cohen's introductory text on Buddhism, for example, echoes Schrödinger's insights in its claim that "Mi mente y el mundo están compuestos por los mismos elementos" (my mind and the world are composed of the same elements),[82] almost a direct citation from Schrödinger's argument in the third chapter of *Mind and Matter*.[83] In *Un hombre amable*, a similar formulation is expressed by Dainez, who defends himself against LaMente's accusation that he has simply invented the zone by stating that "ocurre que el mundo y mi cerebro están hechos de lo mismo. Por eso no están peleados" (it happens that the world and my head are made of the same thing. For that reason they don't fall out with each other).[84]

If Cohen's exploration of immanence and nondualism draws simultaneously on ancient Buddhist philosophy and twentieth-century science, it also situates itself in relation to another constellation of ideas, associated with Romantic theory and literary praxis. Tracing the dialogue established in *Un hombre amable* with Romantic thought on chaos and order in the natural realm and in artistic composition will throw into relief Cohen's use of mathematical and scientific ideas in order to restage or resolve certain literary debates. These include some of the epistemological and ethical quandaries that have troubled a self-conscious postmodern culture, such as the averred narcissism of postmodern irony and reflexivity, and the ethical minefield of representing the Other.

"Form gulping after formlessness": art and chaos in Romantic thought

The poet Wallace Stevens has been identified by Cohen as one of the "six or seven" writers who have influenced him most,[85] and in 1987 he published a Spanish translation of *Adagia*, a collection of Stevens's aphorisms on the nature of poetry.[86] Stevens's poetry has been read as profoundly Romantic in its overriding concern with the relationship between inner, "subjective" experience and the outer, "objective" world. All-pervasive in Stevens's work is the question of whether we can distinguish with any certainty the perceiving self from the world around it. In relation to "An Ordinary Evening in New Haven" (quoted in the epigraph above), David M. LaGuardia suggests that "The poet seeks a relationship between the mind's eye and the reality it perceives but can locate no dividing line between them. Does the mind *know* what is there, or does it *make* what is there?"[87] As Frank Doggett reminds us, the mind in Stevens "is only nature looking at itself"[88] and can therefore take up no privileged position in relation to the matter it perceives. By extension, language – as Stevens asserts in the same poem – is not a medium for expression but part of the same material from which the whole world is made:

> The poem is the cry of its occasion,
> Part of the res itself and not about it.[89]

The provisional universe of Cohen's texts, in constant flux and exceeding all attempts to impose order upon it, bears considerable resemblance to Stevens's world, in which "We live in a constellation / Of patches and of pitches," surrounded by "Thinkers without final thoughts / In an always incipient cosmos."[90] The Romantics' rejection of the orderly Newtonian universe begged for a new kind of poetry that would express and participate in such constant transformation, one that "should forever be becoming," as the Romantic poet and scholar Friedrich Schlegel described it.[91] Both Stevens and Cohen respond to the formal challenge of capturing life in flux, of expressing dynamic change and boundlessness in fixed words on a page: "form gulping after formlessness," as Stevens would sum up the paradox in "The Auroras of Autumn."[92] Dainez voices a similar quest in *Un hombre amable* when he writes: "Que haya para nosotros una forma. Una forma neutra, tolerante, una forma que contenga el caos sin disimularlo" (let there be for us a form. A neutral, tolerant form, a form that contains the chaos without disguising it).[93]

Both Cohen and Stevens repeatedly echo the observations of Schlegel, for whom Romantic irony served both to emphasize the chaotic nature of the universe, unrestrained by Newtonian laws, and (paradoxically) to insist on the power of the mind to impose forms and patterns on it: to construct worlds in which to live, and to render finite and firm what is infinite and subject to continual transformation. As Schlegel maintains, "isn't this entire, unending world constructed by the understanding out of incomprehensibility or chaos?"[94] The source of the Romantic ironist's skepticism is an acute awareness of the provisional nature of such structurings of experience: "Irony is the clear consciousness of eternal agility, of an infinitely teeming chaos."[95] One of the many ways Cohen seeks to dramatize the interplay between chaos and form in his fiction is through the use of unresolved contradictions, signalling the provisionality of all potential explanations and essentialist notions of identity. At every turn, his narrative places disjunction, antinomy, and unresolved paradox above coherence, integration, and reconciliation. In fictions crowded with gurus, disciples, and beliefs of all kinds, Cohen introduces an antithesis for every thesis and refuses to arbitrate between them.

A clear example of this technique in *Un hombre amable* may be seen in the invention of the character LaMente, who acts both as a kind of double for Dainez and as his most feared nemesis. His ontological status is left entirely undecidable. He is first introduced as a spiritual well-being mentor employed by the company Dainez works for, but his "reality" as a character is undermined by repeated suggestions that he may be some kind of spiritual force or mental projection. In her own narrative of events, Dainez's daughter gives him a mythical standing as "un antagónico, un ángel opaco enviado por el mundo de las cosas pesadas para que Dainez frente a él se haga más fuerte" (an antagonist, a dark angel sent by the world of heavy things so that Dainez would become stronger through confronting him).[96] Dainez himself comes to question whether LaMente really exists and to wonder whether he might be an invention of his own. Playing the disciplining role of "los antiguos maestros" (the ancient masters)[97] to a fault, LaMente might represent a Socratic figure, a rhetorical device invented in order to present contradictory positions and to dramatize the process of coming-to-knowledge. This device is thickly overlaid with irony, however, as the status of sage and voyant Dainez acquires in his daughter's narration is placed firmly under erasure: his aloofness and meditative silence may not be the result of enlightenment but of brain damage following a head injury.

Among the many and conflicting theses advanced by both Dainez and LaMente throughout the novel, one in particular does seem to attain the irrefutable quality of a metanarrative: "'Vivir,' dijo LaMente, 'es mantenerse entre contradicciones que ningún analísis puede conciliar'" ("To live," said LaMente, "is to maintain a position between contradictions that no analysis can reconcile").[98] This recognition again accords with the place given to antithesis in Romantic irony as theorized by Schlegel, for whom "Everything that is worth something ought to be simultaneously itself and its contrary."[99] Opposites should be held in tension, not resolved into a final synthesis, with creativity to be found in "the continual self-creating interchange of two conflicting thoughts."[100]

The ethics of irony and reflexivity

> But is incomprehensibility really something so unmitigatedly contemptible and evil? Methinks the salvation of families and nations rests upon it.—Friedrich Schlegel[101]

As Anthony Whiting points out, the inability of the mind to understand a chaotic universe did not become "a cause for despair" for the Romantic ironist, who "celebrates the universe of becoming and change and warns against a universe that is completely available to rational comprehension."[102] It is this celebration that infuses the work of Cohen, much fuller and more joyous than the exaggerated and cynical pageants marking the end of epistemology to be found in much postmodernist literature and theory. In this spirit, Cohen recuperates mathematical uncertainty as crucial to the survival of the zone in *Un hombre amable*. Dainez thinks that he may have access to a number, or a key, that would in some way "complete" the zone, just as a solution was imagined to the square root of minus one and thus imaginary numbers came into being to complete the set of all possible numbers. He fears that the longer he continues his dialogue with LaMente, the nearer he will come to finding such a figure, which will hold some kind of explanatory power over the zone. If he doesn't remain silent, he will give LaMente that key, and

> Con eso LaMente haría un aforismo inolvidable. Empaquetaría el barrio en una frase. Otros llenarían el aforismo de significados. Le clavarían explicaciones. Lo encaminarían a muchos fines. La frase se convertiría en una herramienta, hasta que el uso la estropeara; o bien se convertiría en una joya muy cara.
> Mejor no encontrar ninguna cifra.[103]

> With that, LaMente would invent an unforgettable aphorism. He would package up the neighbourhood in a phrase. Others would load the aphorism with meanings. They would nail explanations to it. They would channel it towards many goals. The phrase would become a tool, until it either wore out through use or turned into a very expensive jewel.
> Better not to find a number at all.

The zone is vulnerable to LaMente's manipulation, who seeks to inject into it "la dureza del mundo, su resistencia, su falta de flexibilidad" (the hardness of the world, its resistence, its lack of flexibility).[104] In contrast, Dainez is attracted by the uncertainty of the methods of finding primes, which can sometimes be found, on testing, not to be primes after all, and whose distribution remains one of the most significant unsolved mysteries in mathematics. This embrace of uncertainty becomes, as we begin to understand, as much an ethical stance as an epistemological one. A notion of freedom, and the lives of the zone's residents, appear to depend on it.

It was the question of the ethics of Romantic irony that fuelled the vigorous critiques delivered by both Hegel and Kierkegaard of Schlegel's theorizations of Romantic literature. If irony, for Schlegel, is "the mood that surveys everything and rises infinitely above all limitations,"[105] this surely results in a position of detachment rather than engagement with the world left down below. For Hegel, rejecting the narcissism of the Fichtean ego that underpinned Schlegel's thesis, the "disengaged" ironist takes up the position of a "divine creative genius" and "looks down from his high rank on all other men," closing himself off from genuine interaction with others.[106] In ironic modes of writing, Romantic inexpressibility did not signal artistic failure but was more commonly reincorporated as a theme of the work itself, a device with which any reader of Keats or Wordsworth will be familiar. As Lilian R. Furst suggests, the Romantic ironist "aims to demonstrate the artist's elevation over his work, his transcendence even of his own creation."[107]

Such critiques of the solipsistic attitude of the ironist fail to take account of Schlegel's refusal to guarantee the self any kind of independent existence from the external world. Notwithstanding, questions over the ability of the narcissistic, transcendent ironist to engage fully with the world around him have been rearticulated many times in subsequent revisitings of this debate. The condemnation of the ironic mode on ethical grounds resurfaces more recently in the criticisms of postmodern reflexivity voiced by Bruno Latour and others.[108] Latour outlines the way in which reflexive texts, in deconstructing the very process of representation, succeed in establishing their own mode as more "truthful," reserving a special claim to truth and honesty for the writer who is able to see through the deceptions of his own fictions. For Latour, this technique has both epistemological and ethical consequences, as "reflexivists spend an enormous amount of energy on the side of the knowing, and almost none on the side of the known. They think that any attempt to get at the things themselves is proof of naive empiricism."[109] Cohen's particular mode of irony and reflexivity challenges the terms of this debate. As we will see, it does so in ways that demonstrate, among other conceptual frameworks, a significant debt both to Schlegelian non-duality and to a more contemporary understanding of chaos and form deriving from theories of emergence.

Cohen's teeming worlds cannot be tamed by our attempts to impose order upon them; however, our invented structures are not for that reason simply dismissed as fictional, and therefore invalid, misleading, and worthless. Like Schlegel, Cohen's characters adopt a contradictory position in relation to such structures, both skeptical and committed: aware of their provisionality and their insufficiency, but equally of their necessity. As Schlegel warns, "It's equally fatal for the mind to have a system and to have none. It will simply have to decide to combine the two."[110] In his "Adagia," Stevens voices a similar insight: "The final belief is to believe in a fiction, which you know to be a fiction, there being nothing else. The exquisite truth is to know that it is a fiction and that you believe in it willingly."[111] This double-think is precisely what characterizes Dainez's relationship with the zone and with the various ideologies expressed by himself and by others in the novel. As I will show, it also forms the basis of Cohen's understanding of the nature of human creativity, and particularly as a form of knowledge that transcends any true/false dichotomy.

The question that dogs Martínez's writing – to what extent our mathematics and logic are sufficient as tools to account for reality – is wholly displaced in Cohen's work, which does not permit any straightforward opposition between form and chaos, or truth and illusion. In Martínez's *Crímenes imperceptibles* (see Chapter 2), the layers of deception are eventually peeled back to reveal the facts: if there is a murdered body, there must be a murderer, and the question only then remains of whether our skills of deduction lead us to the right person or not. Although Martínez emphasizes the gap between truth and proof, and the extent to which aesthetic values affect our logical judgment, he leaves intact the truth-value of the events that spark off the narration. In Cohen, by contrast, misunderstandings or deceptions do not play a role of any importance: ultimately there is little interest on the part of Dainez or any other character/narrator in the truth-value of the zone and what is described as taking place there. Is Roxana really pregnant with the child of a man she has probably imagined? We don't discover. There are no external observers in *Un hombre amable* who might be able to construct a unified or analytical representation of the zone. LaMente recognizes this very well when he protests to Dainez, "quiere que la conciencia se funda con las señales incomprensibles que le manda la vida. Usted pretende romper los límites del pensamiento" (you want your consciousness to merge with the incomprehensible signs that life sends you. You are trying to break down the boundaries of thought).[112]

If irony is often used as a tool to shatter poetic illusion, we find a very different dynamic at work in *Un hombre amable*. There are no illusions here to be dismantled: instead, Cohen's emphasis is always on the creative power of the imagination to engender something that permits new encounters and participates in different ways in the endless creativity of the universe. There is no act of analysis that is not also an act of creation: the processes by which we add bias or transform what we see into something else is evidence of an essentially human creativity. This does not become a cause for lament or cynicism, as we see in the following passage, but simply places an additional requirement on us to adopt that creative responsibility in an ethical manner:

> Mientras miraba la vida de la zona, [... Dainez] se preguntó si no era cierto que algunas formas de mirar, por ejemplo la de él, achataban la realidad y con la realidad a las personas; si no las privaban del grosor donde los gestos, tan volubles, nunca dejaban de complicar las palabras, de obligarlas a multiplicarse.
>
> Era una pena. ¿Sería posible mirar algo sin añadirle ningún prejuicio?
>
> Pero añadir, inventar, era una necesidad humana tan natural que al principio debía haber sido inhumana: la necesidad de hacer algo con lo que presentaba la vida, casucha sin humo o humo sin chimenea, de preguntarse irremediablemente adónde iría ese barquito visto en el horizonte. Como a eso no había escapatoria, más valía rendirse y usar, usar con esmero y confianza los detalles que ofrecía la vida. A él la vida lo había puesto en ese barrio.[113]

> As he watched life in the zone, [... Dainez] wondered if it were true that certain forms of looking, his own, for example, flattened out reality and people along with it; if it deprived them of that thickness in which gestures, changeable as they are, never failed to complicate words, to oblige them to multiply.
>
> It was a pity. Was it possible to look at something without adding any kind of prejudice to it?
>
> But adding, inventing, was such a basic human need that at the beginning it must have been inhuman: the need to do something with what life gave, a hovel without smoke or smoke

without a chimney, to ask oneself the inevitable question of where the boat glimpsed on the horizon was heading. As there was no escape from that, it was better to surrender and to use, with care and confidence, the details life offered. Life had put him in that neighbourhood.

Our propensity always to "add" something to a pre-existing reality might be a cause for epistemological skepticism. In Cohen, however, it also opens the way to a different form of knowledge. As he explains,

> adhiero a algunas ideas de Wallace Stevens, en el sentido de que la única manera de renovar y refrescar el mundo es mediante la imaginación, que es lo que agrega algo a lo que ya estaba. Ese acto no sólo es un acto de creación sino de conocimiento.[114]

> I adhere to some of Wallace Stevens's ideas, in the sense that the only way to renew and refresh the world is through the imagination, which is that which adds something to what was there before. That act is not only an act of creation but also one of coming-to-knowledge.

This kind of knowledge bears no resemblance to the detached, objective exercise of rational analysis that cannot avoid being simultaneously an exercise of power. LaMente – like the voice of a troubled conscience – accuses Dainez of engaging in abstract activities that are divorced from reality or that simply construct a world around him for his own purposes, twisting reality to suit his own whim, like a tyrant.[115] His mind is full of words and numbers, but these cannot hope to speak to, or intervene compassionately in, a reality that LaMente describes as "ugly" and "irreparable."[116] But LaMente's accusations do not ring true: Dainez's commitment to the zone is clear, as he descends repeatedly from his lofty seat above it to mingle with its inhabitants, to defend them (if ineffectually), to enjoy companionship with them, or to suffer rejection or violence at their hands.

If Martínez's creative genius (Roderer) is an archetypal Romantic solipsist – an isolated ego, dismissive of others and incapable of genuine interaction with them – Cohen's is intimately and compassionately involved with those around him, although modestly, humbly, and with neither the desire nor the ability to become their hero or saviour. He is not in a position to judge or impose order or explanations on the world, not because the discipline of mathematics (and poetry, LaMente adds) occupies a pure, abstract realm separated from reality, but precisely because mathematics, poetry, consciousness and the physical world are all made from the same stuff. Dainez realizes that the zone "sólo se entenderá aceptando ser, no un lugar por donde pasan las cosas, sino cosa que sin darse cuenta ocurre en un lugar. Aceptando ser cualquier cosa. Un cualquiera" (can only be understood if we accept to be, not a place through which things pass, but a thing that, without knowing it, happens in a place. If we accept to be whatever. A nobody):[117] in other words, understanding comes by grasping our coextension and consubstantiality with the world and eschewing any privileged position or vantage point in respect of it.

Indeed, it is the ironist's skepticism of the validity of the structures we impose on the world that leads, not necessarily to radical, paralyzing epistemological doubt nor to a cynically detached whimsicality, but to a much more engaged and ethical approach. This view, in fact, was expressed by Schlegel and is summarized very effectively here by Whiting:

> To see the universe only through the patterns the self imposes on it is to turn the universe into a mirror image of the self. Skeptical reduction shatters this mirror and leaves the self confronting a universe that no longer reflects its image. The displacement of the world as self-image does not for Schlegel result in feelings of isolation or alienation. Freed from its narrow focus on itself, the self can turn to the universe at large. "We must rise above our own love," Schlegel writes, "and be able to destroy in our thoughts what we adore; if we cannot do this, we lack [...] the feeling for the universe."[118]

In the same way that Piglia's reflexivity becomes, not an inward-focussed exercise but a way of connecting with the world beyond the text (see Chapter 4), Cohen's irony also defends itself against charges of narcissism and detachment and paves the way instead for a more intimate relationship with the world, based on an understanding of the consubstantiality of creator and created.

The only value to which Dainez is able to give himself wholly is that of "amabilidad" (kindness). In an interview, Cohen identifies this word with the Sanskrit word "maitri," which has been variously translated as "loving kindness" and "unconditional friendship"; speaking specifically of Dainez's embrace of "amabilidad," Cohen adds further definitions: "la convivencia cívica" (civilized coexistence) and "una disposición de apertura" (an attitude of openness).[119] Dainez adopts kindness as the ultimate – or only possible – value by which he might live in a post-ideological world:

> Mientras sigue camino Dainez comprende, y el paso se le aviva, que la amabilidad es un alto valor práctico. No es un ideal, por supuesto, y por eso le gusta. Le gusta mucho, la amabilidad. Y aunque tal vez tampoco sea un valor, seguro que es una virtud. Dainez no ve bien la diferencia entre valores y virtudes. […]
>
> Ni vencedor ni muertito. Un abandono. Una apertura.[120]

> As he sets off again, Dainez understands, and his step lightens, that kindness is a highly practical value. It is not an ideal, of course, and for that reason he likes it. He likes it very much, kindness. And although perhaps it isn't a value either, it is definitely a virtue. Dainez does not see much difference between values and virtues. […]
>
> Neither victor nor dead guy. A withdrawal. An opening.

Interestingly, Cohen also associates "amabilidad"/"maitri" with concrete, physical proximity and a form of intimacy: "una disposición ante las cosas inmediatas, para vencer las mediaciones" (an inclination towards immediate things, so as to overcome mediations).[121] As we will see, *Un hombre amable* extends this theme to a formal experiment, as Cohen seeks to balance the vertigo of recursion, and a continual sliding between the material and non-material, with a commitment to the concrete and the immediate. In this he echoes to some extent Stevens's pragmatism, which leads him to cast out theory in favour of the physical facts and reject previous hypotheses to demand "new ones originating from renewed physical contact."[122] In the sum of the parts, there are only the parts," writes Stevens; "The world must be measured by eye."[123] It is the pragmatist rather than the rationalist, in William James's terms, who rejects the "skinny outline" of abstraction, "so much purer, clearer, nobler," in favour of the "rich thicket of reality."[124]

The overcoming of ironic distance and the cultivation of intimacy become central to Cohen's aesthetic. If Romantic irony performs a continual rise through higher and higher levels of reflection (Schlegel observes that the poet "can raise that reflection again and again to a higher power, can multiply it in an endless succession of mirrors"[125]), then Cohen delights in bringing his ironists back down to earth with a bump. One episode in *Un hombre amable* exemplifies particularly well this short-circuiting of the distance created through ironic modes of narration. His attention drawn to a single chamomile flower growing between stone slabs, Dainez stretches out a hand to pick a petal but is distracted by a vision of himself stretching out a hand towards the flower and then by a vision of himself watching himself stretching out his hand. This regression repeats itself many times until "al cabo, sin esfuerzo, la conciencia rompe la serie" (in the end, effortlessly, his consciousness breaks the series) and all the images press into one to form "un solo Dainez impalpable, o unido ya a la florcita" (a single, intangible Dainez, or one already fused with the little flower).[126] For a moment it appears to him that he and the flower are one and the same, or interchangeable, before he gathers in the whole string of reflexive images he has just seen and returns, suddenly, to the space he was occupying when he first noticed the flower growing between stone slabs.

This is not the simple, unidirectional recursion of "the dreamer dreamed," as in Borges's "Las ruinas circulares." Borges's story is misnamed insofar as the Chinese-box structure never comes full circle, but continues to reach dizzyingly upwards, as the wizard who has imagined his son into being realizes himself to be dreamt up by another, who may in turn be the creation of another, ad infinitum. Cohen's mise-en-abyme might continue spiralling ever-upwards in the same way, but instead the trajectory is reversed and inverted. The ironic distance created through layer upon layer of self-framing is obliterated as the consciousness of the observing subject fuses with the object in the original act of observation (the flower) and then re-merges with the consciousness of the self under observation (Dainez looking at the flower). Dainez returns to his self much as he left it, but perhaps a little more "inseguro" (uncertain) than before.[127]

This vision of immanence acts as a check to any narcissistic version of reflexivity. One is reminded of Borges's citation in "El Zahir" of Tennyson's invocation of the flower:

> si pudiéramos comprender una sola flor, sabríamos quiénes somos y qué es el mundo. Tal vez quiso decir que no hay hecho, por humilde que sea, que no implique la historia universal y su infinita concatenación de efectos y causas.[128]

> if we could only understand a single flower, we would know who we are and what the world is. Perhaps he meant that there is no event, however small, that does not involve the history of the universe and its infinite concatenation of causes and effects.

In a materialist formulation that echoes down the line from Deleuze to Spinoza and beyond, passing here through Borges, Cohen insists that "hay una sola sustancia" (there is just one substance), and that "En el momento que se piensa que la mente y el mundo están hechos de materias distintas, uno no puede ver nada sin ver a la vez su propia conciencia. Entonces pierde su cuerpo y, con él, todo lo que está viendo" (as soon as one starts to think that the mind and the world are made from different materials, one can see nothing without seeing one's own consciousness at the same time. The body is therefore lost, and with it, everything one sees).[129] Cohen's narrator-creator is not poised above the world but one with it. His position is exemplary of the relationship between creator and created world described by Deleuze:

> The author creates a world, but there is no world which awaits us to be created. Neither identification nor distance, neither proximity not remoteness, for, in all these cases, one is led to speak for, in the place of... One must, on the contrary, speak *with*, write *with*.[130]

In a similar way, as I will show, the role of Cohen's narrator is not to impose order on a chaotic mass but to participate in the continual intermutation of order and chaos that characterizes the natural world as well as our artistic depictions of it. Here Cohen draws on the more contemporary relationship between chaos and order suggested by theories of complexity and emergence, in which the two – unlike in Romantic literature and theory – are not necessarily opposed or mutually exclusive, providing a way of understanding literary innovation as participating in the endless creative fluxes of the universe at large.

Complexity and emergence: models of narrative construction

> There is nothing exclusively human about it: culture emerges from the complex interactions of media, organisms, weather patterns, ecosystems, thought patterns, cities, discourses, fashions, populations, brains, markets, dance nights and bacterial exchanges. There are eco-systems under your fingernails. You live in cultures, and cultures live in you.—Sadie Plant[131]

Two illustrations in *Un hombre amable* demonstrate the dynamics of self-organization at the heart of theories of complexity and emergence and, in doing so, also suggest a method of literary composition. The first analyzes the nature of human activity on the dance floor in the zone, as observed by the fascinated Dainez. Cohen de-individualizes the dance-floor frenzy in a string of plural or uncountable nouns: "Manos enguantadas frotan caderas de lycra. Jactancia de las pelvis, braguetazos. Festival de cerveza y saliva, apretones y cachetadas, arrumacos, espasmos, orlón, algodón" (gloved hands rub lycra hips. Pelvic bragging, smacking groins. Festival of beer and saliva, crushes and slaps, pettings, spasms, acrylic, cotton).[132] Dainez's initial focus on the multiple faces, mouths, clothes, and muscles of the dancers gives way to an appreciation that the mobile mass is something more than a group of individuals: it is "un organismo hecho no de unidades pegadas sino de conjuntos, y que tiene tantas conexiones como membranas divisorias" (an organism, not made up of units stuck together but of groups, and which has as many connections as it does dividing membranes).[133] These groups continually shift, folding together and reabsorbing other groups, generating "asimetrías nuevas y jugosas" (new and juicy asymmetries), and the picture is further complicated by individuals drifting through the mass and resisting any categorization, "como áreas confusas de un cerebro que nunca generará una identidad" (like confused areas of a brain that will never generate an identity).[134]

Dainez then understands that

> La pista entera con sus cuerpos es ese cerebro, compacto pero gelatinoso, uno de la unción y múltiple de contracciones, vibrante pero no muy estructurado, quizá ebrio. El amasijo de cuerpos es el cerebro de Dainez, y Dainez está dentro, como la neurona capital en el centro de todas las relaciones, esperando una descarga para que nazca la conciencia. Pero no. La masa encefálica sólo se mueve.[135]

The whole dance floor with its bodies is that brain, compact but gelatinous, one in its anointing and multiple in its contractions, vibrant but not very structured, maybe drunk. The jumble of bodies is Dainez's brain, and Dainez is inside, like the cardinal neuron at the centre of all the connections, waiting for a discharge to spark consciousness into being. But no. The mass of brain matter only moves.

This vision accords closely with some of the observations of emergence theory. Emergence – to borrow Jeffrey Goldstein's definition – describes "the arising of novel and coherent structures, patterns, and properties during the process of self-organization in complex systems." As in the commonly cited examples of swarming bees and flocks of birds, emergent phenomena are "conceptualized as occurring on the macro level, in contrast to the micro-level components and processes out of which they arise."[136] The patterns arising from the chaotic mass of dancing individuals leads Dainez to consider the possibility that there is some central organizing function, like a brain, only to realize that these patterns merely emerge from the blind functioning of elements at the micro-level and are not imposed consciously from above.

As he moves backwards, Dainez loses sight of individuals altogether and thinks "Tal vez lo que llena la pista sea un gran número primo" (perhaps what was filling the dance floor was a huge prime number):[137] in other words, an entity that is elusive, indivisible, and irreducible. If the poetry of Wallace Stevens testified to a world without certainties, in which totalizing visions have splintered into "parts, and all these things together, / Parts, and more things, parts,"[138] adhering to the pragmatic view (cited above) that "In the sum of the parts, there are only the parts,"[139] Cohen's texts demonstrate a rather different understanding, in accordance with theories of emergence and complexity, that the whole is greater than the sum of its parts: that a system has properties that cannot be explained simply with reference to its constituent elements, and that the co-functioning of the parts gives rise to higher forms of order. In an essay, Cohen applies this understanding to the interplay in narrative between the whole and the elements that comprise that whole:

> una narración no está hecha de elementos que se ensamblan, no es un artefacto armado con piezas de meccano, no puede desarticularse. La entidad narración es anécdota, paisaje, personajes, "peripecia moral," pero no una suma económica de estos componentes; y aunque lo fuera, el total es de una índole nueva, así como una palabra es algo más que una suma de letras.[140]

> a narration is not made up of elements that are assembled; it is not an artefact pieced together with bits of meccano; it cannot be dismantled. The narrative entity is the anecdote, the setting, the characters, the "moral vicissitudes," but it is not simple sum of those components; and even if it were, the total has a different nature, in the same way that a word is more than the sum of its letters.

In this respect, Cohen articulates a familiar Romantic preference for organic rather than mechanistic accounts of artistic creativity. However, his understanding of chaos and complexity allows him to take explicit distance from the Romantic apprehension of chaos (and that of many of the postmodern theorists and critics denigrated by Sokal and others[141]) as entirely antithetical to order. As he states, his version of chaos is not the one that, for Novalis, must "shimmer through the veil of order" in a work of art, but a chaos that continually generates ephemeral forms and orders itself.[142] By deconstructing the dichotomy between order and chaos in this way, Cohen effectively reworks the Romantic theme of "the world as a work of art." For Schlegel, "All the sacred plays of art are only a remote imitation of the infinite play of the universe, the work of art which eternally creates itself anew," and therefore the artist can produce only a simulation of the creativity and randomness of nature, constructing an "artfully ordered confusion" that allows us to glimpse the "original chaos of human nature."[143] This opposition between an artificially generated chaos and a real one inevitably casts the artist in the role of imposing a form, even one cleverly disguised as chaotic, on the world. This is a division that Cohen cannot admit: firstly – as we have seen – because it relies on an essential distinction between creator and creation, and, secondly, because it is too crude in its polarizing of order and chaos and its association of chaos with nature and order with art.

A second picture of emergence Cohen gives us in *Un hombre amable* further erodes any distinction between the artificial and natural processes by which complexity is generated. The zone "sings," each voice sending up to Dainez's ziggurat a different musical phrase. Cat miaows, phrases from a televised drama, a scolding voice, laughter from the dance floor, the bellow of Justín's harmonica and the chirping of a cricket: all combine and overlap until a pause signals the end of a series, only to begin again:

> Rayan el aire los crótalos del grillo. *que ese maldito bastardo ha dilapidado la herencia de Candy.* Aterrizan cajas en un camión. Rumor de cordajes en las matas. Uuuoooou y briiich en los dominios de Justín. *me lo tenés que decir, con todo lo que pasó entre nosotros.* Gurubel. Gato. Grillo.
>
> Gurubel, Ruoooouuu. *me lo digas por favor favor quiero que.* Chapoteo. Briiich. Maullido. Plástico, vidrio y chapa. Gurubel. Aplausos, risotada general en el bailongo. Jarcias. Publicidad en la tele: *¿cuando va a darse ese gusto?* Grillo. Gato. Chillido de murciélago.[144]

> The cricket's castanets scratch the air. *that mean bastard has squandered Candy's inheritance.* Boxes land on the floor of a truck. The sound of rigging in the bushes. Uuuoooou and briiich from Justín's dominions. *you've got to tell me, with everything that's happened between us.* Gurubel.[145] Cat. Cricket.
>
> Gurubel, Ruoooouuu. *tell me please please I want to.* Splashing. Briiich. Miaow. Plastic, glass and corrugated iron. Gurubel. Applause, general laughter from the dance hall. Rigging. TV advert: *when are you going to give yourself the pleasure?* Cricket. Cat. Bat screech.

Dainez realizes that he is at the centre of "una música aleatoria cuyo discreto director es un viento arremolinado" (a piece of aleatory music whose self-effacing director is a swirling gust of wind).[146] The action of the wind, picking out different sounds in the zone, creates a system that demonstrates emergent properties – hurricanes are a common example given to illustrate emergence – in which the wind orchestrates the different sounds, gathering them up together, organizing them into segments and marking pauses before the start of the next series. The action of the wind, which does not consciously choose the order of the "instruments" it plays as it has no will of its own, creates new and ever-changing patterns and forms from the different motifs playing out in the zone, such that one series is never identical to another: "Los segmentos cambian de orden, se permutan, se traspolan, se desplazan, nunca se confunden" (the segments swop round, change places, switch to opposite ends, move around, they never fuse together).[147] Although the direction of the wind seems random, we are told that it creates a higher level of organization that brings the different musical elements together without negating their individual autonomy: "en el rocío que moja los objetos del zigurat, y moja a Dainez, el conjunto reverbera con la parsimoniosa autoridad de una mantra" (in the dew that wets the objects of the ziggurat, and wets Dainez, the ensemble reverberates with the unhurried authority of a mantra).[148]

Thus from simple individual motifs, series are formed, and these combine and overlap with each iteration to create such formal complexity that the piece of music as a whole is initially experienced as random and chaotic; however, new forms of order emerge from the seeming disorder. The composition technique brings to mind Messiaen's experiment in *Quartet for the End of Time*, in which two prime-number sequences of 17 and 29 notes are played simultaneously. As they will not coincide again until they have been played 17 × 29 times each, this form creates a wealth of new combinations of sounds from just two original motifs. From the simple to the complex, the complex to the simple: human invention is merely an extension of the creativity of the universe, as studied in theories of complexity and emergence. In Dainez's words, "Real e imaginario. Vieja cupla. Qué tedio. Qué tandem embustero. Un buen invento era tan milagroso como la existencia" (real and imaginary. Old coupling. What tedium. What a phony duo. A good invention was as miraculous as existence).[149]

Only a simplistic, Romantic conception of chaos as the preserve of nature, resistant to (human) order would make it possible to insist, as Frederick Garber does, that the ironist offers only "a skillful mimicry of that anarchy which is always out there," in such a way that "the threat of disintegration" is turned into "the matter of high art," ensuring the triumph of the ironist over the chaos he purports to allow into his work.[150] To accuse Cohen of merely fabricating an illusion of chaos intruding into a narrative that is always in reality under his control would be to reassert precisely those dichotomies between creator and created world, order and chaos that are challenged in his writing. Both art and the world (as art is part of the world and not divisible from it) operate as complex systems that manifest elements of both chaos and order in their functioning, just as the creator is not merely an observer of an external flux of chaos and order but part of that same flux. It is too naïve to assume that our consciousness sets us apart from the rest of the creative universe. We may impose patterns on the world around us but, like Dainez caught up in the crowds on the dance floor, we are also organized into higher systems that transcend us; we do not even transcend our own creations, which act upon us and shape our destinies as much as we program theirs. The impossibility of transcendence gives rise, neither to despair nor skepticism, but to a sense of our participation in an endlessly creative universe that is exhilarating, but brings with it a renewed, if less hierarchical, sense of ethical responsibility.

An ethics of creativity for a post-ideological world

Cohen's explorations of emergence and complexity, when combined with an abiding interest in the ethics of narration, form an effective rebuttal of both Romantic and postmodern critiques of the narcissistic detachment of ironic and reflexive modes of literary narrative. In *Un hombre amable*, Dainez is intensely irritated by the general lament over the rise of insensitivity and emotional numbness that has become fashionable in his hyper-televised information society, which looks remarkably similar to our own. In the face of apocalyptic announcements of the end of ethics – the inevitable consequence, it is claimed, of the demise of idealism – he chooses to climb to his habitual seat on the rubbish dump and bring the zone and its inhabitants into being through the act of thought. The much-trumpeted end of ideology or idealism does not, Cohen suggests, mean the end of ethics at all: Dainez's engagement with the zone is both intimate and compassionate. Nor does his self-consciousness paralyze him. Ignoring the hypocritical hand-wringing that accompanies the noisily proclaimed crisis of values and the end of ideology, he simply gets on with the task of imagining and creating new things.

When no philosophy proves to be of much help and the deceptions and weaknesses of all systems of thought have been laid bare, there always exists the option of going forth to create, with or without their assistance. As Cohen states,

> Mi utopía es constituir nuevas comunidades con los requechos materiales, filosóficos, narrativos y espirituales que encontramos. [...] La oportunidad es ver que nos han dejado ruinas, reducirlas a corpúsculos y empezar de nuevo.[151]

> My utopia is to constitute new communities with the material, philosophical, narrative and spiritual remnants we come across. [...] The opportunity comes from seeing that we have been left ruins, reducing them to corpuscles and beginning afresh.

As in nature, nothing here is wasted; the recycling of material does not point to a lack of innovation but is the chief process by which life is created, with simple molecules and organisms transformed and organized into higher forms, and functioning together in different ways to construct systems of increasing complexity. The implications of this non-hierarchical, rhizomatic vision of creativity for an understanding of authorship are explored further in Chapter 4, which focusses on the supplanting of the Romantic figure of the author in Cohen and Piglia by thoroughly depersonalized, transubjective, machinic, and anonymous forms of authorship, far more fitted for creative rebellion against the political and economic systems within which they are trapped.

Cohen reads Wallace's (Romantic) sense of his consubstantiality with the world around him – which becomes the source of great creativity – against a similar perspective in Ballard, which leads instead to an unremitting and carceral oppressiveness. While for Ballard the merging of mind and landscape produces horror, for Stevens, as Cohen points out, it is a cause for poetic celebration:

la idea fundamental de Ballard, que está en sus novelas apocalípticas, es que entre el paisaje y la mente no hay distancia. Una idea que, de otra manera, está también en Wallace Stevens, cuando dice: "Soy lo que me rodea" o "Una mitología crea su región."[152] La diferencia es que esto para Stevens es motivo de felicidad y de fervor poético y para Ballard es terrible. El hecho de que no exista ninguna distancia entre mente y paisaje significa, para Ballard, que sólo llegando al fondo de la desintegración del paisaje se puede encontrar el pequeño nódulo de realidad a partir del cual se puede salir. Por eso sus personajes se quedan siempre en medio del desastre, no escapan nunca.[153]

Ballard's fundamental idea, present in his apocalyptic novels, is that between landscape and mind there is no distance. An idea that, in a different way, is also present in Wallace Stevens, when he says "I am what surrounds me" or "a mythology creates its region." The difference is that for Stevens, this is a reason for happiness and poetic intensity, and in Ballard it is terrible. The fact that no distance exists between mind and landscape means, for Ballard, that only by reaching right down into the decomposition of that landscape can one find the tiny nodule of reality through which escape is possible. For this reason his characters always remain in the midst of disaster, they never escape.

The general turn towards apocalyptic narratives in science fiction represents for Cohen "una forma más de la culpa y el miedo con que buena parte de la cultura nos paraliza y nos entristece" (yet another form of the guilt and fear with which a great deal of culture paralyzes and saddens us) and has the effect of ageing the genre, including – he admits – his own earlier fiction.[154] By contrast, Cohen's later novels, notably *Un hombre amable* and also *Donde yo no estaba* (2006) and *Casa de Ottro* (2009), are brimming with new beginnings, surprising revelations, transformations, and renewals. The following chapter explores in more detail the critical dialogue his texts establish with Ballard's apocalypticism.

4 | Machines, Metaphors, and Multiplicity: Creativity Beyond the Individual

For David Porush, "cybernetic fictions" are most properly defined as those taking technology and particularly cybernetics as their theme but that also "focus on the *machinery or technology of their fiction*."[1] Recent critical studies have begun to look beyond representations of science or the posthuman in literature to consider how scientific theories or cybernetics may illuminate the workings of the text itself. Metafiction has become an instance of complexity theory, and the act of reading a demonstration of the relationship between noise and information in information theory. There has been a move away from a focus on how literature might *represent* certain scientific theories towards an understanding of how it *manifests* complex structures, incompleteness, or emergence.[2] Many texts by Piglia and Cohen, exemplary of a highly reflexive literary tradition in Argentina, lend themselves particularly well to this kind of approach. In exploring here their use of certain metaphors drawn from mathematics and biology, my purpose is to try to understand more accurately what it means to claim that their fiction (or literature more broadly), in addition to representing machines, is itself a machine: in other words, to find the point at which the "machine is not a metaphor" (Deleuze and Guattari).[3]

The many machines and scientific models constructed in texts by Piglia and Cohen allow them to explore ideas of creativity that are fully depersonalized. The tangled textual hierarchies of *La ciudad ausente* (1992) become open systems, energized by constant flows across the boundaries of the text. Mutation, variation, self-organization, and other biological metaphors are marshalled to provide models for creativity and continual self-renewal in literature. Piglia draws on models of autopoiesis and open systems as a way of thinking about the constant exchanges between the text and its environment in which porous boundaries are paradoxically key to the text's self-definition, preservation, and propagation. Our approach to his work alters significantly when we see the many intertextual references in his fiction, not as hidden messages for the critic to decode, but as the deliberate foregrounding of a method of narrative construction. Intertextuality and reflexivity do not mark the apogee of postmodern narcissism but a manifestation of how meaning is created through resonance and rhizomes. The theory of creativity suggested by the writing machines in *La ciudad ausente* and *Blanco nocturno* (2010) is in many ways a post-Romantic one. It replaces the individual artistic genius with a thoroughly depersonalized art and reworks the old conflict between organic and mechanistic visions of the world to reveal a strikingly new perspective on the relationship between human creativity and the machinic.

Exemplary of Cohen's practice of "realismo inseguro" (unstable realism), the stories of *El fin de lo mismo* (1992) are textual experiments with the kind of provisional and unstable structures that characterize non-equilibrium systems. They demonstrate the extent to which Cohen draws on dissipative structures and theories of chaos and complexity, "no sólo [...] como mito de la época, sino como hipótesis de trabajo para las invenciones de la literatura" (not only [...] as a myth of our times, but as a working hypothesis for the inventions of literature).[4] In this collection, entropy becomes a privileged metaphor, firstly for the potential elimination of difference in a hyper-mediatized, market-governed society, but also, and more importantly, for literature's role in staging an encounter with radical and irreducible difference. Cohen's use of the entropy metaphor therefore diverges significantly from its apocalyptic deployment in the fiction of Ballard, Dick, Pynchon, or Michael Moorcock. Instead, it becomes a way of thinking – alongside Nietzsche and

Michel Serres – about multiplicity, and the creative power of disorder and difference.

In Piglia's unusual couplings of the organic and the machinic, together with his interest in autopoiesis and open systems, we may detect resonances of Deleuze and Guattari's conception of the text as assemblage. Cohen's interest in dissipative systems and entropy as metaphors for the act of literary creation also draw on Deleuze's understanding of the act of writing as becoming-other or becoming-multiple. These frameworks, as I will show, are of considerable use in probing the construction, in work by Piglia and Cohen, of post-Romantic perspectives on subjectivity and writing.

POST-ROMANTIC WRITING MACHINES / PIGLIA

> We will never ask what a book means, as signified or signifier; we will not look for anything to understand in it. We will ask what it functions with, in connection with what other things it does or does not transmit intensities, in which other multiplicities its own are inserted and metamorphosed, and with what bodies without organs it makes its own converge. [...] A book itself is a little machine.—Gilles Deleuze and Félix Guattari[5]

Piglia's theory of literary innovation receives its fullest metafictional development in *La ciudad ausente* (1992). The major part of the novel consists of a series of stories generated by a storytelling machine called Elena who is at the heart of the resistance operating against state control in Buenos Aires. Elena's status as a character is thoroughly enigmatic. She appears at points to be a real machine, complete with nodes and cables, possessing solid physical dimensions – "una forma achatada, octagonal" (a flattened, octagonal form)[6] – and locked up by the state in a closed museum in an attempt to control the threat she poses to the regime. At other points, we understand that this incarceration does not prevent her from continuing to operate in a virtual realm, generating stories that circulate among the inhabitants of Buenos Aires. Elena is the wife of the writer Macedonio Fernández, who appears as a character in the novel and invents a machine to immortalize her memory, but she may also be a psychiatric patient hallucinating in one of the city's clinics. Elena's stories make up much of the text of *La ciudad ausente*; they are linked by a paratext, the story of Junior's investigation into the origins of the storytelling machine.

In referring to its own genesis and evolution, *La ciudad ausente* draws explicit analogies with Gödel's incompleteness theorems, the role of genetic reproduction in evolution, and with biological models of self-organization in open systems. These models are brought to resonate with the Formalist concepts of literary evolution so significant to Piglia's approach to literature and criticism, which have already been discussed in relation to *Respiración artificial* in Chapter 1. The narrative machines pictured in both *La ciudad ausente* and *Blanco nocturno* (2010) dismantle distinctions between the organic and the mechanical in a manner that leads us away from the Romantic opposition of these forces and firmly in the direction of Deleuze and Guattari's synthesizing concept of the machinic. Piglia removes the author as the central figure in literary innovation to explore the question of machinic creativity. His texts operate as machines in the Deleuzean sense, forming new and often surprising assemblages with other texts, producing and being produced by a multiplicity of connections.

Tangled hierarchies

The narrative technique with which Piglia experiments in *Prisión perpetua*, putting signs and stories into circulation within and between different narrative hierarchies (as discussed in Chapter 2), is brought to full expression in *La ciudad ausente* in the central trope of the storytelling machine. J. Andrew Brown argues that, in many ways, *La ciudad ausente* is paradigmatic of cybernetic fiction, as defined by Porush, both in its presentation of Elena as a "truly cyborg narrator" and in "its attention to the idea of language as cybernetically organized"; his analysis of the novel highlights the quasi-hypertextual or virtual properties of the text.[7] Through the storytelling machine, both a character in the novel and the "author" of the short stories contained within it, Piglia creates a proliferating network of textual nodes and nuclei that defy attempts to separate them into clear narrative hierarchies. Recursion, feedback loops, and tangled hierarchies present a problem for a traditional hermeneutics in search of transcendent meaning. But in Piglia – as I will show – this realization leads not to a cynicism with regard to hermeneutical interpretation but to an understanding of the principles of literary creation and the vast potential in literature for self-renewal.

It is often unclear whether narrative strands and events in *La ciudad ausente* are to be read straightforwardly as part of the novel's plot, as the hallucinations or memories (real or implanted) of one or more characters, or as transmissions from some external source. Repeated allusions to Gödel and Tarski reinforce the sense of a continual movement up through an infinity of narrative levels, as each level is subject to self-reference and recursion, and the search for an ultimate meaning or metalanguage is always deferred. The narratives of *La ciudad ausente* are caught up in tangled hierarchies akin to Gödelian "strange loops," in which propositions about the truth-value of logical statements are found within the same system as those statements to which they refer, allowing for the possibility of paradoxical statements such as "this statement is false." Presented as one of the machine's stories, Junior discovers in the museum a tableau of the Majestic Hotel room he has just visited, complete with the wardrobe and the bottle of perfume the woman he met there was searching for. These are details from what we had understood to be the paratext of Junior's search for the truth of the machine, not one of the machine's own texts. A strange loop confuses the distinction between the investigating subject and the object of the investigation.[8]

Motifs from the machine's stories often recur in this way in the story of Junior's investigation into the machine. In a more complex example, the first narrator introduces Junior as the son of Mister Mac Kensey, an English station master whose wife left with his daughter to go and live in Barcelona; later, Junior hears a story that is structurally suspiciously similar (told by the storytelling machine in the museum, here a second-order narrator) but this time about Russo, in which Ríos (a third-order narrator) mentions a mechanical bird kept in the house of an English station master called McKinley, whose wife had also left him. The recurrence, with variation, of narrative nuclei in this way gives weight to the notion that the storytelling machine might actually be the narrator of the entire text, as well as a lower-order narrator. This interpretation is in fact suggested by Piglia himself in an interview, when he proposes that Junior may be just another of the fictional characters invented by the storytelling machine, conceived so that he could come and save her.[9]

Gödel and the creative potential of the undecidable

The fact that the different orders of narration in the novel cannot logically be separated causes a particular difficulty in interpretation and encourages the reader to engage in a fruitless search for an ever-higher order of narration, a more powerful language or metanarrative, which might contain and comment on the seepages between lower-level orders. Nevertheless, Gödel and Tarski – whose undefinability theorem similarly states that, in a given arithmetic system, the truth of that arithmetic cannot be defined within that same system – are not primarily cited in *La ciudad ausente* as evidence for the fallibility of human logic and the failure of the rationalist enterprise but for the creative possibilities that seem to be suggested by the discovery of the limitations of the formalist project in mathematics.

In his account of how the storytelling machine in *La ciudad ausente* came into being, Russo points to the importance of the metaphysical thought of the writer Macedonio Fernández. For Macedonio, "Lo que no es define el universo igual que el ser" (what does not exist defines the universe as much as what does exist).[10] Macedonio's interest in possible worlds becomes a key principle in the machine's construction. As Russo explains,

> Macedonio colocaba lo posible en la esencia del mundo. Por eso comenzamos discutiendo las hipótesis de Gödel. Ningún sistema formal puede afirmar su propia coherencia. Partimos de ahí, la realidad virtual, los mundos posibles. El teorema de Gödel y el tratado de Alfred Tarski sobre los bordes del universo, el sentido del límite.[11]

Macedonio planted the possible within the world's very essence. For that reason we began to discuss Gödel's hypotheses. No formal system can prove its own consistency. That was our starting point, virtual reality, possible worlds. Gödel's theorem and Alfred Tarski's treatise on the boundaries of the universe, the concept of limit.

There is no direct link, in mathematical or philosophical terms, between Gödel's theorem and virtual reality or possible worlds. Piglia draws on Gödel's findings obliquely to suggest that the limitations of formal logic give rise to new possible orders, in which, as for Macedonio, fantasy and reality are not opposed to each other; it is the discovery of the limit of axiomatic logic that allows us to imagine other worlds that are not governed by that logic or to posit realms of existence in which truth is undecidable. The association Piglia establishes between Gödelian logic and the invention of fiction and new worlds would have been even more explicit if he had carried through the original plan of giving Gödel's name to the creator of the storytelling machine in the novel.[12]

Piglia's (mis)reading of Gödel bears a resemblance to Lacan's. For Lacan, the undecidability of statements that cannot be reduced to axiomatic truth, and open up a faultline within formal logic, can be identified with the Real.[13] As Guillermo Martínez explains, an analogy is drawn in Lacan's work between the discourse that emerges from analysis and a logical system that is found to have "fallas" (flaws) or "aberturas" (gaps, fissures): it is these that provide a point of access to the unconscious and should therefore constitute the analyst's focus.[14] This process, by which a failing in logic exposes a truth that cannot otherwise be expressed, is perhaps most clearly seen in Piglia's "La loca y el relato del crimen." Renzi applies the skills of a linguistician to dissect the transcript of the madwoman's testimony, stripping away the repeated forms to discover "Lo que no entra en ese orden, lo que no se puede clasificar, lo que sobra, el desperdicio" (what doesn't fit in the scheme, what cannot be classified, what is left over, redundant).[15] In what cannot be categorized, cannot be communicated, lies the truth about the identity of

Larry's murderer and points to corruption at the heart of the system. In best post-structuralist manner, the redundant, or that which cannot be proved or categorized, threatens the integrity of the whole: it cracks open the system of the text.

Self-reference, open systems, autopoiesis

These fissures in logical systems, opened up in *La ciudad ausente* by means of self-reference, may destroy any illusion of coherence; however, they are also crucial to the renewal and the self-transforming potential of the literary text. The proof of Gödel's incompleteness theorem rests on the possibility of a statement that refers to itself but whose truth-value is undecidable within the terms of the system. Similarly, in Piglia, self-reference demonstrates the incomplete, and therefore open and dynamic, nature of the system. Junior discovers that the state wants to neutralize the machine and take it out of circulation, as:

> Algo estaba fuera de control. Se había filtrado una serie de datos inesperados, como si los archivos estuvieran abiertos. [...] Habían empezado a entrar datos sobre el Museo y sobre la construcción. Estaba diciendo algo sobre su propio estado. [...] Filtraba datos reales [...].[16]

> Something was out of control. A series of unexpected facts had leaked in, as if the archives were open. [...] Details about the Museum and its construction had started entering the loop. The machine was saying something about its own state. [...] Real data was seeping in [...].

Self-reference here is not, therefore, a kind of narcissism, but the point at which reality seeps into the text, at which it cannot remain hermetically sealed off from the real world. As Ana explains to Junior, "Ha empezado a hablar de sí misma. Por eso la quieren parar. No se trata de una máquina, sino de un organismo más complejo" (it has begun to speak about itself.

That's why they want to stop her. This isn't a machine, but a more complex organism).[17] Reflexivity here is inextricably associated with the machine's nature as an open system, engaging in exchanges with external reality across its boundaries: "Los hechos se incorporaban directamente, ya no era un sistema cerrado, tramaba datos reales" (events were being incorporated directly, it was not a closed system anymore, reality was getting into the plots).[18] Piglia's use of Gödel's theorem throws light on his paradoxical claim that self-reference is one of the greatest expressions of literature's imbrication with the social:[19] (very roughly) following Gödel, it is the point at which the system demonstrates its incompleteness and its interactions with other systems from which it had been assumed to be independent.

Another metaphor suggested in *La ciudad ausente* for this interdependence is drawn from biology rather than mathematics. First theorized by Humberto Maturana and Francisco Varela, autopoiesis refers to the processes through which a living cell or organism produces the elements it needs to maintain its bounded structure. It therefore differs from an "allopoietic" system, which uses elements to create something other than itself. As N. Katherine Hayles observes in her study of the implications of their work for the field of cybernetics, the autonomy ascribed to the organism in the autopoietic model is held in tension with "structural coupling," which describes the interaction of that organism with its environment.[20] Varela would go on to place greater emphasis on that interaction in his theory of "enaction," which, while remaining faithful to the principles of autopoiesis, posits "the active engagement of an organism with the environment as the cornerstone of the organism's development."[21] The storytelling machine of *La ciudad ausente* mimics these processes, maintaining and reproducing itself by means of a constant exchange of matter and energy across its boundaries, assimilating other fictions and reality itself into its own stories. Piglia's texts, systems, and models invariably demonstrate the dynamic self-reference that Ira Livingston identifies as underlying both biological autopoiesis and the operations of the reflexive text, in which "the point at which the text closes back on itself is also where it connects with everything that sustains it."[22]

The autopoietic system becomes a useful model for thinking about the relationship in art between self-reference and openness to other systems, two orientations that are more often seen as incompatible, the first charged with narcissism or aesthetic separatism. In his account of self-organizing processes in nature, Erich Jantsch explains clearly how the metabolic exchanges that take place between an organism and its environment are "self-referential" in the sense that an autopoietic system "is primarily geared to self-renewal."[23] Intertextuality becomes just the most clearly visible example of the way in which the text is engaged in a complex and continually evolving network of relations with everything that it is not, relating productively with its environment as part of the process of self-renewal. The wealth of intertextual references in *La ciudad ausente* – to Macedonio Fernández, Lugones, Faulkner, Dante, Poe, and several other authors – defines the novel as an open system, one that draws energy from transactions taking place across its borders, feeding on pre-existing texts, which are then subjected to a process of transformation. Joyce's *Ulysses* and *Finnegans Wake* provide several of the motifs circulating in the novel, and there is mention of the names of many of Joyce's characters, usually slightly distorted or misspelled, Buck Mulligan appearing here as "Bob Mulligan" and Anna Livia Plurabelle sometimes referred to as "Ana Lidia."[24] Such richness in intertextuality provides fertile hunting-ground for the literary critic, duped into uncovering each allusion and treating it as a clue to a hidden story or theme, as if the novel's meaning could be rendered through detective investigations of this kind.

This approach is also encouraged by the repetition of narrative motifs. The experience gained by the machine through composing different stories means that they do not simply proliferate in a dispersed manner, each one moving further away from the original nucleus. In fact, we are told that the "key" to understanding the machine's workings is that it learns as it narrates, conscious of the stories it has already told, and that "quizá termine por construirles una trama común" (perhaps it will end up constructing a common plot for them).[25] However, the recurring elements and motifs are presented here as materials for future stories, not clues to some overarching narrative already in existence. This is an important distinction. What is revealed therefore is not a hidden meaning that may be accessed through *interpretation* but a principle of *construction*. This emphasis on defining the text according to how it has been constructed rather than how it might be interpreted is precisely that which interests Piglia most in the Formalist approaches of Shklovsky and Eichenbaum.[26]

If – as Jameson maintains – for a Formalist critic a work "speaks only of its own coming into being, of its own construction" and of the "formal problems" it attempts to resolve,[27] this description is of clear relevance to *La ciudad ausente*. The novel is most effectively read, not as a representation of cybernetic society or even as an exercise in anti-totalitarian textual politics, but as a solution to a formal problem: how to encapsulate in a single, linear form the idea of iterability and endless mutation, or how to construct a text with multiple entry points. We become alert to the manner in which the text is created from fragments of other texts, by means of operations of appropriation, transposition, and transformation. Like Scheherazade of the *Arabian Nights*, mentioned in the novel, what holds these micro-stories together is obviously an artifice, a formal device. The subject of *La ciudad ausente* is the act of storytelling, and this produces what Tzvetan Todorov in his analysis of the *Arabian Nights* calls an "a-psychologism," in which narrative does not exist to illustrate character but characters exist to bring forth narratives.[28]

Our approach to the novel – and to Piglia's work in general – changes radically when we view the many intertextual references in his fiction, not as hidden messages for the critic to decode, but as the deliberate foregrounding of a method of narrative construction. This approach is the one Piglia models in his own critical work, as can be appreciated, for example, in his analysis of the role of Homer's *Odyssey* in Joyce's *Ulysses*. In spite of the best efforts of Jungian critics to treat the mythical references as symbols to be interpreted, Piglia insists that the role played by the *Odyssey* in Joyce's novel is really as a formal device that allows him to order his proliferating material, a way to lend some coherence to the plot of the novel. It should be understood as "una etapa necesaria en la construcción de la obra, como el molde de hierro de una escultura que desaparece, retirado o escondido por el material" (a necessary stage in the construction of the work, like the iron mould of a sculpture that disappears, removed or hidden by the material).[29]

Blanco nocturno and the dream-text: from interpretation to construction

This notion of literary construction emerges even more explicitly in *Blanco nocturno*. At the heart of the novel, a rather unconventional twist on the detective genre, we find another writing machine. During his investigation of a murder, the journalist Renzi encounters an Arltian figure of the mad inventor, Luca Belladona, who locks himself away in an old car factory, in the middle of nowhere, to pursue a crazed quest to construct a different kind of machine. The walls of the factory are covered with words and phrases, underlined or circled, linked together with arrows and diagrams. Every morning, Luca combines and recombines the images and phrases of his dreams with those from previous nights, treating them as if they were fragments of a single narrative, until the pieces fit together naturally. A laboratory-like room houses the machine proper, a cylinder with little boards on which Luca writes words and draws images related to his dreams. A series of nickel-plated cogs move the plates into different positions to create new possibilities for relations between the different phrases, and therefore new possible meanings. It is, in effect, a writing machine, functioning in a very similar way to the storytelling machine of *La ciudad ausente*, which subjects initial narrative nuclei to processes of transformation, creating ever-new versions.

Explicitly, here, these nuclei derive from Jungian archetypes. As Luca explains, *Man and His Symbols* (1964) expounds Jung's theory that the content of dreams, studied systematically, can be seen to follow a certain order. Although they evoke different scenes and images every night, dreams nevertheless correspond to a "modelo común" (common model) that orchestrates the emergence, disappearance, and recurrence of certain contents over time, "como si fuera un solo relato que se iba armando en fragmentos discontinuos" (as if it were a single story gradually assembled from discontinuous fragments).[30] There is a clear echo here of the "trama común" (common plot) that links the stories of the machine in *La ciudad ausente*. In the same way, while evoking theories of interpretation and analytical approaches to the dream/text, Piglia is not positing the existence of a hidden truth that might "explain" the text but a principle of textual construction that points to the existence of narrative archetypes. Luca's machine does not reveal past traumas or analyze concealed truths: he believes, instead, that it may be used to predict the future.

The presence of Jung's theories in Piglia's novels does not, ultimately, endorse a "depth psychology" approach to understanding the meaning of texts. Dreams and symbols do not await an analyst's interpretation, symptomatic of deeper drives or hidden narratives. Instead, they become materials for construction. Again, Piglia's interest in Jungian archetypes takes us back to Russian Formalism. Piglia's narrative nuclei function very much like the archetypal tales identified by structural anthropologists and Formalist literary critics such as Vladimir Propp: the original stories from which others are generated, in all their variations. Both the machine in *La ciudad ausente* and the one in *Nocturno blanco* produce multiple variations in this way, drawing on a stock of common narrative figures. Like Propp, who discovered thirty-one basic narrative units in his analysis of Russian folktales,[31] Piglia is also interested in the primordial narrative elements and functions that underpin the construction of stories. Indeed, he goes much further than Propp, reducing them to just two: "en el fondo todos los relatos cuentan una investigación o cuentan un viaje" (essentially, all stories narrate an investigation or a journey).[32]

The operation of the machines in *La ciudad ausente* and *Blanco nocturno*, drawing on pre-existing forms and shuffling narrative elements to produce new patterns and series, establish literary creativity very much as an *ars combinatoria*. As Ítalo Calvino suggests in his imaginative recreation of the evolution of storytelling, from just a few "prefabricated elements," such as Propp's narrative functions, "unlimited combinations, permutations, transformations" become possible.[33] The machines do not simply run preset programs but have a creative power of their own. Fed first with the story "William Wilson," the machine in *La ciudad ausente* captures the *form* of Poe's narrative but alters the content. Every story in Piglia generates a potentially infinite number of others. Unlike the Freudian unconscious, a repository of repressed desires, Jung's account of the unconscious emphasizes its creative capacity, with the collective unconscious acting as a reservoir of archetypes, which are then processed in different ways by the personal unconscious. Luca believes that his recent ability to construct completely original objects directly from his imagination derives from the operation in his dreams of "cierta fuerza *suprapersonal*" (a certain *supraindividual* force) that "interfería activamente en forma creativa y llevaba la dirección de un designio secreto" (actively interfered, in a creative manner, and put a secret plan into motion).[34]

Inventions of all kinds abound in *La ciudad ausente*, but they do not emerge from nothing: Piglia rejects the possibility of creation *ex nihilo*. Russo shows Junior a pocket watch that transforms itself at the touch of a button into a tiny chess board: it is the first chess-playing machine to be made in Argentina, using the watch's microscopic cogs and wheels to program the game and its hours for memory. He tells him: "Inventar una máquina es fácil, si usted puede modificar las piezas de un mecanismo anterior. Las posibilidades de convertir en otra cosa lo que ya existe son infinitas. No podría hacer algo de la nada" (Inventing a machine is easy, if you can modify the parts of a previous mechanism. The possibilities of converting one thing into another are infinite. I couldn't make something from nothing).[35] The storytelling machine is similarly pragmatic in its recyclings and transformations: "Se las arregla como puede. Usa lo que hay y lo que parece perdido lo hace volver transformado en otra cosa. Así es la vida" (she gets by in whatever way she can. She uses what is there and what seems lost she brings back, transformed into something else. That's how life is).[36]

Genetic recombination and the role of chance

Piglia draws significantly on the role of genetic reproduction in evolution as a metaphor for the creative recombinations of literature. The machine, once programmed with "un conjunto variable de núcleos narrativos" (a variable set of narrative nuclei)[37] produces an endless series of variations, stories that are manifestly related to the original but have been transformed in some manner. As Dr. Arana declares in the novel, "El código genético y el código verbal presentan las mismas características" (the genetic code and the linguistic code share the same features).[38] Like the myriad permutations of just four nucleotides that make up the DNA of every living organism, the meanings that can be generated from the words and structures of language are for practical purposes inexhaustible. As a model of creativity, the language of genetics cuts up the flows and rivers of Romantic inspiration into a series of discrete entities that are endlessly copied and recombined in new ways. Piglia's storytelling machine works rather like the tarot cards in Calvino's *The Castle of Crossed Destinies* (1973), in which a finite number of figures can be combined in almost infinite ways, each taking on a different meaning when placed in a different order or within a different constellation, and forming in this way "a machine for constructing stories."[39] Calvino argues that the "triumph of historical continuity and biological continuity" in the nineteenth century (Hegel and Darwin) has been replaced by the knowledge that "the endless variety of living forms can be reduced to the combination of certain finite quantities" in the form of the acids and bases of DNA.[40] This vision permeates our thought and our understanding of the world, such that "the process going on today is the triumph of discontinuity, divisibility, and combination over all that is flux."[41]

In biology, it is an imperfection in the transcription of the genetic code that allows for the mutations that drive evolution; similarly, Piglia's stories evolve and thrive precisely because of their minute deviations from other texts in the series and their encounters with chance. Central to the concept of creativity in *La ciudad ausente* is the idea of a crucial error in translating or transforming texts that allows variation to occur. The text identified by Junior as "la frase inicial de la serie" (the initial phrase in the series) is a brief biographical sketch of Stephen Stevensen taken from "Encuentro en Saint-Nazaire," with some sentences paraphrased and others reproduced verbatim.[42] As Junior reads further, it transpires that this narrative has undergone a series of transformations, as the narrator is invited, not as a writer to a *Maison des écrivains* in France, but as a doctor to an *estancia* owned by a scientific community in Argentina. He reflects that "Las imprecisiones formaban parte de la construcción de la historia. No se podía ajustar a un tiempo fijo y el espacio era indeciso y a la vez detallado con precisión minuciosa" (the imprecisions formed part of the story's construction. It could not be fitted into a fixed time and its space was undecided and, at the same time, detailed with meticulous precision).[43] Many of Piglia's stories hinge on a tiny but decisive error that can change an entire destiny: we are introduced in the novel, for example, to a Japanese soldier who, determined to carry out his duty and convinced that the war was eternal, obediently remained in the jungle to fight the American forces for thirty years. In this case too, "salvo por un dato casi microscópico (la firma de paz en un papel), todo su universo era real" (with the exception of one almost microscopic detail, the signing of a peace treaty on a piece of paper, his whole universe was real).[44]

This focus on the role played by chance and microscopic variation in evolution again inspires a method of composition: minute alterations to the narrative premises of one story lead to the construction of another. Piglia's understanding of evolution always emphasizes the contingent and the accidental, and therefore also resonates with the Foucauldian genealogical approach that, far from attempting to "restore an unbroken continuity" between past and present, highlights instead "the accidents, the minute deviations – or conversely, the complete reversals – the errors, the false appraisals, and the faulty calculations" that shape existence.[45] The emphasis on chance and error also recalls the importance of these in Formalist accounts of literary evolution. In Tynyanov's words, what critics label as *"an exception to the system, a mistake"* often turns out to be *"a dislocation of the system"*; the "opposing constructive principle," which leads to innovation, "takes shape from *'chance'* results and *'chance'* exceptions and errors."[46]

In the figure of Russo in *La ciudad ausente*, the role of inventor-scientist and storyteller-artist are conflated, much in the same way as they are in Canterel, the protagonist of Raymond Roussel's *Locus Solus* (1914), in which increasingly complex machines provoke the telling of ever-more elaborate tales. Roussel's mechanistic compositional technique, which makes use of puns as formal constraints, is criticized by Porush for its stultifying effect, "designed to produce a literature that recaptures the merely haphazard elements of language within a larger structure of logic, an artistic positivism that leaves nothing to chance."[47] Drawing on twentieth-century advances in genetic biology, Piglia's text-as-machine is designed to operate in a very different manner: order is not imposed from above but emerges from a complex sequence of chance events and a form of collective memory.

Berg comments perceptively on Piglia's construction of newness, not as rupture, but as the rediscovery of distant filiations, or the unprogrammed forging of connections between hitherto unrelated elements:

> La novedad ya no debería ser entendida como lo hacían las vanguardias históricas de principios de nuestro siglo, es decir como una ruptura que borra las huellas del pasado, sino como la introducción de paradojas en los discursos existentes. Una política vanguardista contemporánea podría ser ésta: encontrar paradojas, alianzas o parentescos allí donde no se ven, introducirlos allí donde no están.[48]

> Novelty should no longer be understood as it was by the historical avant-gardes of the beginning of our [twentieth] century, as a rupture that erases the traces of the past, but as the introduction of paradoxes in existing discourses. A contemporary avant-garde approach could be as follows: to find paradoxes, alliances or relations of kinship that are not visible, to introduce them if they do not exist.

Forging new alliances, tracing oblique and distant family relationships, recycling and refunctioning existing forms: this is not only the language of biological evolution but also that of Formalism. It is in this respect that *La ciudad ausente*, apparently so different in style and focus, can be read as a direct continuation of *Respiración artificial* (see Chapter 1). Piglia finds in Borges the model of a writer who is always a reader, reading against other writers, betraying what he reads to appropriate it for his own ends. In Borges's "inclinación deliberada a leer mal, a leer fuera de lugar, a relacionar series imposibles" (deliberate inclination to read badly, to read out of context, to relate impossible series together)[49] lies a notion of creativity that is fundamental to Piglia's own work.

The machinic, beyond organic vs. mechanical

As a theory of creativity, Piglia's understanding of the expressive power of genetic recombination is decidedly post-Romantic. So, too, is his overhaul of the old conflict between organic and mechanistic visions of the world, proposing in its place a series of affinities between human creativity and the machinic. Piglia does not respect the distinctions between the organic and the mechanical that underpin Coleridge's theory of aesthetics and much of the Romantic rupture with Classical artistry. For Coleridge, the role of the imagination is to bring multiplicity into unity, forming – as in nature – a self-evolving whole that is greater than its parts; herein lies the contrast between "imagination" and "fancy," which can only employ an "aggregative power,"[50] bringing together existing materials in different combinations, much like a mechanical apparatus, which can be dismantled and reassembled. Edward Young had drawn a similar distinction between the natural and the mechanical in his *Conjectures on Original Composition* of 1759:

> An *Original* may be said to be of a *vegetable* nature; it rises spontaneously from the vital root of Genius; it *grows*, it is not *made*: *Imitations* are often a sort of *Manufacture* wrought up by those *Mechanics*, *Art*, and *Labour*, out of pre-existent materials not their own.[51]

By contrast, in Piglia's machines, recombination emerges as the primary creative operation. Moreover, the renewed power of literature derives from the consistent commingling and co-functioning of the organic and the mechanical in his work. The machines of *La ciudad ausente* and *Blanco nocturno* are strikingly life-like, or even fused in some way with human memory and consciousness, like Russo's mechanical bird, which appears to breathe, or the tiny boards of Luca's machine, made to move *"como si aleteara un pájaro"* (as if a bird was flapping its wings).[52] Conversely, human creativity is pictured as a system, like Elena, "de tubos y de cables" (of tubes and cables),[53] in which newness is produced through a network of relations, both logical and metaphorical, and in which – as Croce says in *Blanco nocturno* – "Nada vale por sí mismo, todo vale en relación con otra ecuación que no conocemos" (nothing means anything in itself, everything means something in relation to another equation we don't know).[54]

As Martínez points out, at the heart of the formalist quest to demonstrate that mathematics followed a finite system of axioms – definitively shown to be incorrect by Gödel – was the attempt to prove that all mathematical demonstration could be carried out mechanically.[55] Gödel's theorem has often been used to "prove" that machines will never be able to match human intelligence. Roger Penrose, for example, draws on Gödel in his argument that human consciousness is non-algorithmic and cannot therefore be reduced to the operations of a computer.[56] Human intelligence is distinguished by the ability to move fairly effortlessly between a hierarchy of systems – moving from speaking about a subject to speaking about the language used in speaking about that subject, for example – whereas artificial intelligence is limited to the correct execution of a specific set of operations within a system. Douglas Hofstadter observes that "the thought processes involved in doing mathematics, just like those in other areas, involve 'tangled hierarchies' in which thoughts on one level can affect thoughts on any other level. Levels are not cleanly separated, as the formalist version of what mathematics is would have one believe."[57]

In Piglia, the capacity for reflexivity and the ability to transcend mechanical rules in order to create something new is associated as much with *machinic* intelligence as the human variety. Calvino imagines something very similar when he posits the idea that a machine could be used to produce literature, and not just of a logical, classicist variety. Given recent advances in cybernetics towards producing machines capable of learning, he suggests that "nothing prevents us from foreseeing a literature-machine that at a certain point feels unsatisfied with its own traditionalism and starts to propose new ways of writing, turning its own codes completely upside down."[58] We have come full circle: instead of a Romantic rebellion of the artist against mechanization, we can now imagine a machine that satisfies that same human need to shake up the system. The storytelling machine of *La ciudad ausente* operates very much in this manner, performing acts of resistance to authoritarian control and defying literary convention in its radical reworking of divisions between the real and the virtual.

The machine in *Blanco nocturno* is in fact described as being *more* inventive than nature. In Luca's account of the objects he has created, he differentiates clearly between the products of machines and the products of nature, insisting on the originality of the first and the imitative, second-hand quality of the second. Nature's products are not really *products* as such, but "una réplica natural de objetos anteriores que se reproducen igual una y otra vez. Un campo de trigo es un campo de trigo" (a natural replica of previous objects that are reproduced identically again and again. A wheat field is a wheat field).[59] By contrast, machines are "instrumentos muy delicados; sirven para realizar nuevos objetos inesperados, más y más complejos" (very delicate instruments; they are used to make new and unexpected objects, of greater and greater complexity).[60] Unlike nature, machines can produce new objects for which there is no previous model available simply to copy.

Although Piglia does not use a specifically Deleuzean lexicon, his machines are strikingly homologous to Deleuze's, for whom "machinic [...] does not mean either mechanical or organic."[61] Claire Colebrook gives a succinct summary of the difference between the mechanical and the machinic in Deleuze and Guattari's work: "A mechanism is a self-enclosed movement that merely ticks over, never transforming or producing itself. A machinic becoming makes a connection with what is not itself in order to transform and maximise itself."[62] For Deleuze and Guattari, both living organisms and technological apparatuses can function as machines if they engage in processes of becoming through being connected with other machines in ever-evolving assemblages. Those connections produce further connections, none of which are organized by any transcendent figure. Piglia's texts are machinic in Deleuze and Guattari's sense, functioning as an assemblage together with other assemblages, forming and being formed by multiple connections that are often creative in their unpredictability.

A dream no longer in need of its dreamer

In the same way that Piglia's theory of literary creativity rescues recombination and machinic production from their denigration at the hands of the Romantics, his notion of authorship thoroughly undermines Romantic notions of the individual genius. *La ciudad ausente* creates a number of explicit intertextual links with Foucault's famous essay "What is an Author?" of 1969. One of the most obvious of these is Piglia's use of the figure of Scheherezade in *The Thousand and One Nights*, who postpones death through the telling of stories and is also cited by Foucault in his essay. Foucault's central argument is that the author in modernity has become a function "by which one impedes the free circulation, the free manipulation, the free composition, decomposition, and recomposition of fiction."[63] Our critical emphasis on the author as the originator of meaning in a text, "as a genius, as a perpetual surging of invention," effectively reduces its possible meanings and therefore contains what Foucault refers to as "the great danger with which fiction threatens our world," which is the possibility of transgressive discourses and the proliferation of meanings.[64] Literature, like Scheherazade's narratives, can "ward off death,"[65] but only by metaphorically killing off its author and becoming anonymous and infinitely iterable.

The Romantic figure of the artist-genius places limits on the text's possible meanings, its capacity to elude or transform an original set of premises, and therefore its potential resistance to orthodoxy. The machinic qualities of Piglia's storytelling cyborg in *La ciudad ausente* are precisely those that open up the free circulation of fiction. As we saw in Chapter 2, the correspondence between creativity and the depersonalization of literature in Piglia's work complicates the more conventional relationship established in apocalyptic (Romantic) science fiction between machines and dehumanization. Idelber Avelar, in his very insightful reading of the novel, argues that the storytelling machine

> metaphorizes the possibility of creating new stories, but "new" and "create" need to be understood here in a most antiromantic sense. The machine handles combinations, plagiarism,

apocryphal narratives, and disinteriorized affects. Piglia depersonalizes mourning and desubjectivizes affect.[66]

This depersonalization unties the text from its author and frees it to circulate in a virtual space.

In "Las ruinas circulares," Borges imagines a man who dreams up another but who discovers himself in turn to be created through another man's dream. Piglia severs these chains of ontological dependency and creates a dream no longer in need of its dreamer, which is free to pursue multiple forms of embodiment. The machine's peculiar power in *La ciudad ausente* rests on an ability to insert her stories into the consciousness of her readers and listeners to the extent that they merge with those individual pasts and become indistinguishable from them: "ella produce historias, indefinidamente, relatos convertidos en recuerdos invisibles que todos piensan que son propios" (she produces stories, indefinitely, narratives that become invisible memories that everyone thinks are their own).[67] Iterability and anonymity, rather than the individual subjectivity of the author, become forces of radical creativity and unexpected forms of resistance against the discourses of authoritarianism.

That this depersonalization is much more readily associated with the inhuman and the workings of oppression than it is with creativity and freedom is evidence of the persistent legacy of Romantic notions of authorship in our own era. Susan Stewart refers to "the terror of the doll," which, if animated, "would only cause the obliteration of the subject – the inhuman spectacle of a dream no longer in need of its dreamer."[68] M. H. Abrams laments the "systematic dehumanizing" of literature that characterizes the "Age of Reading," such that "the text forfeits its status as a purposeful utterance about human beings and human concerns, and even its individuality, becoming simply an episode in an all-encompassing textuality." In this dissolving of the text, "the relations between authors which had traditionally been known as 'influence' are depersonalized into 'intertextuality,' a reverberation between ownerless sequences of signs."[69]

The much more positive relationship established between depersonalization and creativity in Piglia's work bears distinct traces of Formalist approaches, which were of course highly influential in structuralist and post-structuralist thought. In *Respiración artificial*, as we saw in Chapter 1, Piglia draws on the Formalist understanding of literary evolution as a discontinuous, dialectical process that skips generations, takes up oblique or broken lines, and creates unexpected alliances. In *La ciudad ausente*, he takes a step further in imagining innovation and renewal in literature as the Formalist "dialectic play of devices"[70] that transcends the individual altogether. The Formalists set themselves the task of accounting for literary evolution "outside individual personality" as Boris M. Eichenbaum put it.[71] Victor Erlich explains that the literary genius "was reduced to the status of an agent of impersonal forces," citing Shklovsky's representation of the creator as "simply the geometrical point of intersection of forces operative outside of him.'"[72]

J. Andrew Brown holds back from categorizing *La ciudad ausente* as a "cybernetic fiction" for the reason that, although Junior becomes a virtual reader of sorts, the novel as a whole "is still a traditional book; it does not allow the actual reader options like a hypertext narrative would, nor does it create for him or her a virtual reality."[73] It is of course true that the novel takes the form of a consecutive series of printed pages and therefore does not correspond to the strictest definition of the term "cybernetic fiction." However, as we saw in Chapter 2, evident in Piglia's work is an understanding of literature as the constructor *par excellence* of virtual reality, implanting artificial experiences in the reader and creating affects that did not exist before. The discussions above have focussed on the sustained enquiry in Piglia's texts into the nature of biological and artificial processes that are the primary focus of cybernetics. Even more powerfully, though, the texts themselves exemplify the kind of creative machines envisioned by cybernetics, which transcend the division between the human and the mechanical.

Porush argues that as the machine metaphor has become more and more prevalent in our culture, to the extent that it has come (in formalism and cybernetics, for example) to represent the workings of language and our own consciousness, it acquires the status of "something even more powerful than a metaphor." Borrowing from Umberto Eco's definition of the "icon" as "a model of relationships," Porush proposes that we consider the machine in literature as an icon, "capable of crystallizing, reflecting and embodying not only a complex system of meanings (determinism, logic, order, system) but the act of making meanings itself."[74] If Piglia's fiction amply demonstrates the status of the machine as icon in the manner Porush describes, it is equally evident that it draws on an updated version of that "model of relationships," in which the machine does not – as in so much literature from the eighteenth century onwards – signify determinism, mechanism, and the clockwork universe but rather the dynamic interconnectedness of all things, the interdependence of the human, natural, and technological realms, the thorough imbrication of the material and the virtual, and the complexity that confounds simple accounts of causality. This rescues the machine from the more arid or formulaic of modernist experiments with literary composition as the application of techniques, liberating the text to operate as a Deleuzean assemblage together with other assemblages, endlessly creating meaning through myriad connections, most of which are not programmed by the inventor.

ENTROPY AND METAPHOR / COHEN

> Zebra-streaked, tiger-striped, variegated, motley, fleck-speckled, bedizened, star-spangled. We invent, we produce like the Demiurge, in and through the mix.—Michel Serres[75]

Entropy, as stated in the first two laws of thermodynamics, increases as the temperatures in an isolated system become more uniform over time. From the discovery of these laws, scientists moved quickly to speculate about the heat death of the universe: William Thomson (Lord Kelvin) was the first to posit the exhaustion of energy in the universe in his paper of 1852, "On a Universal Tendency in Nature to the Dissipation of Mechanical Energy." The idea was extended and popularized by Hermann von Helmholtz and William Rankine, but it was not until the New Wave of science fiction in the 1960s and 1970s that it was thoroughly mined for its fictional potential by North American and British writers such as Philip K. Dick, Thomas Pynchon, J. G. Ballard, and Michael Moorcock. What Pynchon was later to refer to as the "thermodynamical gloom" of his early short story on the theme, "Entropy" (1960), chimed all too convincingly with the pessimism of Beat literature and the most apocalyptic strains of North American science fiction.[76]

Pynchon and Ballard are key referents in Cohen's fiction and critical essays; however, their use of the entropy metaphor is substantially reworked within Cohen's highly reflexive texts to serve as a trope for creativity. This transformation is particularly evident in *El fin de lo mismo*, a collection of short stories published in 1992. At first sight, entropy appears to be employed in some of these fictions as a metaphor to narrate a familiar trajectory towards homogenization, stasis, and death, marking the potential elimination of all difference in Cohen's hyper-mediatized, market-governed societies. However, it is also resignified as the potential source of newness and unpredictability and often completely refigured for much more positive ends, specifically to point to the creative power of literature in staging an encounter with radical and irreducible difference. Entropy here becomes more than a metaphor: literature does not simply appropriate the idea of entropy to express the nature of certain cultural or social phenomena; instead, it is itself caught up in the very dynamics of entropy, and therefore constantly manifests, produces, or arrests those same phenomena.

For Eric Zencey, entropy acts as a "root metaphor" in the sense given to the term by Stephen Pepper in *World Hypotheses* (1942). Zencey identifies several ways in which the picture of flows of energy given to us by thermodynamics is taken up across the disciplines – biology, psychology, history, economic theory – and particularly how it comes to shape a view of the universe as an "incipient chaos" in which we live "in a state of ontological anomie."[77] As John Bruni observes, the earliest treatments of entropy in literature, such as that of H. G. Wells in *The Time Machine* (1895), "tended to restage images of exhaustion" present in the work of Flaubert and Baudelaire.[78] In New Wave fiction, entropy is often used as a metaphor for cultural and social decline in an ultra-urbanized, war-mongering, high technology world.

Entropy is a recurrent motif in Moorcock's novels, and particularly in the Jerry Cornelius series; it is often associated with the dissipation of identity and memory. Cornelius fails in his mission to combat the forces of decay and entropy, becoming caught up in them instead. In Ballard's catastrophic worlds, the dissolution of identity results in a merging of the subject and the environment around him, in which the oppositions we normally use to order experience – internal and external, subject and object, mental and physical – are thoroughly dismantled. This movement from tension to dissipation, towards maximum entropy, is central to Ballard's apocalyptic vision.

That the future promises not progress but stasis, and the end of genuine difference and innovation, is an idea pursued with equal vigour by many theorists of the postmodern. In the commodification of newness in postmodern culture Jameson observes a paradox, which is "the equivalence between an unparalleled rate of change on all the levels of social life and an unparalleled standardization of everything."[79] Jameson employs a lexicon shared with the science of entropy and thermodynamics when he describes the manner in which "the supreme value of the New and of innovation, as both modernism and modernization grasped it, fades away against a steady stream of momentum and variation that at some outer limit seems stable and motionless," leaving "the realization that no society has ever been so standardized as this one, and that the stream of human, social, and historical temporality has never flowed quite so homogeneously."[80] The temporality that structured modernization has been replaced with "an appearance of random changes that are mere stasis, a disorder after the end of history."[81]

Pynchon, who acknowledges his debt to the metaphorical use of entropy by Henry Adams and Norbert Wiener,[82] draws in "Entropy" – and in other texts – on their understanding of entropy as heat-death and exhaustion. The world of "Entropy" appears at times to be full of activity and complexity ("a *stretto* passage in the year's fugue") and at others to be listless and directionless, characterized by "private meanderings" and "aimless loves."[83] But it is set on a course of entropy, until such point as the moment of equilibrium is reached and heat-transfer becomes impossible, with the temperature reaching a steady and stable 37 degrees Fahrenheit and effecting "the final absence of all motion" in a perpetual state of limbo.[84] This elimination of difference in the physical world evokes the more general social and cultural torpor produced by American consumerism which, as Callisto states, enacts "a similar tendency from the least to the most probable, from differentiation to sameness."[85]

The homogenizing forces of consumerism and mediatization are also, as we will see, figured as entropic in Cohen's fiction. However, Cohen's understanding of entropy owes much more to the re-reading of the second law of thermodynamics presented in Erwin Schrödinger's *What is Life?* (1944) and *Mind and Matter* (1958), and Ilya Prigogine's work on dissipative structures, published in texts such as *Order out of Chaos: Man's New Dialogue with Nature* (1984) and *The End of Certainty: Time, Chaos and the New Laws of Nature* (1997, both written with Isabelle Stengers). Schrödinger argues that life is constantly re-energized by using resources from outside, exporting entropy or importing "negative entropy" (or "free energy") to produce a higher order from disorder. This does not contradict the second law of thermodynamics – that entropy and disorder increase in a closed system – precisely because the universe is not a closed system. This is the key distinction that allows Cohen to borrow entropy as a model, not only on occasion to suggest the sense of exhaustion with which it is associated in most anglophone fiction, but also, and more insistently, to posit an endlessly renewable production of difference. Indeed, the very instability of metaphors such as entropy in Cohen's fiction becomes one of several techniques through which literature may introduce uncertainty and generate the kind of heterogeneity that combats the very process of entropy.

The etymology of entropy (from the Greek "tropos," meaning transformation or turning) already suggests transformations of the kind effected by metaphor as a literary trope. Many of the narratives of Cohen's *El fin de lo mismo* discussed below do not simply appropriate entropy as a trope for certain social, economic, or cultural phenomena but exploit the tautology of this operation to explore what the processes of entropy can reveal about the nature of metaphor itself. In his literary and critical work, Cohen develops a theory of metaphor that dispenses with Platonic divisions and hierarchies and draws instead on models of multiplicity and metamorphosis developed in recent scientific and philosophical thought. Along the way, as we will see, he constructs a role for the critic in an immanent, rhizomatic world of continual becoming that has nothing to do with the traditional explication or exegesis of texts.

Becoming-inhuman in "Lydia en el canal"

> He counted the materials of the landscape: the curvilinear perspectives of the concrete causeways, the symmetry of car fenders, the contours of Karen's thighs and pelvis, her uncertain smile. What new algebra would make sense of these elements?—J. G. Ballard[86]

The protagonist of Cohen's "Lydia en el canal" experiences an intensely chaotic relationship with the physical architecture of her world. She fails to tame the strange geometry of the new apartment to which she has been transferred on becoming a widow: its volumes, surfaces, reflections, and angles "no se unían con el cuerpo en un sistema duradero" (did not join with the body in a durable system).[87] This experience is associated with bereavement: Lydia feels that the presence of another body – that of her husband, for whom she is grieving – would be needed to conquer this unfamiliar territory. Objects change form, harden and threaten to collapse on top of her, in what appears to be an extension of an inner discord between body and thought: at one point, Lydia's body is described as fleeing from her and disintegrating, while, at another, it is her untamed thought that escapes and spins with such violence that the floor gives way and a centrifugal force crushes her against the wall.

"Lydia en el canal" establishes an important dialogue with Ballard's *The Atrocity Exhibition* (1970), the first novel Cohen translated into Spanish.[88] The apartment sex scenes between Lydia and Tranco strongly echo those between Tallis and Karen Novotny in Ballard's novel. Tallis and Karen watch each other's bodies interact with the angles and surfaces of the apartment, and "the sexual act between them was a dual communion between themselves and the continuum of time and space which they occupied."[89] The "act of love" for them becomes "a vector in an applied geometry."[90] With a similar consciousness of geometrical confusion and (dis)harmony, Lydia is shaken by "las inestables alianzas del espacio, la fugacidad de sus cuplas" (the unstable alliances of space, the fleetingness of its bonds)[91] but finds brief respite during intercourse with her neighbour Tranco, watching how "alrededor de los dos cuerpos, la turba de objetos de la pieza se ordena en un pachorriento mandala" (around the two bodies, the mob of objects in the room ordered itself into a calm mandala).[92]

"Lydia en el canal" exemplifies the unstable, chaotic realms of Cohen's narrative worlds. Caught up in unpredictable forces, his characters struggle and usually fail to impose any order on the continually transforming matter and energy of the universe. Lydia's predicament is also similar to the peculiar condition suffered by Aubade in Pynchon's "Entropy," in which all perceptions of the world around her are experienced as sound, a discordant cacophony from which fragments of more ordered and harmonious music emerge. She has a heightened sense of the continual battle between order and disorder that governs the world around her and struggles to order and reorder the perceptual information she receives, to keep formlessness and meaninglessness at bay:

> The architectonic purity of her world was constantly threatened by such hints of anarchy: gaps and excrescences and skew lines, and a shifting or tilting of planes to which she had continually to readjust lest the whole structure shiver into a disarray of discrete and meaningless signals. [...]
> That precious signal-to-noise ratio, whose delicate balance required every calorie of her strength, seesawed inside the small tenuous skull [...].[93]

However, if Aubade is ultimately powerless to prevent the resolution of these tensions into an irreversible stasis, the geometric and atmospheric anomalies of Cohen's worlds often present a means of liberation for his protagonists. Unlike Aubade, his characters often learn to come to terms with their frightening, unhomely environments, and to understand that they form part of the constant flux of these, not positioned above or beyond them. The moment of epiphany that reveals to them their shared nature with the universe gives them a particular sense of meaning and destiny.

Indeed, Lydia's coming-to-terms with the world around her, her passage through grief to a renewed sense of belonging in an alien landscape, is not achieved by means of shoring up her individual identity or reestablishing the boundaries of her self, but through an embrace of the interconnectedness of all things, herself included. Smoking a cigarette by the canal, she observes that "las hilachas del humo parecían anudar síntomas dispersos" (the loose threads of smoke seemed to tie scattered signs together):[94] they link together the greasy reflections of the water, the moss on the sunken barges, the angles of plexiglass, and the blackened columns of the bridge, and all of these with herself, as she takes another drag and feels the smoke at the back of her throat. Focussing on another image, that of a virus, she meditates on the "communion" that brings together bodies invaded by viral cells, including her own.[95] This revelation is part of the process that leads to a possible integration for Lydia in the unhomely environment in which she finds herself.

Of the stories collected in *El fin de lo mismo*, "Lydia en el canal" most closely follows Ballard in the psychopathological origin of the unusual couplings between characters and the urban landscape. In *The Atrocity Exhibition*, insistent references to the merging of the contours of human bodies with the geometries of concrete overpasses and underpasses and multistorey car parks are clearly associated with the protagonist's narrative perspective, and Dr. Nathan finds that he is suffering from a specific condition, a "perpetual and irresistible desire to merge with the object in an undifferentiated mass."[96] Lydia's experience of disorder in the physical environment and of repeated transgressions of the boundaries separating subject and object are, if not linked with a complicated version of sadism as in the case of Ballard's protagonist, clearly the result of intense grief, and the symptoms abate as she gradually begins to come to terms with her loss.

However, Cohen parts company with Ballard on a very significant point. In *The Atrocity Exhibition*, we are led to understand that Travis's distorted perspective is the result of over-exposure to the traumas of technological warfare and the most inhuman traits of the post-Vietnam era. It is a reaction,

Dr. Nathan suggests, against the natural order, perhaps partly attributable to the power of thermonuclear weapons "in bringing about the total fusion and non-differentiation of all matter."[97] Travis therefore reacts against "the phenomenology of the universe, the specific and independent existence of separate objects and events."[98] Cohen reverses this association: it is instead the *natural* world in which all matter is fused or interrelated, and his characters attain their highest point of sanity when they recognize their oneness with the universe, not the supposed independence of subjects, objects, and events.

That we should not understand this "natural" world to exclude technology, however, is made clear from the particular forms of "becoming" Cohen narrates, and the language used to express these transformations. Pynchon pursues a musical analogy throughout "Entropy" to suggest a delicate balance between form and chaos, meaning and noise, modulation and resolution, and the complex relationship Aubade conceives with the tensions between these in the world around her. Cohen's story, in comparison, is more radical in its use of style to suggest this tension and the transference and negotiation of agency between subject and object. An insistent use of transitive verbs ascribes intentions, desires, and emotions to the objects around Lydia to the extent that her keys and clothes often seem to be more alive than she does and to have a greater sense of conscious, purposeful activity. It is a technique that Cohen would put to much more extensive use in his novel *Casa de Ottro* (2009), which explores zones of indiscernibility and exchange between human subjects and inanimate objects and conveys something of the forms of becoming that Deleuze and Guattari have described as "becoming-molecular" or "becoming-inhuman."[99]

While Deleuze and Guattari favour the use of free indirect discourse in literature to express the nature of language as a "collective assemblage"[100] – used extensively in the work of Woolf and Joyce, for example – this technique is conspicuously absent in Cohen. Cohen's own expression of dispersed subjectivity and the nature of language and discourse as "collective assemblages" is most strikingly to be found in a conceit employed in many of his novels and short stories, the "Panconciencia." A kind of virtual information network that allows users to access other citizens' minds, the Panconciencia is a trope for the flows of perception and experience across the boundaries of the subject. Connecting up, the narrator of *Donde yo no estaba* (2006) hears a murmur in crescendo, "el vocerío del multiverso interior" (the clamour of the interior multiverse) and understands that "Mi historia personal ya no era cosa solitaria" (my personal life was no longer a solitary thing).[101] The Panconciencia invokes Deleuze and Guattari's assertion that "Language in its entirety is indirect discourse," and that "Direct discourse is a detached fragment of a mass and is born of the dismemberment of the collective assemblage; but the collective assemblage is always like the murmur from which I take my proper name, the constellation of voices, concordant or not, from which I draw my voice."[102]

Cohen's Panconciencia conceit imagines a (virtual) technological interface that mediates these intersubjective flows. As in Piglia's fiction, technology here is neither antagonistic towards the human nor a substitution for it. Indeed, "becoming-inhuman" seems to play a vital role in preparing human subjects for an encounter with each other. As is clearly the case in "Lydia en el canal," a process of becoming-other with inanimate objects or non-human organisms makes it possible for Cohen's characters to break out of their isolation and discover a sense of proximity with other humans. In *Casa de Ottro*, Fronda's gradual understanding that life flows through the objects around her as well as herself leads to a renewal of her relationship with both the cyborg and human inhabitants of the house; likewise, as we will see, an encounter with the sea's cycles of preservation and destruction brings the protagonist of "La ilusión monarca" to desire communication with his fellow prisoners. Lydia, gradually coming to terms with the sharp angles and aggressive intrusions of her material environment, eventually understands that her self-exclusion from it and from the community of peculiar and rather menacing youths around her will only lead to greater danger and misery, and she begins to interact compassionately with them. "No se puede ser condesa a cien yardas de un carruaje" (you can't be a countess a hundred yards from a carriage),[103] she repeats to herself. She realizes that her destiny is here and that, if she shares their space, she is also part of them. In contrast to Ballard's fiction, the merging of the human with the inhuman in Cohen's, while it may be symptomatic of trauma or produce a traumatic experience itself, nevertheless precedes a transformation in which the human becomes more fully human. As in Deleuze's vision, "The human becomes more than itself, or expands to its highest power, not by affirming its humanity, nor by returning to animal state, but by becoming-hybrid with what is not itself."[104] Cohen's fiction marks a significant departure from the novels of Pynchon, Burroughs, and Moorcock in its treatment of dispersed subjectivities. In the latter three, the dissipation of identity and the increasing erosion of difference between human subjects and their environment are associated with the effects of trauma or an inexorable slide towards entropy, numbness, and stasis. In Cohen, by contrast, human subjects find their home in the chaotic flux that binds together the natural and artificial elements of their environment. This reversal lays the ground, as I will show, for Cohen's resignification of entropy as a mechanism to produce difference and creative conflict rather than sameness and the depletion of energy.

Entropy and dissipative structures in "El fin de lo mismo"

The chaotic and disordered geometries of "Lydia en el canal" are resignified in other stories of *El fin de lo mismo* as a source of creativity and resistance to the homogenizing effects of capitalism. "El fin de lo mismo," the title story of the collection, imagines a world that is highly unstable and subject to extreme hyperinflation. Bodies, goods, and money are caught up in a frenzied circulation in which the rate of exchange rockets daily, generating such uncertainty and panic that "El tejido del progreso se deshilachaba, pinchado por las navajas de los hambrientos, roído por la vehemencia disciplinaria de los profesionales inseguros" (the fabric of progress was fraying, pierced by the knives of the hungry, eaten away by the disciplining vehemence of insecure professionals).[105] Even the physical world is affected, the river misshapen, cracks and protuberances appearing in the sky. Tensions are exacerbated by the heat of the summer, a constant 37 degrees in the shade (the reference to Pynchon's "Entropy" cannot be accidental). "Tanto desarreglo podría haber resultado en un gran alumbramiento" (this much disorder could have resulted in a great birth), Cohen's narrator observes,[106] articulating the insight – proper to theories of complexity and emergence – that disorder is always an opportunity for a system to reorganize itself at a higher level. But instead, the vertigo induced by inflation robs Gumpes and his fellow citizens of their energy and restricts them to progressively more cramped spaces, as they have to downsize to smaller and shabbier apartments.

In such circumstances, can they be blamed for swapping uncertainty for stability, even if it comes at the price of homogenization, stasis, and the incursion of the authorities into their private lives? To arrest this inevitable drift towards entropy comes Olga, a woman with three arms. With her "torso de disonancia perfecta" (torso of perfect dissonance),[107] Gumpes considers Olga to be "la guardiana de la inestabilidad" (the guardian of instability) and therefore worthy of his love in a world that threatens to eliminate all difference and fizzle out into numbness.[108] However, an unexpected twist sees Olga propelled into sudden fame in a spate of interviews and magazine covers; as Miguel Dalmaroni observes, the scandal of her third arm is effectively defused by the mass media, which swallows up all possible anomalies into itself.[109] The power of dissonance is neutralized, as the forces of entropy flatten out difference and everything tends towards sameness.

When entropy comes as predicted, however, it is not the cataclysmic heat-death of the universe but merely a gentle adjustment in the atmosphere: the water stagnates a little more in the backwaters of the river, April is perhaps a little less fresh than usual, and business and consumption slow down. This state of entropy is for Cohen not the end, but merely a passing stage: what no one had foreseen, we are told, "es que la entropía es desorden; y que, al calor de los escombros del progreso, la ciudad ya incubaba nuevas alteraciones, anomalías brutales y asombrosas;" (is that entropy is disorder; and that, in the heat of the ashes of progress, the city was already incubating new disturbances, surprising and brutal anomalies).[110] This is simply a stage of relative calm and rest before new divergences and disruptions arise to challenge the somnolence of the status quo. For this reason my reading of the story would not trace a move from the fantastic to the realistic as definitively as Dalmaroni's does: Cohen leaves us with the full expectation that new anomalies are about to emerge.

Disorder for Cohen always signals the possibility of re-organization at a more complex level, a state of potential creativity and energy; his sophisticated grasp on the implications of thermodynamics and information theory allows him to unshackle the entropy metaphor from its more commonly apocalyptic use in Pynchon and Ballard. Along with uncertainty, chaos, emergence, and dissipative structures, entropy is one of the scientific tropes Cohen draws upon in his construction of a theory of "realismo inseguro" (unstable realism), which describes a series of aesthetic strategies suited to the "realistic" portrayal of a complex, emergent, ever-evolving universe. He introduces these theories not simply to reflect on the nature of the physical world in which we live or the narratives we construct about it – chaos "como mito de la época" (as a myth of our time), for example – but insistently "como hipótesis de trabajo para las invenciones de la literatura" (as a working hypothesis for the inventions of literature).[111]

The key element of this hypothesis rests on the notion of the creativity and energy available in dissipative structures, which make use of chaotic processes and flows across their borders to produce new kinds of order. In a universe far from equilibrium, Prigogine maintains, the operation of such systems "leads to new collective effects and to a new coherence."[112] Drawing on Prigogine's understanding, Cohen distinguishes between "la novela agónica" (the dying novel), which attends to the apathy of its mass audience, and "las narraciones de lo real incierto" (narratives of the uncertain real): while the former represents the lukewarm universe of entropy, he claims, the latter are "estructuras caóticas alejadas del equilibrio. Son incendios, son oleajes" (chaotic structures that are far from equilibrium. They are fires, waves).[113] Flames and waves are prime examples of turbulent and chaotic processes that defy the homogenizing effects of entropy. Both are favoured images in Michel Serres's quest – highly relevant to Cohen's own, as will become clear – to "think a new object, multiple in space and mobile in time, unstable and fluctuating like a flame, relational."[114]

As Cohen observes, if dissipation suggests chaos and dissolution, the opposite of structure, herein lies the central paradox of Prigogine's vision: a dissipative structure is able to maintain stability precisely by constantly opening itself up to flows from the environment, as "se autoorganiza, se realimenta en contacto con agentes aleatorios y se transforma por bifurcación, amplificación y acoplamiento. Cada turbulencia genera nuevos órdenes" (it self-organizes, it feeds off aleatory agents and transforms itself by bifurcation, amplification, and connection. Each instance of turbulence generates new orders).[115] In Cohen's work, this becomes a picture of how literature may generate new forms and ideas through an encounter with difference and the unpredictable. Elsewhere, he proposes that good technique in short-story writing should involve dealing with "lo improcedente, lo intempestivo, lo superfluo y lo que otras técnicas desechan" (the improper, the untimely, the superfluous and whatever is rejected by other techniques).[116] The economical and measured in style, the concise, and the clear: these are impositions of form that cannot remain open to the unexpected or the excessive and cannot therefore create new orders or produce new visions. Instead, Cohen's strategy in the narratives that make up *El fin de lo mismo* – together with many of his other texts – responds to what he understands to be the task of literature: "incorporar el caos a la forma sin disfrazarlo de otra cosa" (to incorporate chaos within form without disguising it as something else).[117]

Cohen's less apocalyptic understanding of entropy leads to a resignification of the breakdown of the subject/object division that characterizes most fiction on the theme. As we saw in "Lydia en el canal," the dissolving of the self does not connote a loss of identity but its rediscovery, a consciousness of the true nature of subjectivity as dispersed within the complex system of the universe it inhabits. The integrity of the subject is violated and transversed by external forces, but this does not eradicate agency: this is clearly the case in "El fin de lo mismo," as Olga's assymetric body causes a radical dislocation in the physical structures and objects around her, unbalancing the system's gradients and introducing an instability that momentarily re-energizes it and decreases entropy. This (rare) ability of individuals to arrest entropy by introducing dissent and resisting homogenization again marks Cohen's vision as more optimistic than Ballard's. As open systems rather than closed ones, the worlds of Cohen's fiction thrive on the disorder produced by entropic forces, which submit the status quo to constant transformation and reorganization.

Resonance in "Aspectos de la vida de Enzatti"

The characteristics of "realismo inseguro" are very much in evidence in "Aspectos de la vida de Enzatti," another narrative from *El fin de lo mismo*, in which Cohen draws on the physics of acoustics to create a picture of literature's construction of meaning through resonance, rather than reference. An extended exploration of the relationship between sound and harmonics directly links Cohen's interest in dispersed subjectivity with the textual practice of "realismo inseguro."

Lying in bed, Enzatti believes that the "system" of the night, with its "armonías equívocas" (ambiguous harmonies), depends on his remaining at the centre of it, articulating it.[118] As he sits up, he is keenly aware that he has altered the balance of the system; however, he is also subject to its "fuerzas mañosas, arbitrarias" (crafty, arbitrary forces). He and the night are part of a single system whose elements co-interact and co-evolve, shaping each other: if at first it is the silence of the night that is fractured, it soon becomes Enzatti who is full of "rajaduras" (cracks).[119] Enzatti has been woken by a shout that pierces the night air and draws him into the street, searching for its source. The many vibrations and resonances set into play by the production of sound become a means in this story to reflect more generally on the invisible connections and forces that link subjects and objects across time and space in a complex system in which every alteration has an effect on multiple networks. This sense of the intangibility of the forces that hold a system in tension and produce form is reinforced by references in the text to magnetic fields.

Every sound, Cohen's narrator explains, creates secondary vibrations, or harmonics; never pure or singular, "un sonido es él y el racimo de sonidos simultáneos que arrastra o desencadena. Eso dice la física" (a sound is itself and the cluster of simultaneous sounds that it carries with it or triggers. That's what physics says). In a more poetic vein, Cohen describes the complex interaction between fundamental notes and overtones in terms that ascribe agency to objects and forces in preference to human subjects: "El grito surca el cráneo y los armónicos se expanden, se arremolinan, chocando con cosas dormidas que, obnubiladas, se alzan a la vigilia tintineando" (the shout cuts through the skull and the harmonics expand, whirl around, colliding with dormant objects which, befuddled, rise jingling into wakefulness).[120] Neither can the listener remain inert or a passive witness to this frenzy of frequencies: Enzatti too is caught up in the system of vibrations that traverse his body and that he alters as well as receives. The sound of the shout echoes impossibly, fantastically, until everything seems to be drawn into the "revolution" it has unleashed.[121]

If the shout traverses space to construct a web of multiple connections in the present, it also assembles "un revuelo de sonidos antiguos" (a tumult of old sounds) in Enzatti's head.[122] The main thread of "Aspectos de la vida de Enzatti" is interrupted by four sections that recount previous episodes in his life at different ages. The form of the narrative has an aleatory feel: the interspersed sections are not clearly related to each other or to the main "plot," although certain points of resonance may be discernible. In many of them Enzatti experiences a sense of the transience of time and the provisionality of the material, together with a disconnection with the world around him, alternating with the sudden revelation of connections and coincidences not previously seen.

In the section entitled "31 años," for example, the improbability that Enzatti's only surviving parent will regain consciousness cuts him loose into the world: "caminaba suelto, como supurado por el mundo, sin origen ni explicación" (he walked alone, as if oozing from the world, without origin or explanation).[123] Leaving behind the "visiones desunidas" (disunited visions) of limbs, machinery, and syringes in the hospital,[124] Enzatti meditates on a contrasting image of unification – the surface shine of a wine glass in a nearby bar, which brings together a miscellany of people and objects in its reflection – and notices that "sobre el vidrio convexo se acumulaban sin disputas las partes de ese mundo suspendido, el bar y zonas de la calle" (amassing themselves on the convex glass, without quarrelling, were all the parts of that suspended world, the bar and areas of the street).[125] "29 años" relates the temporary and unexplained disappearance from sight of Enzatti's girlfriend, who remains present to the touch of his arm around her shoulder as they walk down the street but becomes invisible, only to rematerialize a few moments later; this leads him to wonder to what extent the "essence" of

Annabel resides in substance or something more intangible, and to glimpse the importance of the immaterial bonds that unite them, while reassuring himself of her bodily presence. In "36 años," in contrast, Enzatti is surprised, looking back at steps leading to a balcony on a street, that they look exactly the same as they had done less than a minute earlier. This impression of the stubborn durability of things is itself transitory, however, and he writes an elegy to the moment, which has now gone; and yet he keeps the poem safe, hoping that in the future he will discover it again and feel some form of continuity and inexorability, "una anomalía persistente, irremediable" (a persistent, irreparable anomaly).[126]

While these "flashbacks" have no explanatory function within the diegesis, their presence testifies to the rich, divergent, multiple, and unpredictable nature of the connections that unite sensations and experiences across time as well as space. They are linked by references to events or impressions as "arbitrario" (arbitrary),[127] "aleatorio" (aleatory),[128] and "gratuita" (gratuitous).[129] Placed within the main narrative, their overall effect is to produce a sense of the radical reorientation of perception, to question or sever the continuities and connections we take for granted – such as the persistence of a person's identity over time – and to establish new or surprising associations not obvious to the eye.

Resonance, then, becomes, not simply a picture of the intrinsic connectedness of things, the vibrations that can trigger change even in far-flung corners of a system, but a mode of literary construction. It is one that leads away from realism's hierarchy of referent and representation and towards what Cohen calls "Un arte de superficies" (an art of surfaces): a plane of immanence. This does not refer, as he hastens to point out, to an art that is in any way superficial, but "un arte que se hace ahí donde todos los efectos lindan con las cosas y el lenguaje, y resuenan unos en otros. Es dispersivo, porque tiene una ilimitada capacidad de relación" (an art made at the point where all effects adjoin things and language, and each echoes in each. It is dispersive, because it has an unlimited capacity for relationality).[130]

Cohen cites Rupert Sheldrake's theories of morphic fields and morphic resonance in defining this field as one of relations rather than material objects. Sheldrake, a former biochemist, has since worked largely in the field of parapsychology; his major theories have been dismissed by mainstream scientists. Much of his work has been written in response to what he perceives as the limitations of the mechanistic approach to developmental biology. According to his hypothesis of "formative causation," each kind of cell or organism has a "morphogenetic field" that shapes their development, representing "a kind of pooled or collective memory of the species": "Thus a developing foxglove seedling, for example, is subject to morphic resonance from countless foxgloves that came before, and this resonance shapes and stabilizes its morphogenetic fields."[131] Although no evidence for the existence of such fields has been found, Cohen takes inspiration from Sheldrake's insistence that "La materia ya no constituye un principio de explicación fundamental, mientras que los campos y la energía sí" (matter no longer constitutes a fundamental explanatory principle, while fields and energy do).[132] He finds that "Morfogénesis es una palabra adecuada a la manera en que los relatos resuenan entre sí y entre ellos y el mundo" (morphogenesis is an accurate word to describe the way stories resonate with each other and with the world).[133]

While Sheldrake's morphic resonance takes place between very similar organisms, Cohen's version is deliberately less selective in its reach, bringing into relationship objects that may otherwise be dissimilar and disconnected to form a picture of multiplicity and complexity rather than unification and simplicity. Enzatti understands that if the shout – real and human, rather than imagined – has called him, "no es para instalarlo en la claridad sino presentarle diversas formas del enigma" (it is not to settle him in clarity but to present him with different forms of the enigma).[134] For this reason, perhaps, we are told that the vibrations caused by the shout continue long after Enzatti has rescued its author, a man who has fallen through the floor of a garage. As he departs from the scene, "Sonidos díscolos chocan entre sí, confundidos" (unruly sounds collide with each other, confused), and Enzatti realizes that the most important thing is that they should not be silenced through any kind of clarification.[135] This confusion is part of an encounter with the unknown. As he reflects, "Lo que zumba en el cráneo de Enzatti y lo conmueve, y lo debilita, no es solamente lo olvidado que regresa. Es lo desconocido" (that which buzzes in Enzatti's skull and moves him, and weakens him, is not merely the forgotten returning. It is the unknown).[136]

In place of the finished, the rounded, and the neatly explained, Cohen's "realismo inseguro" chooses to deal in "los excursos, los tiempos muertos, las descripciones impertinentes, las analogías, las referencias múltiples y el poder transformador de la resonancia" (excursions, dead time, irrelevant descriptions, analogies, multiple references, and the transforming power of resonance) in search of "un ámbito donde el suceso hace fulgurar todos los niveles de la realidad y todas las realidades" (a field in which the spark of an event causes all levels of reality and all realities to light up).[137] The "site" of resonance, Cohen explains, is the metaphor:

> La metáfora vincula entidades de diversa especie creando entidades distintas de los términos vinculados: es la contigüidad entre realidad material e imaginación, el lugar donde el acontecimiento se cuenta mejor. Es el motor privilegiado de la autogeneración del texto-mundo. Es la forma proliferante, el "sostén" de la estructura difusiva; reúne pero no encierra. Estructuras difusivas, campos de resonancia donde los acontecimientos se relacionan en paralelo y lo que parece agotarse en una causa siempre se realimenta con una relación más, son las novelas de Thomas Pynchon, pero también, por ejemplo, las de Julien Gracq.[138]

The metaphor links entities of different kinds, creating different entities from the terms it links: it is the contiguity between material reality and imagination, the place where the event is best recounted. It is the principal engine for the self-generation of the text-world. It is the proliferating form, the "support" for a diffusive structure; it brings together but it does not enclose. Dissipative structures, fields of resonance where events relate to each other alongside each other, and what seems to be fully exhausted by one cause is always re-energized by another set of relations: that is what Thomas Pynchon's novels are about, but also, for example, Julien Gracq's.

If "Aspectos de la vida de Enzatti" gives us a glimpse of this world, in which new links and pathways are constantly being traced across a field of resonance, two other narratives in *El fin de lo mismo* take up the task of modelling in greater detail how these particular metaphors of resonance and dissipative structures can be used to account for creativity in literature and literature's role in destabilizing the ruling social order.

Realismo inseguro in "Volubilidad"

> Writing has no other end than to lose one's face.—Gilles Deleuze[139]

In "Volubilidad" we move into a more explicitly reflexive realm, in which Cohen's vision of a world held in tension between the forces of entropy and those of self-organization, the tension between formlessness and form, becomes an allegory: not just for the relationship between sociopolitical power and resistance (as in "El fin de lo mismo"), but also for the role of literature in contemporary society. The story's protagonist, Maguire, suspects himself to be the subject of the fantasies of a fellow-passenger on the subway train he takes to work every morning. These fantasies take the form of projections of Maguire performing a wide variety of different jobs: window-cleaner, magician, waiter, taekwondo instructor, and many more. Over time, these projections multiply until they are an almost constant presence in his life. It appears at least possible that they have been instigated by the state-owned "Oficina Intersubjetiva" (Intersubjective Office) in order to exacerbate Maguire's already rather provisional and shifting sense of personal identity and to frighten him into making "un esfuerzo de cohesión" (an effort towards cohesion).[140]

In this society's current and paradoxical phase of post-industrial growth, the greatest socioeconomic advance is available to citizens who stay put in one place; those who have a tendency to move about, to avoid tying themselves to a single point, get left behind. This is an environment in which fixity, solidity, and clarity are valued: the more easily identifiable an object or a person, the greater the likelihood of their continued existence in social reality. By contrast, the versatile, fickle, or unstable – those of "carácter disperso" (a dispersed nature)[141] – do not bind themselves so fully to career ambition and socioeconomic ascent and therefore do not contribute so obviously to economic growth; labelled "indefinidos sociales" (social indefinites), these marginal figures are subject to a series of measures taken by the state to force them to acquire greater cohesion as subjects and to re-enter consumer society. Once settled back into the system, the "derroche de energía" (waste of energy)[142] they had represented can be channelled more efficiently towards productive ends.

If the imprecise, the undefined, and the redundant are not so easily caught up into the inexorable cycle of production and consumption, then it is their proliferation that becomes the business of literature. In a society in which almost absolute power is wielded by a sinister coalition between politics and information, the role of literature is to introduce noise, from which alternatives might arise. The accelerating post-industrial growth experienced by the societies of *El fin de lo mismo* produces certain reading preferences among their populations that might remind us of those of the mass market in our own society. In "Volubilidad," Cohen introduces a reflexive commentary into the narrative, exploring the question of which aspects of the story would fulfil those mainstream narrative expectations and which would not. For example, after his encounter with the social worker, Maguire takes a series of actions that appear to show his willingness to reintegrate into the socioeconomic sphere. However, a heavy note of irony is introduced by inserting a metafictional observation before the list of his next moves: "En un marco narrativo apto para el agitado ocio posindustrial, los pasos que Maguire da a continuación resultan satisfactorios y coherentes" (within a narrative framework suited to the hectic leisure-time of postindustrial society, the steps Maguire then takes prove to be satisfactory and coherent).[143] And indeed, Maguire soon abandons this pretence of social conformity.

If the mass market demands plots that demonstrate clear causality, with all ends neatly tied up, it also demands characters that are easily identified and categorizable. Like many of Cohen's characters, Maguire is simultaneously more than and less than an individual. His multiple selves add up to something that is paradoxically much less than a person, often emotionally blank or unreactive. As he practises the same invasive technique of fantasy-projection on his ex-girlfriend and star television newsreader, who initially stands firm against his attempts to disperse her identity, we are told that "un nuevo desvío traicionó entonces las expectativas que el lector posindustrial habría puesto en su historia. Y es que Maguire no estaba decepcionado. Maguire no estaba nada" (a new change of course then betrayed the hopes the postindustrial reader had placed in his story. And that was that Maguire wasn't disappointed. Maguire wasn't anything).[144]

A little later, another comment contrasts the value of predictability in mass-market narrative with the more creative role chance plays in genuine imagination. The expectations of the postindustrial reading public are met by chains of events that are entirely foreseeable; "No obstante Maguire, también lector de su historia, descubrirá pronto que a la imaginación le encanta el azar. O, lo que es parecido, que el gran público no va a interesarse por su historia" (nevertheless, Maguire, also a reader of his own story, will soon discover that imagination loves chance. Or, which amounts to the same thing, that the general public is not going to be interested in his story).[145] Meaning and narrative drive in "Volubilidad" are consistently shaken by events that may (or may not) be accidental or coincidental. The unexpected appearance in Maguire's hostel of the fellow-passenger he suspects to be responsible for the projections does not contravene the conventions of realist fiction: such narrative "coincidences" often shape the plot of detective stories, for example. But the passenger is accompanied by another girl he recognizes from the same train carriage, and Maguire considers that "la casualidad que los enfrentaba había añadido innecesariamente a la chica" (the coincidence that brought them together had unnecessarily added the girl).[146]

Cohen's narrative thus provides a metacommentary on the differences between his own fiction and that of the mass market, demonstrating his allegiance to the techniques of "la narración de lo real incierto" (the narration of the uncertain real), which "no cree en las virtudes indispensables del acabado, la redondez, los cabos atados, las coincidencias explicadas, los motivos desvelados, los proyectos nítidamente cumplidos o frustrados, las causas exhaustivas, ni en la flaca gratificación del desenlace" (does not believe in the indispensable virtues of the finished, roundness, all the ends tied up, coincidences explained, motives revealed, projects neatly fulfilled or frustrated, causes comprehensively listed, nor in the thin satisfaction of the final dénouement).[147] Just as Maguire's capacity to "disgregarse" (disintegrate) becomes a measure of his resistance to society's definition of progress,[148] so we are asked to understand the instabilities and divergences of Cohen's own narrative as a sign of its critical distance from, and challenge to, dominant social and cultural discourses.

In some respects, this sounds rather like a typical postmodern resort to textual indeterminacy as the key to disarticulating discourses of authority: if everything is a text, then language is the only battleground and the play of signification the only weapon against monologic discourse. However, if Cohen's texts are freed from the imposition of unitary meaning, this is not via a Foucauldian-Barthesian "death of the author," in which signification is severed from authorial control and becomes endlessly deferred. Cohen's authors and narrators do not disappear from their texts but disperse into them, in a way that produces new encounters. The multiple, composite nature of the self does not occasion a postmodern crisis of representation but becomes a starting-point for new forms of knowledge and ways of relating to the world around.

Maguire's dispersive identity not only performs an act of political resistance: it also performs a "becoming-other," or "becoming-multiple," which for Deleuze is intrinsic to the act of writing. "Volubilidad" acts as a precursor to the monumental *Donde yo no estaba*, a kind of fictionalized diary/autobiography in a Deleuzean mode and Cohen's most sustained and radical treatment of the process of "becoming-other." The narrator of this novel is engaged in a personal quest, presented as one of supreme ethical import, to "despersonalizarse" (depersonalize himself), and to work towards "el adelgazamiento del ser" (the slimming-down of one's being). This involves a recognition that "el yo es una prenda sin contenido" ("I" is a garment with nobody inside),[149] and the recommended procedure to follow is "ingerir lo que de sus personas suelten otros, y en el mismo acto evacuar parte de uno" (to ingest what other people let go of and, at the same time, to evacuate part of oneself).[150]

An important difference emerges between this understanding of the self-transforming process of writing, on the one hand, and, on the other, a mistrust of writing as a way of imposing meaning on the world (or constructing a world into existence) that often underlies Marxist and psychoanalytical approaches to literature as well as various schools of ideological criticism (feminism, postcolonialism, etc.). As Deleuze describes it,

> To write is certainly not to impose a form (of expression) on the matter of lived experience. [...] Writing is a question of becoming, always incomplete, always in the midst of being formed [...]. Writing is inseparable from becoming: in writing, one becomes-woman, becomes-animal or -vegetable, becomes-molecule, to the point of becoming-imperceptible.[151]

Writing therefore involves participating in the multiple acts of becoming taking place in the world around us and accepting, in Colebrook's précis, "the challenge of no longer acting as a separate and selecting point within the perceived world, but of becoming different with, and through, what is perceived."[152] This again takes us away from a post-structuralist emphasis on the situated (if unstable) nature of subjectivity and cultural meaning. Maguire's projections, like those of O'Jaral (see Chapter 2), are not impositions of the self onto the other but evidence of the multiple and dispersive nature of the self. As Deleuze argues, the fabulating function of literature "does not consist in imagining or projecting an ego."[153] Quite the reverse: it is a process in which the self becomes other and understands its place in the flux of becomings of which the world is comprised. Cohen's distance both from conventional psychoanalytical or symptomatic approaches to the text, and from their suspicion of literature as a form of anthropomorphism or self-projection, is worked out most thoroughly in the remaining narrative of *El fin de lo mismo*, "La ilusión monarca."

"La ilusión monarca": metaphors of multiplicity

Of the narratives that comprise *El fin de lo mismo*, it is "La ilusión monarca" that demonstrates most clearly the power of metaphor as the "engine" of art, creating fields of resonance in which meaning is never closed off or exhausted but continually renewed and re-energized. If "Aspectos de la vida de Enzatti" theorizes the power of resonance to create unusual topologies, linking disparate elements across time and space, "La ilusión monarca" gives this idea full expression as a model for literary creation. Cohen's story assembles a constellation of texts and images, multiply connected in a constantly evolving galaxy in which any new event flashes and reverberates through the whole, and those reflections and echoes found in the most distant places return to spark the original stimulus in a never-ending play of meaning. The sea, the subject of "La ilusión monarca," does not simply refer to a mass of water but to the history of its representation in art and literature, Romantic and modern. However, Cohen's narrative takes us far from the usual, rather glib postmodern celebration of multiplicity and mixture in which all difference is eventually flattened into sameness and all texts refer to nothing but other texts. This story, like many others by Cohen, represents instead a serious, committed attempt to stage an encounter with difference, and to understand the dynamics of such an encounter and its capacity to engender newness.

The characters of "La ilusión monarca" struggle to attach a meaning to their existence, living in virtual isolation in a prison built on a beach. The prisoners are restricted to a confined area comprising a cell block and a section of the beach, flanked with walls reaching far into the sea. They are fed at intervals through hatches and forbidden to approach the guards, but no other discipline is exercised on them. In the absence of all societal structures and conventions, the prisoners form tribal groups for protection and sociability, which engage violently with other groups and with those individuals who, like the protagonist Sergio, choose to remain on the margins.

The prisoners' attempt to read meaning into their situation mirrors our own interpretative efforts as readers and makes them redundant. They suspect that they have been placed beside the sea as a method of psychological torture, as they are faced daily with a possible escape route that is nevertheless extremely risky: nearly all those who attempt to swim their way to freedom eventually return as corpses washed up by the tide, often with mysterious wounds. One of the prisoners, Jolxen, seems to confirm the prisoners' suspicions that the prison is some form of social experiment by claiming to be one of its designers, a sociologist contracted by the government to test the effects of anxiety on individuals in a controlled situation. But it is at least as likely that he is deluded or deceitful; this interpretation is neither confirmed nor dismissed. Other hypotheses suggested include the idea that the prison exists to provide a space for the circulation of goods within the economy.

To these interpretations, the text's critics have added their own. Annelies Oeyen, while she acknowledges that the narrative is "un texto ambivalente" (an ambivalent text), reads it very much in an allegorical key.[154] The isolated prison recalls the concentration camps of the dictatorship, the bodies washed ashore re-enact the fate of many of the disappeared, and the society both within and beyond the prison bears the hallmarks of the uncertainties and new forms of exclusion of Argentina's neoliberal 1990s.[155] This leads Oeyen quite naturally to a psycho-sociological reading of the story: "Cohen presenta una fantasía que sirve de catarsis y alivio ante la incertidumbre cotidiana de la experiencia argentina" (Cohen presents a fantasy that serves as a cathartic relief from the daily uncertainty of Argentine experience).[156] Escape from the prison is not a question of leaving the country, "sino a través de una salida hacia sí mismo que devuelve la perdida fe en su entorno" (but through a journey towards oneself that restores a lost faith in one's environment): the response to uncertainty is not emigration but a journey of discovery within the self that makes it possible to regain trust in the country.[157]

Although Oeyen's analysis is perhaps over-zealous in its quest to anchor the story in a single time and place, the explicit use of the enclosed-world-as-microcosm-of-society device in Cohen's narrative certainly opens itself up to any and all interpretations of this kind. Although unnamed, the country in which the prison is located certainly bears resemblances to post-dictatorship Argentina. These are evoked through references to the failure of the nation to construct a coherent sense of identity for itself, to the riches of the land and a glorious past now eclipsed by heavy debts, and to the dual tendency of the state towards violent disciplinarianism and the sudden abandonment and neglect of its citizens. The problem is that these readings are all too consciously *invited* by the text. Its sheer openness to multiple metaphorical readings, together with its diegetic concern with the process of metaphorization itself, undermines the validity of proposing any one reading, including those suggested in the text itself.

It is the sea, the prisoners' constant reminder of a possible but perilous escape route, that acts as the point of condensation for many of the story's metaphors. The prisoners ascribe to it myriad and conflicting qualities: "El mar es un potrillo indeciso. Al mar hay que dominarlo" (the sea is a hesitant foal. The sea has to be controlled);[158] "El mar es una puta remilgada" (the sea is a fussy whore); or, more puzzlingly, "El mar es un clarinete ortopédico" (the sea is an orthopaedic clarinet).[159] In this way, the sea becomes something different to each: "El mar es la ilusión monarca, todo le cabe" (the sea is the monarch of illusions, everything fits into it).[160] One is reminded of the ocean in Stanislaw Lem's *Solaris* (1961), which appears to have no essence or substance of its own, but instead produces powerful projections of the characters' own fears and desires. Closer comparisons with Lem's ocean will open up some of the complexities of Cohen's approach to metaphor in this narrative.

On one hand, Cohen's insistence on the utter indifference of the sea reinforces Lem's critique of the anthropomorphizing approach that we cannot lay aside in our quest for knowledge, which domesticates the other or provides a familiar point of reference to increase our understanding of the unfamiliar (the task of metaphor). The prisoners' clichéd metaphors bring them no closer to understanding the radical otherness of the sea:

> Por mucho que algunas asombren, todas en el fondo son frases consabidas, refritos mal logrados de frases ya viejas, que el mar ni siquiera oye. Con frases como ésas los presos podrían pasarse siglos sin entender qué pretende el mar de ellos, siempre y cuando pretenda algo.[161]

However surprising some of them may sound, they are all in the end habitual phrases, badly rehashed versions of already dated phrases, which the sea doesn't even hear. With phrases like these, the prisoners could carry on for years without understanding what the sea expects of them, if indeed it expects anything at all.

The sea remains impassive to their existence, imperviously material and resistant to interpretation. When Sergio swims out to sea, he understands that "cualquier frase sobre el mar, cualquier cábala es mentira" (every phrase about the sea, every speculation, is a lie).[162] The sea knows nothing of the prisoners, and if they choose to enter it in the hope of escape, it is because they need to find a direction to move in: "Así los actos cobran sentido" (that way, acts gain meaning).[163]

Thus "La ilusión monarca" demonstrates the delusional nature of anthropomorphizing metaphors and insists on the irreducible materiality of the sea, which transcends all human attempts to organize it into a coherent narrative and remains totally other to human society. However, unlike Lem, Cohen is not principally concerned here with the limitations of our knowledge and our inability to encounter the Other without projecting ourselves onto it. "La ilusión monarca" becomes instead an exploration of the creative power of metaphor and "a meditation on pure multiplicity," as Serres defines his own project in *Genesis* (1982),[164] a book that becomes a significant node in the textual and tropological network that Cohen's text creates. Although metaphor's rendering of an unfamiliar thing in terms of a more familiar thing inevitably limits and distorts the knowledge gained, Cohen's narrative also redeems metaphor for the insight it affords into the processes of transformation and recombination that govern the literary text as much as the natural physical world. If an understanding of these processes leads to greater knowledge of the human condition and our place in the universe, metaphor should not always provoke epistemological skepticism. In this manner, Cohen departs significantly from the Nietzsche-inspired suspicion, prevalent in postmodern theory and criticism, that what we take as "truth" is nothing but "a mobile army of metaphors, metonymies, anthropomorphisms."[165]

Anthropomorphic analogies and metaphors, far from being wholly discredited as tools that are far too blunt to produce genuine knowledge, play a crucial role in establishing the indivisibility of man and nature, one of the central tenets of Romanticism. Jules Michelet's *The Sea* (1861) exemplifies the Romantic principle of analogy – linking the particular with the general, the individual with the nation, the physical and the moral – that also underpins much of Cohen's work. Michelet's sea, like Cohen's, is a "majestic and indifferent" entity:[166] "If we have need of it, it has no need of us. It can do admirably without man."[167] We feel a heightened sense of our own transience, confronted with its immortal and unchangeable existence, feeling ourselves to be an "ephemeral apparition" in comparison to "the grand immutable powers of Nature."[168] And yet the sea shares our nature – "Ocean breathes as we do – in harmony with our internal movement" – and, in reminding us of our mortality, it points us to the divine spirit that animates all creation: "it compels us to count incessantly with it, to compute the days and hours, to look up to Heaven."[169] For Michelet, a "grand, sympathetic, and pregnant dialogue" unites all of creation with itself and with its Creator, but the harmony and fertility that characterize the world result not from agreement but from a "gigantic struggle," a constant tension between Life and "its sister, Death," and between forces of preservation and destruction at every level of existence.[170]

The sea in "La ilusión monarca" pullulates and pulsates to the rhythm of Michelet's, according to the same principle of conflict and disorder: "Todo está ahí, esforzándose, luchando, ocupado, todo se mezcla, se enfrenta, se plagia, devora" (everything is there, striving, fighting, busy, everything mixes, clashes, copies, devours).[171] The sea's "energía criminal" (criminal energy) litters the shore with marooned jellyfish each day; many more deaths and decompositions are signalled only by "los olores que exhala" (the smells it gives off).[172] If the sea is anthropomorphized, it is to show its commonality with man: both are systems that ingest and expel, create and destroy, protect and lay waste, give birth and die. Sergio, engulfed in the sea's waves, becomes part of this cycle as the half-digested sardine head he vomits becomes food for a passing shoal of sardines. As Edward K. Kaplan notes, "Michelet's relentless anthropomorphism is far from being a sheer stylistic quirk; rather it points to the divine impulse shared by humanity and nature."[173] Likewise, Cohen's use of analogy emphasizes the structural similarity of all living things. The difference, of course, is that Cohen does not posit a divine originator who breathes life into his creation, but locates life in the push and pull of forces that, if blindly functioning, are nevertheless able to create new forms out of disorder and conflict.

For Michelet, as Serres observes, the sea is the "prebiotic soup," "the matter from which all other material things originated."[174] In his exploration of how matter is generated or animated, Michelet makes imaginative use of a number of different theories of mechanics circulating at the time; his most original contribution to the theme, in Serres's view, stems from his use of the principles of thermodynamic circulation.[175] Serres notes the precision with which Michelet uses the vocabulary of "a boiler, a source, and a steam engine" to represent circulation in the sea, the mixing of the "soup" from which all matter emerges.[176] As he explains, "there can be no mixture without a movement to disperse the solute through the solvent. […] There must be fire to prepare the soup, and a pot to prepare it in, and it has to boil."[177] Cohen uses a similar image in "La ilusión monarca" of the soup that mixes as it is heated; his sea is also a model of turbulence and disorder that confounds any attempt to move through it in a straight line, and indeed rids Sergio of all sense of direction or goal, and all desire to escape. Everything in the sea "se intercambia y disuelve" (exchanges and dissolves) in a continual process of transformation.[178]

When in one of many descriptions of the sea, Cohen's narrator draws our attention to "esta vaga claridad a lo Turner" (this hazy Turneresque light),[179] the direct comparison seems almost redundant. The text repeatedly returns to the shifting hues and forms of the sea and sky, the shimmering play of light on surging waves, in ways that strongly evoke Turner's seascapes. For Serres, Turner's art marks the transition "from simple machines to steam engines, from mechanics to thermodynamics," showing the transforming power of fire to change the form of matter and the fundamental roles of chance and disorder, dramatizing hot and cold matter in fusion: "On the one hand clouds of ice, on the other clouds of incandescence."[180] From the precise drawing of forms and forces, Turner takes us towards a different understanding of matter in flux, which forms "aleatory clouds" and in which "the stochastic is essential": "The instant is not statically immobilized, fixed like a mast; it is an unforeseen state, hazardous, suspended, drowned, melted in duration, dissolved."[181] For this reason, Serres avers, "Turner is not a pre-impressionist. He is a realist, a proper realist."[182] Cohen's descriptions of the sea are imbued with a similar sensitivity to matter in constant movement. His sea, which "a cada instante se pulveriza en violencias" (at every instant atomizes itself in acts of violence),[183] also enters into a continual play of heat and light with the sky in descriptive passages that could easily refer to a Turner painting. It rains, and the horizon is hidden by clouds of vapour; "repentinos bultos de carbón revientan, lentos, dejando escapar hilos espermáticos, floraciones de nata y de yogur, lirios ardientes donde el sol hace sentir su fuerza" (sudden masses of coal burst, slowly, allowing the escape of spermatic threads, flowerings of cream and yoghurt, burning lilies where the sun makes its force felt).[184]

Nietzsche's Dionysian sea, another precursor to Cohen's, also draws inspiration from the dynamics of difference and sameness at play in entropy, as expressed in various versions of the two laws of thermodynamics formulated by Rudolf Clausius (1850) and others. In a fragment published in *The Will to Power*, Nietzsche finds in the sea a metaphor for the world itself, a "monster of energy," "a sea of forces flowing and rushing together."[185] Aligning his description with the first law of thermodynamics, which states that the energy within a system may change form but remains constant, Nietzsche describes a world "that does not expend itself but only transforms itself." Strictly finite in extension, it is nevertheless full of contradictions, opposing forces and turbulence, "eternally changing, eternally flooding back [...] with an ebb and a flood of its forms." It is noteworthy, however, that Nietzsche also departs significantly from mid-nineteenth-century scientific principles – and from their articulation in much twentieth-century literature – by insisting on what we would now identify as emergent phenomena in complex systems. Nietzsche's sense of nature "striving toward the most complex," as simple forms, through turbulence, give rise to more complex ones before dissolving again into simpler ones, together with his vision of the sea's forces flowing "out of the stillest, most rigid, coldest forms toward the hottest, most turbulent, most self-contradictory," evoke the dynamics of emergence, which would initially seem to defy laws of entropy. Life-affirming creativity, not the heat-death of entropy, marks Nietzsche's "Dionysian world of the eternally self-creating, the eternally self-destroying."[186]

The "blissful ecstasy" of the Dionysiac, which breaks down the *principium individuationis*," results in a dissolution of subjectivity that Nietzsche compares to the experience of intoxication and brings humans together in a "mysterious primordial unity."[187] This sense of oneness works to "annihilate, redeem and release" the individual,[188] much as it does in Cohen's fiction. When Sergio in "La ilusión monarca" finally swims out to sea, the intensely sensorial experience of his body's immersion in water teeming with life initially leads him to lose a sense of his self. He feels that "puede que no sea él quien nada" (it may not be him who is swimming),[189] and the immensity and the sameness of the sea surrounding him has a decentring effect in which his outer limbs seem disconnected from his body and his body itself fragmented and dispersed. A lexicon of exchange, dissolution, transformation, disintegration, and recombination predominates, as – like an endlessly turning kaleidoscope – narrative figures trace the dissolving of one transient form into another. In the sea Sergio both loses himself and finds himself in a way that strongly evokes the effect of Dionysian art for Nietzsche.

Dionysian art convinces us of the eternal creativity of nature, which endures despite all changes in appearance and all destruction. In Nietzsche's words,

> For brief moments we are truly the primordial being itself and we feel its unbounded greed and lust for being; the struggle, the agony, the destruction of appearances, all this now seems to us to be necessary, given the uncountable excess of forms of existence thrusting and pushing themselves into life, given the exuberant fertility of the world-Will; we are pierced by the furious sting of these pains at the very moment when, as it were, we become one with the immeasurable, primordial delight in existence and receive an intimation, in Dionysiac ecstasy, that this

delight is indestructible and eternal. Despite fear and pity, we are happily alive, not as individuals, but as the *one* living being, with whose procreative lust we have become one.[190]

This vision thoroughly permeates Cohen's description of Sergio's experience at sea, in which he senses both the "eternal lust and delight" and the "terrors" of existence painted by Nietzsche and feels the simultaneous pain and pleasure of discovering himself to be caught up in a conflict and a creativity that extends far beyond him, lost in a centreless, directionless, pulsating mass of energy. The sea returns Sergio to the shore a changed man. The prison seems little more than a theatre set to him now, and the only question of significance is "cómo sumergirse mejor en el mundo cuando salga, cuál la fácil brazada, estar de veras donde esté; no qué hacer, no adónde llegar, sino cómo seguir estando" (how to submerge himself better in the world when he gets out, which is the easy stroke, how to really be where one is; not what to do, not where to arrive, but how to continue being).[191] The destruction of the individual, for Cohen as for Nietzsche, leads paradoxically to a greater sense of one's place in the world and of one's connections with others. A cynical loner prior to his experience in the sea, Sergio now seeks out community to communicate what has happened to him.

The play of waves and forces in Nietzsche's Dionysian world allows us to glimpse its nature as "at the same time one and many."[192] A similar use of the analogy of the turbulent sea to theorize multiplicity connects the work of Nietzsche with Serres, and both of these with Cohen. Turning to a different analogy from the history of art, Cohen describes how "El mar se desmenuza en cien mil puntos de Seurat" (the sea breaks down into a hundred thousand of Seurat's dots):[193] like Seurat's pointillist works, the unity of the sea is an illusion that hides a multiplicity. The sea might appear uniform, cohesive, and enduring, but it is in fact "una ilusión de continuidad" (an illusion of continuity): "el mar no es una superficie ni está hecho de una pieza" (the sea is not a surface, nor it is made of one piece).[194] As he reflects elsewhere,

> En la forma que tiene de aparecérsenos, la realidad nos engaña. Los sentidos nos presentan una multiplicidad exorbitante que

impide ver la unidad de todo lo real, o bien dan a las apariencias una solidez duradera de la que la realidad carece.[195]

In the form in which it appears to us, reality deceives us. Our senses present us with an exorbitant multiplicity that prevents us from seeing the unity of all reality, or alternatively they give appearances a lasting solidity that reality does not possess.

Serres's *Genesis* also draws on the sea to explore multiplicity, finding in turbulence a way of thinking the multiple without reducing it to the unitary. Turbulence is "an intermediary state, and also an aggregate mix," bringing together order and disorder, and mixing or associating the one and the multiple by putting into play both a "systematic gathering together" (the unitary) and a "distribution" (the multiple).[196] Turbulence gives us a vision of the world that is not governed by laws, uniformity, and structures but by intermittence, mixture, and noise:

> The world is empty here and full there, sometimes being and sometimes nothingness, here order, there chaotic, here occupied, there lacunary, sporadic, and intermittent, as a whole, here strongly foreseeable, there underdetermined, here temporal and there meteorological – here, I mean, predictable or reversible and there an estimate and aleatory, here universe, there diverse, here unitary and there multiplicity, all in all when all's said and done a multiplicity. The cosmos is not a structure, it is a pure multiplicity of ordered multiplicities and pure multiplicities.[197]

Both Serres and Cohen attempt in this way to think about multiplicity from perspectives that do not start or end with postmodern pluralism and to understand chaos and indeterminacy in ways that do not inevitably lead to postmodern skepticism.

The positive charge acquired by entropy and multiplicity as forces of creativity in Cohen – following Nietzsche and Serres – is set into relief if we examine the rather different representation of these in another node in this network of tropologies, Henry Adams's *The Education of Henry Adams* (1918). In Adams's presentation of the dialectic of unity and multiplicity, multiplicity is always associated negatively with chaos and disorder; he traces "a movement from American unity of purpose to self-serving multiplicity" and predicts "a world torn apart, grinding down to entropic inertia."[198] Tony Tanner notes the recurrence of sea imagery in *The Education*, evoking in turn the violence of war, a fear of the void and darkness, and a sense of drifting and purposelessness.[199] Like hundreds of thousands of young men, Henry Adams is cast into "the surf of a wild ocean" to be beaten about by "the waves of war";[200] a different sort of confusion is generated later in politics, in which "All parties were mixed up and jumbled together in a sort of tidal slack-water."[201]

Philipp Schweighauser, in his comparison of the treatment of unity and multiplicity in the work of Adams and Serres, observes that the sea is one of a number of tropes shared between them.[202] However, if in Adams the turbulence of the sea becomes a metaphor for the chaos of war, in Serres it acquires much more positive connotations: it is the source of noise and ultimately of life itself. Schweighauser focusses on the crucial difference in their representation of Venus/Aphrodite. Adams associates Venus with unity and harmony; for Serres, on the other hand (in company with Lucretius), Aphrodite is "born of this chaotic sea, this nautical chaos, the *noise*."[203] If disorder is the universal principle that gives rise to newness, for Serres "it is necessary to rethink the world not in terms of its laws and its regularities, but rather in terms of perturbations and turbulences, in order to bring out its multiple forms, uneven structures, and fluctuating organizations."[204]

The sea-as-metaphor in Cohen's work sets off an expanding series of vibrations in those tropes and texts that are to be found in t(r)opological proximity to it. Metaphors may unite two different fields of reference, but they also resonate across a plane of immanence in which trope and referent are not distinguished in a hierarchical fashion but form part of a dense, rhizomatic network. This, then, becomes a way of thinking about multiplicity that does not posit relations of "influence" in literature in linear or directly causal terms, or understand the relationship of literature and the rest of the world as one of reference, but brings together an aggregate of texts, perceptions (of texts and of reality), and experiences (of texts and of reality) in such a way that each encounters the others in an intermittent, turbulent manner, thereby remaining simultaneously multiple and part of a larger system in which forms constantly evolve.

Cohen's conception of the role of metaphor in articulating that multiplicity contrasts directly with its traditional function in Western metaphysics. If, as Heidegger reminds us, "The idea of 'transposing' and of metaphor is based upon the distinguishing, if not complete separation, of the sensible and the nonsensible as two realms that subsist on their own,"[205] this opens the door for a Platonic mistrust of the changeable world of the senses in favour of the unchanging world of Ideas. Cohen's immanent vision does not allow us to distinguish so easily between the sensible and the nonsensible; moreover, the true nature of the world, visible and invisible, becomes one of transformation: there is nothing *behind* its changes in appearance.

Nietzsche's definition of truth as "a mobile army of metaphors, metonymies, anthropomorphisms"[206] is often cited to demonstrate the failure of man's quest for knowledge. Yet in Nietzsche, man's "fundamental human drive" to form metaphors[207] is, as Jos de Mul argues, "nothing less than a metaphor for nature's constant metaphorical transformation of itself," without which "Being itself would not be able to exist."[208] At the service of the artist, metaphor continually remakes the world, unfixing rigid concepts.[209] Nietzsche's own radical and contradictory use of metaphor resists all attempts to fix a single interpretation of his work. Likewise, Cohen's own analogies and intertextual references create a shifting, mobile network in which metaphors such as entropy often change in use from one narrative to another as they are brought into new discursive combinations.

"La ilusión monarca" does not tell a tale of the irresistible lure of anthropomorphism and our doomed quest for meaning in a senseless or unfathomable universe. We are not so caught up in language that we cannot experience that radical otherness that compels us to clutch at metaphors in the first place. Metaphors do not distort; they transform. They do not reduce meaning but set up a series of vibrations that produce new and often unpredictable patternings and permutations. This is what Cohen refers to as the transformative power of resonance, which is the proper subject of enquiry of his "realismo inseguro."[210]

As we have seen, entropy emerges in Cohen's work as a privileged metaphor for literary creativity, and returning once more to Serres's essay on Michelet may throw some light on this choice. Underlying the many different theories and models Michelet draws upon – from geometry, physics, chemistry, biology, and so on – Serres identifies two "completely stable structural analogies."[211] These are *reservoirs* (points of condensation and concentration) and *circulation*. This is tantamount, as Serres explains, to saying "a set of elements plus operations upon these elements"; in defining the object of the text in this way, however, he is not "defining a structure" but "defining structure itself; for the definition of structure is indeed a set of elements provided with operations."[212] Serres shows that asking questions about reservoirs and circulation such as "What is in the reservoir?" and "How do the elements circulate?" will eventually "reconstruct the entire set of interpretative organons formed in the nineteenth century."[213]

And this, Serres suggests, is the reason that his analysis of Michelet's text cannot be considered to have explicated it in any way:

> there can no longer be any question of explicating Michelet by any one or other of these interpretative organons, or by the sum total of them, since the most general conditions for the formation of these very organons are explained clearly and distinctly in the book *The Sea* itself. All I can do is apply these same organons to one another. [...] The object of explanation explains in turn the set of methods that were to explicate it.[214]

The critic cannot explicate the text because "the strategy of criticism is located in the object of criticism," and this, Serres insists, is not a unique characteristic of Michelet's text but fully generalizable: "The text is its own criticism, its own explication, its own application."[215] Any transcendent approach to criticism is therefore redundant.

Serres renders plausible the idea that entropy and thermodynamics might be privileged tropes for literary construction, as they do not represent or explain a particular structure so much as *define structure itself*: the very laws that govern the condensation and circulation of elements within a text. Cohen's narratives suggest a very similar strategy of criticism: metaphors of entropy, dissipative structures, resonance, and turbulence in *El fin de lo mismo* lead us to ask how these texts represent and stage an encounter with difference, how they imagine and perform relations between texts, and between texts and the world, and how they attempt to conceive multiplicity. These are the metaphors that enable Cohen, like Nietzsche, to theorize a world that "lives on itself: its excrements are its food"[216] as a picture of art, which participates in the same, endlessly self-producing, cycle: "The world as a work of art that gives birth to itself."[217] They also allow him to carve out an alternative path that diverges from contemporary society's definition of (socioeconomic) progress, as well as from postmodernism's inability to theorize the new.

In the intricate association of creativity and destruction, energy and disorder in the narratives of *El fin de lo mismo*, we can detect further echoes of Ballard's work, especially in the erotic intensity with which he treats the car crash in *The Atrocity Exhibition* and the later *Crash* (1973), which becomes a site of sexual liberation and energy as well as trauma and violence. Among the many "ecos ballardianos" (Ballardian echoes) that Jorge Bracamonte perceptively observes in Cohen's novels is a shared recourse to science and technology as a source of metaphors.[218] However, Bracamonte's comparative study of the two authors does not touch on what I consider to be crucial differences in the formation of such metaphors. Cohen's much greater reliance on the physics of chaos and complexity allows him to resignify the relationship between disorder and creativity in more unambiguously positive terms and to relocate these dynamics within the natural world rather than emphasizing, as Ballard does, the cruelty of man-made technologies. The trauma and alienation that mark the violent fusion of human bodies and urban environment in Ballard are reversed in Cohen's immanent vision, one in which organic and inorganic matter, conscious and unconscious energies, are bound together according to *natural* laws, in which chaos and turbulence are not the exception but the rule.

Julián Jiménez Heffernan argues that the repeated metafictional references to entropy and metaphor in *The Crying of Lot 49* demonstrate Pynchon's awareness of the fact that "entropy is not simply a trope, but a metatrope, for it harbors a reference to the tropological gesture par excellence: transformation, transference, metalepsis."[219] However, Pynchon's treatment of metaphor, and of the metaphor of entropy, remains much more ambivalent than Cohen's. Peter Freese, among other critics, points to the shift in Pynchon's understanding of entropy that is evident in the passage from "Entropy" to *The Crying of Lot 49*, in which Pynchon places the thermodynamical version of entropy as heat death in tension with the use of entropy in information theory to describe the loss and distortion of information in communication ("noise"). In this context, Freese asserts that the Tristero, a secret communication system discovered by Oedipa, "should be understood as a promising sign of renewal and reordering."[220] Similarly, Thomas Schaub claims that Pynchon's introduction of the information-theory version of entropy allows him to suggest that "Oedipa's sorting activities may counter the forces of disorganization and death."[221] Yet *The Crying of Lot 49* leaves crucially undecidable the question of whether metaphors aid perception or distort it, whether they help us make sense of the world and connect ourselves to it or feed a dangerous paranoid obsession with plots and conspiracies: the "act of metaphor" is both "a thrust at truth and a lie."[222] Freese may be right in suggesting that Pynchon's novel itself, with its dense weavings of plot and metaphor, counters entropy's disorderings as it "constitutes the negentropy activity that imaginative humans might pit against the running-down of their universe,"[223] but this promise of meaning is only promoted in the most uncertain of ways within the text itself. Both Pynchon and Cohen create texts that exploit the wealth of the rhizomatic relationships through which metaphor produces endlessly varied and infinitely mutating meanings. However, while Pynchon, as Heffernan observes, "is constantly alerting us to the slipperiness of figurative diction,"[224] Cohen's choice to embed his treatment of metaphor within the dynamics of chaos and the metaphysics of multiplicity renders his work much less equivocal in its celebration of the creative power of metaphor.

Conclusion | Literature and Science, Neither One Culture nor Two

I have argued throughout this book that mathematical and scientific ideas are primarily adopted in the work of Martínez, Piglia, and Cohen as metaphors for the self-renewing capacity of literary creativity and evolution. This reflexive strategy differentiates their use of such metaphors from that of an earlier generation of British and North American writers, including Ballard and Pynchon; it also diverges from the more positive explorations of complexity and emergence in more recent anglophone fiction of the 1980s and 1990s. Peter Freese and David Porush have observed the rise of a new generation of science-fiction writers in the United States who, like Cohen, have abandoned visions of heat-death and found inspiration instead in Prigogine's dissipative structures, turning entropy "from a messenger of death into a harbinger of rebirth."[1] For both Freese and Porush, this new direction is epitomized by the work of Lewis Shiner and Bruce Sterling. However, these novels are still written very much from within a skeptical postmodern framework: order may emerge from chaos, but the increasing complexity of the universe leaves the characters overwhelmed, stripped of all certainties and disorientated. Although Shiner's *Deserted Cities of the Heart* (1988) imagines a radical new order arising from the ashes of the old world, for his characters, "seeing the pattern" in the chaos around them and feeling a sense of belonging in the universe, being "a part of the all," is only fleetingly possible, under the influence of life-threatening magic mushrooms.[2]

By contrast, metaphors such as entropy and complexity are almost always associated in the work of Piglia and Cohen with the creative work of literature; crucially, this places us as co-creators in the universe, not hapless observers of processes we cannot understand. Deleuze and Guattari suggest that if life creates "zones where living beings whirl around, [...] only art can reach and penetrate them in its enterprise of co-creation."[3] Art and literature become a privileged means of participating in the creative fluxes of the universe.

ARGENTINE LITERATURE: THE REFLEXIVE TRADITION

How might we account for this divergence in the use of scientific ideas in contemporary Argentine literature? I have already argued, in the Introduction, that the work of Martínez, Piglia, and Cohen does not carry forward visions of the relationship between literature and science that we might find in Borges, Cortázar, Arlt, or more distant predecessors from the nineteenth century in Argentina. However, the acutely reflexive tradition of Argentine literature is an extremely important influence on the contemporary writers studied here and may go some way, in tandem with the widespread diffusion in Argentina of the work of Prigogine and other theorists of chaos and complexity, to account for the rather different uses to which scientific theories are put in these texts.

Important continuities mark the influence of Borges on the three writers discussed here. Although their engagements with mathematics and science do not have the primary aim – as they do in Borges – of undermining claims to universal truth, they do draw powerfully on his understanding of literature's self-generative capacity: the idea that – as Jaime Alazraki puts it – "books grew out of other books."[4] Martínez's detective fictions owe a clear debt to the web of intertextualities woven in Borges's stories; Borges's de-individualized, Spinozan fictions (one man is all men, we are all William

Shakespeare) are reincarnated in Cohen's sense of the indivisibility of the world, as well as in Piglia's desubjectivized narrating machines.

It is Borges's incipient sense of the way in which mathematical theories may be appropriated for the theory and practice of metafiction that holds the greatest interest for these writers. Hayles observes that self-referential loops, which for Cantor represented a vexing problem in logic, become for Borges – in "La biblioteca de Babel," for example – a rich opportunity to bring into question the existence of an external reality.[5] Piglia seizes on exactly the same potential that is inherent for him in the work of Gödel that, while demonstrating the limits of a certain kind of axiomatic logic, allows him to postulate the existence of virtual reality and other possible worlds.[6] In Piglia, however, there is much less emphasis on the failure of logic to account for the universe and a much greater interest in the infinite potential of literary recombination that Borges's fictions explore. The myriad permutations of the alphabet that make up the library of Borges's "La biblioteca de Babel" give rise to a weary sense of meaninglessness; in Piglia's *La ciudad ausente*, the inexhaustible permutations of narrative nuclei are a source of resistance against authoritarianism and proof of the endless self-generating creativity of literature. In a similar way, Borges's textual labyrinths and puzzles are – at best – futile exercises and – at worst – veritable death-traps for the intellectual, while for Martínez in *La mujer del maestro* and *Acerca de Roderer* they may also be stimuli for innovation.

While their fiction and critical work stands out in its generation for its clear and recurrent engagement with scientific theories, Martínez, Cohen, and Piglia share many concerns with other contemporary Argentine writers who have approached the question of the relationship between science and literary creativity. The influence of Prigogine is evident in Mempo Giardinelli's *Equilibrio imposible* (1995), a flamboyant tale of the kidnapping of a family of African hippos brought to the Chaco region by the government to solve a local ecology problem. J. Andrew Brown develops a reading of the novel that hinges on its epitaph, a citation from Prigogine on the difference between equilibrium and non-equilibrium systems:

> Un mundo en equilibrio sería caótico, el mundo de no equilibrio alcanza un grado de coherencia que, para mí al menos, es sorprendente [...]. No hay sistema estable para todas las fluctuaciones estructurales, no existe fin para la historia.[7]

> A world in equilibrium would be a chaotic one; a non-equilibrium world attains a level of coherence that, for me at least, is surprising [...]. There is no stable system for all structural fluctuations, there is no end to history.

Brown demonstrates that the plot twists of Giardinelli's classic crime-and-pursuit novel can be read as a series of Prigoginian bifurcations or unpredictable choices. These are chaotic in nature in the sense of being undetermined but generating patterns and new kinds of order at a higher level.[8] The characters become aware that their roles are taking on an increasingly literary or cinematic quality: the criminal lovers escaping from the police, the textbook escape from prison, the daring rescue by helicopter. In the bizarre final pages of the novel, the remaining pair become caught up in a different dimension, that of literature, taking their place alongside Captain Ahab, Sancho Panza, Kafka, and Woolf before being swept up to safety in Jules Verne's hot air balloon. They are gathered up into a metaliterary sphere where disorder and unpredictability suddenly take on the serenity and coherence of a new kind of order. While Giardinelli's novel clearly experiments with the intersections between metafiction and self-organization/complexity, he does so in a way that diverges from Cohen's vision. The end of *Equilibrio imposible* seems to present literature as a place of stability, meaning, and equilibrium: elsewhere, too, he posits literature as a refuge from the anxiety with which we are condemned to pursue an elusive stability, one of "esos pequeños valores que todavía le dan sentido a la vida" (those little values that still give meaning to life).[9] For Cohen, by contrast, literature is the place of turbulence, and any state of equilibrium – as we saw in "El fin de lo mismo," for example – is emphatically a fleeting one, immediately subject to further disorder.

Piglia and Cohen also share certain notions of creativity and dynamic change with César Aira. Aira's interest in procedure and process in (avant-garde) art allows us to trace some analogies with Piglia's writing machines; the frequent clonings, hybridizations, and mutations of his fiction construct a universe in which forms are constantly in transformation. Aira's sustained exploration of the (Deleuzean) concept of the continuum, which – drawing on Leibniz – folds mind and matter, or fiction and metafiction, together, leaving no "outside," bears a notable resemblance to the connectionist vision of Cohen's texts. Of all other contemporary writers in Argentina, however, it is perhaps with the dramatist Rafael Spregelburd that Martínez, Piglia, and Cohen find the greatest affinity. In plays such as *Fractal* (2000), *La estupidez* (2003), and *La paranoia* (2008), Spregelburd has experimented with fractal geometry, chaos theory, and Prigoginian thermodynamics as ways of structuring a piece of theatre as well as reflecting on the complexity of the universe, and he often draws on such theories in his critical work.

Martínez, Piglia, and Cohen share with these writers – and with so many of their predecessors in Argentine literature, stretching back through Borges and Cortázar to Arlt and even to Holmberg and Sarmiento – an interest in incorporating the non-literary within literature as a crucial part of their metafictional interest in the construction and evolution of literature itself. They interrogate the wider, social meanings and consequences of scientific developments and discourses, but they do so in a way that brings to the fore literature's own significance within society, and its own modes of circulation and evolution.

The remaining parts of this Conclusion will focus first on the implications of the theories of creativity developed in the work of Martínez, Piglia, and Cohen for literary and critical debates before returning to the broader question of the relationship between the "two cultures" of literature and science. From a discussion of the particular dialogue these texts establish with Romanticism's complex legacies for postmodern thought, I will then turn to another set of legacies, this time from Russian Formalism, to suggest how the texts studied here permit us to perceive points of articulation between these and Deleuzean approaches to literature. The radical (re)invention of textual genealogies that has become a hallmark of contemporary Argentine literature and criticism brings into view both the Formalist understanding of literary evolution as discontinuous and conflictive and Deleuze and

Guattari's concept of the literary text as an assemblage, co-functioning with other assemblages in topological (rather than historical) proximity to it. In turn, both of these frameworks share some affinities with the processes of change studied by theorists of complexity as, in Sadie Plant's words, "Complex systems do not follow the straight lines of historical narration or Darwinian evolution, but are composed of multiple series of parallel processes, simultaneous emergences, discontinuities and bifurcations, anticipations and mutations of every variety."[10]

ROMANTIC INDIVIDUALISM AND THE CREATIVE UNIVERSE

Martínez's fiction gives ironic treatment to the concept of Romantic individualism that established, in Paul de Man's words, "the cult of the self as the independent and generative center of the work, the Promethean claim to confer upon the human will absolute attributes reserved to divine categories of Being."[11] The figure of the inspired and rebellious genius is appropriated in *La mujer del maestro* and *Acerca de Roderer* in an account that proposes dialectical rationalism as a model for literary creativity and evolution, eroding differences between artistic vision and scientific discovery by showing how each is engaged in a struggle within and against tradition. Piglia and Cohen, for their part, entirely reject notions of Romantic individualism and strive instead to depersonalize authorship. In Piglia's fiction, the figure of the author becomes a veritable obstacle to the potential meanings of the text, and the narrative nuclei of his texts circulate freely within and beyond the text with no reference to the individual author as origin or genesis. In Cohen, both text and author are dispersed within their environments, and their creativity is part of a greater flow and exchange of energy in the system of the universe as a whole.

However, both Piglia and Cohen retain and extend a Romantic vision of the communion of all living things and the coparticipation of the human mind and creativity with the life of the natural world. Joseph Carroll asserts that "In place of the appeal to the creative power of gifted individuals, postmodernism transforms the individual into a passive vessel for the circulation of cultural energies."[12] These texts contain nothing as lifeless as a "passive vessel," though: even their hard objects and machines pulsate with a life that transcends any distinction between the natural and the artificial; they do not dispense with agency but disperse it across the boundary between subjects, or between subjects and objects. The life that these texts engage in is creatively and exuberantly abundant. Their vision has much in common with Deleuze and Guattari's conception of "becoming-inhuman," a non-transcendent perspective that they find to be exemplified in Kafka's fiction: "Instead of being an image set over against the world, such as a mind that receives impressions, we recognise ourselves as nothing more than a flow of images, the brain being one image among others, one possible perception and not the origin of perceptions."[13] Rosi Braidotti draws significantly on Deleuze and Guattari in the "philosophical nomadism" she defends for its model of the body as not wholly human but "an abstract machine, which captures, transforms and produces interconnections."[14] As Braidotti argues, the act of locating subjectivity in a dynamic process of becomings, composed of "non-human, inorganic or technological" forces, opposes both "contemporary bio-technological determinism" and "the anthropocentrism that is in-built in so much evolutionary, biological, scientific and philosophical thought."[15]

The commitment to immanence in Cohen's texts, and to some degree in Piglia's, undermines the elevated, transcendent position of the Romantic ironist. Although the act of creation is nearly always the subject of these texts, this reflexivity does not, as in Romantic literature, become an expression of the writer's "total freedom, his right to manipulate, to destroy as well as create," such that even an avowed failure in creativity "aims to demonstrate the artist's elevation over his work, his transcendence even of his own creation."[16] In both Piglia and Cohen, literature is not primarily or solely a projection of the self but a space of encounter with the other that directly shapes our experience. By participating in literature's becomings, by approaching the perspectives of characters, animals, machines, biological systems, and inanimate objects, we recognize that our selves are not stable entities and that there is no point of transcendence from which we may perceive and interpret life. This perspective grants us a vision of a literature that does not betray or obstruct our experience of an abundant life lying beyond it but participates fully, conscientiously, and joyously within it.

In the various theories of creativity and newness developed in texts by Martínez, Piglia, and Cohen, some important differences may be observed in relation to the teleological understanding of history that, via Hegel in particular, informed much Romantic theory. Martínez's work articulates a strong adherence to Hegelian dialectics, as filtered through Marxist-Leninist thought. His model of newness derives from the competition between rivals, from the bitter oneupmanship and double-dealings of writers seeking fame and fortune in *La mujer del maestro* to the struggle to outwit one's enemies in *Crímenes imperceptibles* and the overturning of established systems of thought in *Acerca de Roderer*. Innovation springs from the individual quest for distinction and entails striving against what has come before, simultaneously negating and preserving elements of tradition, but ultimately usurping its position of prominence. If this is a picture of the dialectical advance of science, it is one that is indebted to a Hegelian view of the unfolding of history as a dialectic between opposing forces that produce change when one overcomes the other. Indeed, one might note – along with Ernan McMullin – that the claim that science advances by means of a dialectical process "has always been a staple of Marxist-Leninism."[17] McMullin finds the application of the Hegelian model of history to science unconvincing, in part because science does not always demonstrate the progressively fuller embodiment of reason that Hegel claimed for successive realizations of the Spirit in human civilizations;[18] Hegel is, he argues, "still working with something like the classical Aristotelian understanding of science [...] as demonstration leading to necessary and unchanging truth."[19] Although he consistently undermines such a notion of truth, Martínez does hold to a belief in a dialectical process that will inspire the advance of both science and literature.

The teleological drive of Hegel's vision of history, mapped by Martínez onto the development of scientific knowledge and artistic creativity, is entirely absent in Piglia and Cohen. Piglia decries the violence implicit in the Hegelian overthrow of each historical period by its successor, which appears in *Respiración artificial* to generate an endless series of massacres and civil wars. However, he retains a vision of the dialectical process of historical and literary change, not as the linear march of Hegel's optimism, towards ever-greater progress and reason, but according to the Formalist model of opposition and refunctioning. Although contradiction is the source of newness in both cases, the latter dispenses with any notion of teleology: newness arises from accidents, throwbacks, mutations, and unprogrammed configurations and serves no other purpose than change itself and the renewal of forms.

Interestingly, in the models of self-organization explored by Piglia, and especially by Cohen, we may perceive a return to the origins of the dialectic in Hegel's thought, which derived from his observation of the self-organizing principles of nature. In his powerful vision of a transient universe in which everything is constantly in a state of becoming, his organicism and his search for alternatives to dualism, Cohen is perhaps more rigorously Hegelian than Martínez; indeed, recent scholars have noted some parallels between dialectics and emergentism.[20] The science of emergence and self-organization has no need of notions of progress, reason, truth, or transcendence in its theorizations of change. It lends itself superbly well to Cohen's exploration of multiplicity and the encounters between the self and the other that perpetuate an endless process of transformation. Unlike in Martínez, contradiction and opposition in Cohen do not provide the opportunity for a transcendent synthesis; instead, it is the absence of such resolution, the endlessly unfinished process of fusion and interchange, between the self and everything that it is not, that allows newness to emerge, located precisely at the point of tension between order and disorder.

FROM METAPHOR TO METAMORPHOSIS

If Cohen's work may be seen to return in some ways to Romanticism, it might be more accurate to speak of a shared resort to Eastern concepts of immanence to challenge the Western enslavement to transcendence, a "specifically European disease" in Deleuze and Guattari's book.[21] It is transcendence that posits a world outside of our perceptions and mistrusts language and images as they are assumed to obscure a real world lying beyond their mediation. Here the writers discussed in this study part company. Martínez does retain a belief in a reality beyond our formulations of it, voicing a suspicion that language and our systems of knowledge often prove more helpful in concealing than revealing that truth. While Piglia frequently points to the power of language in shaping our perceptions, neither he nor Cohen view language as a mediator that stands between us and real experience: for both of these writers, language is that which brings experience into being.

Cohen describes "depth" as "el malentendido romántico más persistente" (the most persistent of Romantic misunderstandings), and one that "trabaja contra las libertades que legó el romanticismo" (works against the freedoms bequeathed by Romanticism).[22] Deleuze and Guattari's objection to ideological and psychoanalytical criticism is based on their conviction that "Cultural forms, like literature, do not *deceive* us; they are ways in which desire organises and extends its investments. This can work positively, when intensities and affects are multiplied to produce further possibilities for experience."[23] A similar approach is articulated by Cohen:

> La tarea de la novela es reencantar el mundo, disolver la falaz dictomía entre razón e imaginación. Creo que la literatura tiene un papel fundamental en la lucha contra el control y a favor de la expansión de los sentimientos. Es una gran engañifa pensar que viendo documentales o programas de investigación vamos a lograr que el poder no nos engañe. El engaño viene a través de la falta de ambigüedad de las palabras. Con el lenguaje, cuando la gente cree que al pan, pan y al vino, vino, estamos sonados. [...]
>
> No se trata de hacer arte político, sino política con el arte, como dijo alguna vez un artista conceptual. Lo primordial es darle otras posibilidades de vida al lenguaje, encontrar resonancias que permitan evadirnos hacia una realidad más real de la que conocemos.[24]

> The task of the novel is to re-enchant the world, to dissolve the false dichotomy between reason and the imagination. I

believe that literature plays a fundamental role in the battle against control and for the expansion of sentiments. We are being conned if we think that by watching documentaries or investigative programs we can manage to avoid being deceived by power. Deception comes in the lack of ambiguity in words. With language, if people believe that a spade should be called a spade, we're in trouble. [...]

It's not about doing political art, but doing politics with art, as a conceptual artist once said. The essential thing is to give language other possible ways of life, to find resonances that allow us to escape to a reality that is more real than the one we know.

Piglia does retain certain ideas associated with a "depth model" of analysis, notably in his use of Jungian notions of archetypes and inheritance, but he does so most often in order to challenge individualism and to bring issues of construction rather than interpretation to the fore. For him, as for Cohen, language is not to be mistrusted as that which shields or bars us from the world beyond or encodes an ideology waiting to entrap us in old ways of thinking; instead, it is the source of new perceptions and possible forms of existence.

What Deleuze and Guattari most value in Kafka's writing is his rejection of metaphor in favour of metamorphosis:

> It is no longer the subject of the statement who is a dog, with the subject of the enunciation remaining 'like' a man; it is no longer the subject of enunciation who is 'like' a beetle, the subject of the statement remaining a man. Rather, there is a circuit of states that forms a mutual becoming, in the heart of a necessarily multiple or collective assemblage.[25]

From the pitfalls of metaphor to the power of metamorphosis: from a transcendent perspective on the literary text as a set of (dubious) transformations of a reality beyond it – according to which, Deleuze states, "Something always has to recall something else"[26] – we move to an immanent perspective according to which the text forms new proximities, stages new encounters, and creates new experiences. Instead of reading the sea in Cohen's "La ilusión monarca" or Luca's dreams in Piglia's *Nocturno blanco* as symbols of something else, we may read them as apertures to new kinds of perception and transformation.

As Piglia writes in *Blanco nocturno*, "El conocimiento no es el develamiento de una esencia oculta sino un enlace, una relación, un parecido entre objetos visibles" (knowledge is not the revealing of a hidden essence but a link, a relation, a similarity between visible objects).[27] The role of criticism is to explore the act of creation, not to interpret the text as a series of signs; to consider how literature creates by forming and transforming links between things, not to approach it suspiciously as a cunning promulgator of concealed ideological agendas. Above all, it is to recognize our own implication in the text's vision, not as the compromised, positioned reader of deconstructive criticism, but as a reader whose experience has been altered, enlarged, and enriched by an encounter with the text. If, as Deleuze and Guattari argue, "artists are presenters of affects, the inventors and creators of affects," they "make us become with them, they draw us into the compound."[28]

DELEUZE AND THE FORMALISTS ON LITERATURE AND NEWNESS

The ideas of creativity and literary evolution developed in and through these texts resonate strongly with Formalist theories in the case of Martínez and Piglia; the affiliation of these ideas in turn to the more recognizably Deleuzean vision of Cohen's texts allows us to trace some important correspondences between Formalist and Deleuzean thought.

Both Deleuzean and Formalist approaches can be read as challenges to what Tynyanov called the "individualistic psychologism" that has dominated literary history in the West, attempting instead to understand literary history as the evolution of forms, functions, and systems.[29] Deleuze and Guattari's concept of the assemblage bears a marked similarity to the manner in which

Formalists such as Eichenbaum, Shklovsky, and Tynyanov, discontented with wholly intrinsic approaches to literature, attempted to model the literary sphere as distinct and autonomous but continually co-functioning with other systems, closely related to them but not determined by them. The symbiotic co-functioning of Deleuze's assemblages ensures that "It is never filiations which are important, but alliances, alloys; these are not successions, lines of descent, but contagions, epidemics, the wind."[30] Indeed, there are strong echoes in Deleuze and Guattari's work of Formalist ideas on the discontinuities and ruptures that characterize literary evolution, not least when they celebrate the Anglo-American "way of beginning" in literature, which does not (unlike the French tradition) "search for a primary certainty as a point of origin," but instead attempts "to take up the interrupted line, to join a segment to the broken line, to make it pass between two rocks in a narrow gorge, or over the top of the void, where it had stopped."[31] Such writing is aligned in Deleuze and Guattari's philosophy with rhizomes, multiplicities, and "lines of flight": the possibility of evading the rigid, binaristic structures of "arborescent" thought.[32]

Both the Formalists and Deleuze explicitly reject a notion of the literary text as a repository of possible meanings for the critic to tease out, which bears witness to a prior (social or psychological) experience beyond it: instead, the text becomes a machine that *produces* experience, affects, and meanings. This is fundamental to the utopian dimension of both Formalist and Deleuzean thought on art: just as, for the Formalists, art has the power to shake us out of old perceptions and allow us to experience newness, so for Deleuze and Guattari, literature's potential to act politically derives from its anti-mimeticism, its expression of what is not yet. The task of the literary critic thus shifts from one of decoding referents to one of exploring textual construction, of observing how the text-as-machine co-functions with other machines, and of creating new meanings by bringing the text to function in different assemblages. The Formalist struggle to combine elements of the mechanistic with the organic in theorizing the literary text is resolved in more sophisticated terms in Deleuze and Guattari's machines, so different, in their potential for creativity and the dynamic relationship they set in motion between the human and the non-human, from the Enlightenment conception of man as a machine, which made of humans mere cogs in a deterministic universe.

The connection between Deleuze and the Russian Formalists is perhaps not so surprising when one considers a shared precursor in the work of Bergson. The influence of Bergson's anti-monism on the theories of Shklovsky and Tynyanov is argued in persuasive detail by James M. Curtis, who particularly notes the importance of Bergson's distinctions between seeing and recognition for the Formalist understanding of art as the deautomatization of perception but also embeds the approaches of both Shklovsky and Tynyanov within Bergson's noncontinuous, heterogeneous time and space.[33] In turn, of course, the dialogue between Bergson's philosophy and modern physics (especially quantum mechanics) has been the subject of a number of studies,[34] and if – in Deleuze's words – Bergson considered that "la science moderne n'a pas trouvé sa métaphysique, la métaphysique dont elle aurait besoin" (modern science hasn't found its metaphysics, the metaphysics it needs),[35] many scholars have considered Deleuze's work, and particularly his exploration of virtuality and multiplicity in the monumental *Difference and Repetition*, as an attempt to supply that missing metaphysics.[36]

Bringing Deleuze's ideas to co-function with Formalism in the manner that I have been suggesting shifts our focus a little: in addition to perceiving a line in philosophy and literary theory (uniting Bergson and Deleuze) that responds to the need to think through the implications of modern physics in those spheres and to develop a new metaphysics, we might also posit that some of these ideas do not originate, or solely originate, in modern science. They also arise from a desire to theorize the workings of literature, which was of course the primary aim of the Formalists. It has certainly been my contention in this book that, while the work of Martínez, Piglia, and Cohen often illuminates the insights of contemporary science and experiments with different ways of embedding them in literary and critical discourse, it does so principally in order to reflect on the theory and practice of literature and critical thought.

SCIENCE AND LITERATURE: NEITHER ONE CULTURE NOR TWO

Nonetheless, in Cohen's texts in particular, the repositioning of literary creativity within the greater creative flux of the universe allows us to theorize the relationship between literature and science in a way which avoids falling into the error of constructing them either as "two cultures" antagonistic towards each other, or "one culture" really engaged in the same enterprise. What these texts allow us to glimpse, instead, is a dynamic relationship between the two that is aptly evoked by the concept of rhizomes developed by Deleuze and Guattari, or by Serres's explorations of synthesis and multiplicity.

As argued throughout this book, Martínez, Piglia, and Cohen do not adopt the Romantic-postmodern view of science as a bastion of reason against the imagination, pursuing outdated claims to objectivity in a world of uncertainties. Science in these texts does not stand for the known, the mechanistic, or the absolute, but for the creative possibilities of the as-yet-unknown and the wonderful adventure of the new. They respond instead to a different (and equally Romantic) attitude towards science: the genuine desire to forge a science and philosophy of life that informed the contributions of Schelling, Goethe, and others to the *Naturphilosophie* project. The specificity of literature is not located, therefore, in a rejection of science and technology. Unlike for the Romantics or for apocalyptic anglophone science fiction, the "enemy" in these texts is not a mechanistic science devoid of ethics. This role is more frequently played by the discourses of epistemological failure and cultural decline sponsored by postmodernism, together with the homogenizing effects of consumer-driven societies. In this battle, science may be an ally: scientific theories of chaos, complexity, and emergence appear to provide more delicate and precise tools with which to think about multiplicity and creativity than flattened-out, undifferentiated postmodern accounts of diversity, multiculturalism, or textual-play-as-political-resistance. N. Katherine Hayles finds in modern physics the most rigorous modelling of what she calls the "field concept," the notion of interconnectedness that traverses a number of scientific models and theories. In contrast to the

Newtonian idea of an atomistic reality, "a field view of reality pictures objects, events and observer as belonging inextricably to the same field; the disposition of each, in this view, is influenced – sometimes dramatically, sometimes subtly, but in every instance – by the disposition of the others."[37] This vision is evident in Cohen's depictions of resonance and his theory of "realismo inseguro," as well as in the complex relationships between virtual and material realms in Piglia's textual machines.

According to J. Andrew Brown's hypothesis, Argentine literature throughout much of the nineteenth and twentieth centuries overwhelmingly registers a "test-tube envy," borrowing from science's legitimizing authority, either to shore up the status of literature itself or as a bid to supplant that authority. However, this is not the dynamic that we see primarily at play in the work of Martínez, Piglia, and Cohen. Science and its notational systems do not occupy a place of institutional authority in the work of these writers. Those mathematicians and scientists who feature in their narratives are almost always marginalized, or mad, and their interest is inexorably drawn to the pseudo-scientific, the unproven, the entirely hypothetical, the uncertain, or the unknowable. Nor is literature presented as an antidote to scientific advance. Instead, both literature and science are shown to be caught up in similar (or even the same) processes of creation and evolution. These texts find in science an endlessly creative pursuit of the new and a remorseless questioning of the established. It is the Formalists' conception of science "as a contest among competing theories" that perhaps marks most closely the spirit in which science is interpellated in these works.[38]

If science is more commonly drawn in as an ally, it is nevertheless the case that all three writers insist on the specificity of literature, which extends our experience in very different ways, and rejoice in its current position at the margins of society. In Martínez's words, it has the ability to "revelarnos algo del mundo que *no* sabíamos, de alzar otro mundo en el mundo, de darnos una nueva forma de ver y de percibir" (reveal to us something of the world that we *didn't* know, to erect another world within this one, to grant us a new way of seeing and perceiving), affording us a specific way to "hacernos parte de algo que no hubiéramos podido aprehender con ninguna de nuestras otras facultades intelectuales" (participate in something that we could not have grasped with any of our other intellectual faculties).[39] Piglia and Cohen vigorously defend literature's position at the margins of society. Cohen notes shrewdly that, as writing is unprofitable in the current economic system, society offers the writer a particular role to play as a form of compensation: "el papel de quien tiene la palabra legítima en el ágora, el sabio de la sociedad" (the role of having the voice of authority in the Agora, the wise man of society).[40] In return, however, "se le exige que la literatura sea comprensible, fresca, que comunique" (society demands that literature should be comprehensible, fresh, that it should communicate). In effect, it should perform the function of providing "una especie de airbag de la sociedad" (a kind of airbag for society), dealing with those metaphysical questions that each society needs to ask in order to convince itself that it is not indistinguishably glued to material things.

In place of this immediate and easily comprehensible literature, Cohen offers one that is markedly more provisional and that refuses to exercise any such kind of transcendence. Both Piglia and Cohen work to renew language from within, which is for Deleuze the effect that literature should have on language, opening up "a kind of foreign language within language,"[41] becoming "a nomad and an immigrant and a gypsy in relation to one's own language,"[42] in order to make "the standard language stammer, tremble, cry, or even sing."[43] This also accords, of course, with the Formalist concept of art as the renewal of perception. The "becoming-other of language" is evident in Cohen's many (and unglossed) neologisms, the frequent shuttling between first- and third-person in the fictional "autobiography" of *Donde yo no estaba*, and the agency granted to inanimate objects in *El fin de lo mismo*; in the many immigrants of Piglia's texts who stumble ungrammatically through Spanish, the constant language-switching in "La isla," and the anachronisms and displacements of epistolary discourse in *Respiración artificial*; or in the use of parody and montage in Martínez's texts, wrenching language from its original context of enunciation.

It is clear that this creative renewal of language is understood as part of a broader gesture towards non-referentiality. We might find echoes here of de Man's insistence on the figural and rhetorical nature of literary language, and his critique of any approach that posits a straightforward division between the text as ideology and a "real" world beyond it. To be polemical, literature needs to remain marginal and irreducible to straightforward communication, to become "minor" in Deleuze's terminology. In combating contemporary (consumer) society's own fictions, the best recourse of literature is – in Cohen's words – to "exhibirse como ficción pura, manifestar desinterés palmario, inconducencia, afán derrochador de juego, a lo sumo de especulación" (flaunt its status as pure fiction, to display a palpable lack of interest, unproductivity, a profligate zeal for gaming, at least for speculation). Resisting the temptation to capture or reflect reality, and above all to interpret it, literature finds its end in itself and declares that "los relatos nacen de los relatos" (stories are born from stories).[44]

But perhaps more than all of these strategies, the "becoming-other" of both language and literature takes place in these texts' appropriation of the discourses of science and mathematics: Piglia's "becoming-machine" and his citations of Gödel in experiments with literary recursion; the tensions in Martínez's work between formal logic and Romantic excess; Cohen's textual renderings of the dynamics of chaos, complexity, emergence, and entropy. Deleuze asserts that "To write is to become, but has nothing to do with becoming a writer. That is to become something else."[45] It is the point at which literature engages with what is not literature that it becomes most fully itself. The models Piglia and Cohen adopt from biology and physics, such as autopoiesis and self-organization, speak to the dynamics of literary construction and evolution; they also map out how exchanges work across disciplinary boundaries. These models imagine, like Deleuze's machines, "a 'proximity' grouping between independent and heterogeneous terms"[46] in which organisms and systems retain their specificity precisely through the nature of their interactions with other systems and their environment.

Sadie Plant argues that, as theories of chaos and complexity "leak out" from the sciences to the arts and humanities, an "emergent connectionist thinking" is beginning to erode distinctions between the disciplines.[47] This "connectionism" has not been welcomed on all sides; neither has it always been practised with the rigour that such interdisciplinary work would require. Although Plant suggests that cultural studies has the "greatest potential" for dealing with such interconnectivity, it has not fully risen to the challenge, principally because it "confines itself to conceptualisations of culture as a specifically human affair. Some notion of individual or collective agency is assumed to play a governing role in all cultural formations and productions."[48] For Plant, this is an illusion that has been dismantled by recent science and its adoption in critical theory. At the heart of the collapse of those disciplines with which modernity attempted to order knowledge, she finds the demise of "the modern integrated, unified individual,"[49] together with the corrosion of boundaries between the human, the natural, and the machinic. As she asserts,

> Complex biochemical processes function within, across, and in-between what were once conceived as autonomous agents, corroding the boundaries between man, nature and the tools with which he has mediated this relationship. The histories written as the histories of humanity can no longer maintain their independence from emergent processes in the economies and complex systems with which they interact, and attempts to define culture in the ideological, humanist and sociopolitical terms which have provided its post-war framework merely perpetuate a distinction between the human, the machinic and the so-called natural which underwrites modernity's techniques of policing knowledge and reality.[50]

Serres chooses a geological metaphor to account for the multiple, complex and shifting channels of communication that may connect the humanities and the sciences, choosing as an image the sea route that links the Atlantic and Pacific Oceans across the archipelagoes and ice floes of the Canadian Arctic. "Le plus souvent, le passage est fermé, soit par terres, soit par glaces, soit aussi parce qu'on se perd. Et si le passage est ouvert, c'est le long d'un chemin difficile à prevoir" (the passage is most frequently closed off, whether by land or ice, or because one loses the way. And if the passage is open, it is along a path that is difficult to predict).[51] Although Serres's work is one of synthesis, it avoids containing or fixing multiplicity within a solid, unitary structure, aiming instead to explore what he calls "a *syrrhèse*, a confluence not a system, a mobile confluence of fluxes."[52] He is not interested in finding a common language or a shared set of concepts that might bring the humanities and sciences together, as:

> Universal metalanguage is comfortable and lazy.
> Conversely, the best synthesis only takes place on a field of maximal difference – striped like a zebra or a tiger, knotted, mixed together – a harlequin's cape. If not, the synthesis is merely the repetition of a slogan.[53]

The form Serres favours for such synthesis is often the encyclopaedia, in which strict taxonomies and totalizing unities are replaced by a web of inter-references, and "The traditional idea of evolution towards progress becomes instead a journey among intersections, nodes, and regionalizations."[54] It is in Piglia that we can see the clearest embrace of a form that Calvino also refers to as "the contemporary novel as an encyclopaedia, as a method of knowledge, and above all as a network of connections between the events, the people, and the things of the world."[55] Calvino suggests an important role for contemporary literature in attempting, "far beyond all hope of achievement," a kind of synthesis of different forms of knowledge that retains the singularity of each within a broader vision of multiplicity: "Since science has begun to distrust general explanations and solutions that are not sectorial and specialized, the grand challenge for literature is to be capable of weaving together the various branches of knowledge, the various 'codes,' into a manifold and multifaceted vision of the world."[56] By working across disciplinary boundaries between literature, mathematics, and science, Martínez, Piglia, and Cohen construct a particular role for literature as a space for such encounters, countering the ever-greater tendency towards the specialization of knowledge. This does not mean the destruction of all specificities into an uncritical and amateurish morass of intellectual compromises: autopoiesis and self-organization provide useful models of the capacity of an organism to sustain its own form and identity through constant exchanges with other organisms and its environment. Neither, at the other end of the spectrum, are we permitted to posit a literature that is independent of that environment.

For both Deleuze and the Formalists, it is paradoxically the autonomy of literature that allows it to engage with other spheres around it: autonomy, as Jakobson insisted, does not mean separatism.[57] Again, the science of chaos and complexity provides illuminatingly precise ways of thinking about such interconnectedness.

If these texts continually construct unexpected genealogies for themselves, rewiring literary history as they connect themselves to it to form multiple junctures, it is patently the case that they inspire, in turn, the tracing of similarly unusual filiations. These cannot be reduced to simplistic notions of influence but are better understood according to Cohen's model of resonance. One such connection links Shklovsky and Tynyanov with Deleuze (perhaps via Bergson); another charts points of affinity between Schlegel, Wallace Stevens, Buddhist nondualism, and theories of emergence. Another might locate in Bloch – a significant node in Piglia's web of filiations – a crucial point of convergence between Formalist ideas and complexity theory. Christian Fuchs claims that "What Bloch calls a novum is called emergent qualities in the sciences of complexity"; Bloch's understanding of matter as "a dialectically developing, producing substance" looks back to Spinoza's conception of nature as self-producing at the same time as it anticipates modern scientific theories of self-organization.[58] This line might in fact re-entwine two approaches I have sometimes contrasted here, a commitment to the dialectical development of knowledge (as expounded by Martínez, in a Formalist vein) and the immanent vision proper to Romanticism as well as theories of emergence (pervasive in Cohen's fiction).

The forging of such genealogies – some outlandish, some less so – inevitably obscures difference while revealing hidden homologies. My intent has not been to "explicate" these texts in relation to scientific principles or literary tropes but to recreate and to multiply the encounters they make possible with other texts and other systems. The lineages suggested by these texts and/or traced here do not enjoy the status of metanarratives but are provisional and subject to continual rupture and realignment; the process of constructing them is vital to artistic creativity and the production of new knowledge. Analogies and metaphors can be dangerously "mistaken," as Serres reminds us, "but we know no other route to invention."[59]

All three authors write with Serres's synthesizing spirit, finding unexpected proximities and isomorphisms between literature and science in their exploration of creativity. The many models and metaphors that circulate in their fiction and critical essays do not hold the status of metalanguages; instead, they attempt – in fluid, provisional ways – both to account for the multiplicity and complexity of experience and to produce new encounters between different forms of knowledge. Hayles reminds us that the conventional studies of influence in literary works are "wedded to the very notions of causality that a field model renders obsolete."[60] For this same reason, we should not "be misled by a causal perspective into thinking of correspondences between disciplines as one-way exchanges."[61] Ultimately – to return again to the autopoietic metaphor – it may be that each discipline borrows from the other to transform, renew, and perpetuate itself, but from that process emerge new forms of experience and invention.

If this is the case, it is perhaps ironic that the challenge to Romantic individualism mounted particularly by Piglia and Cohen only reconfirms the enduring power of another Romantic invention: the self-positing question of literature itself. In their seminal study *The Literary Absolute*, Philippe Lacoue-Labarthe and Jean-Luc Nancy contend that literature in the modern sense dates from Romanticism, which posits "*theory itself as literature* or, in other words, literature producing itself as it produces its own theory."[62] The highly reflexive and self-conscious texts of the three writers discussed here respond to the demands of what Lacoue-Labarthe and Nancy identify as "the *critical age par excellence*," that is, our age, stretching back to Romanticism, in which literature "devotes itself exclusively to the search for its own identity."[63] If it is true, as they argue, that our own age is still immersed in the project of Romanticism and that "we have not left the era of the Subject,"[64] it is also manifestly the case that in their return to certain ideas of creativity bequeathed to us by Romanticism, Martínez, Piglia, and Cohen revisit and re-open new ways of thinking about subjectivity, creativity, and literary evolution that both challenge and invigorate the Romantic projects of theory, literature, and literature as theory.

Bibliography

Abrams, M. H. "How to Do Things with Texts." In *Critical Theory Since 1965*, edited by Hazard Adams and Leroy Searle, 436–49. Tallahassee: Florida State University Press, 1986. http://www.scribd.com/doc/28320582/Critical-Theory-Since-1965.

Adams, Henry. *The Education of Henry Adams*. Project Gutenberg Ebook, n.d. http://www.gutenberg.org/files/2044/2044-h/2044-h.htm.

Aira, César. "La nueva escritura." *La Jornada Semanal* 162 (April 12, 1998). http://www.literatura.org/Aira/caboom.html.

Alazraki, Jaime. *Borges and the Kabbalah: And Other Essays on His Fiction and Poetry*. Cambridge: Cambridge University Press, 1988.

Alí, María Alejandra. "La pasión escrituraria de Ricardo Piglia. *La ciudad ausente*: De la novela a la ópera." *Recto/Verso* 2 (2007): 1–10.

Alsen, Eberhard. *Romantic Postmodernism in American Fiction*. Amsterdam: Rodopi, 1996.

Antonelli, Mirta. "La figuración de la historia nacional en la novela realista: Del árbol genealógico al archivo." In *Actas: VI Congreso Nacional de Literatura Argentina*, edited by Pampa Arán de Meriles. Córdoba: Universidad Nacional de Córdoba, 1993.

Avelar, Idelber. "Cómo respiran los ausentes: La narrativa de Ricardo Piglia." *MLN* 110, no. 2 (1995): 416–32.

———. *The Untimely Present: Postdictatorial Latin American Fiction and the Task of Mourning*. Durham, NC: Duke University Press, 1999.

Ballard, James G. *The Atrocity Exhibition*. London: Fourth Estate, 2006.

———. *La exhibición de atrocidades*. Translated by Marcelo Cohen and Francisco Abelenda. Barcelona: Edhasa, 1981.

Barth, John. *The Literature of Exhaustion and the Literature of Replenishment*. Northridge, CA: Lord John Press, 1982.

Bauman, Zygmunt. *Intimations of Postmodernity*. New York: Routledge, 1992.

Beer, Gillian. *Darwin's Plots: Evolutionary Narrative in Darwin, George Eliot and Nineteenth-Century Fiction*. Third ed. Cambridge: Cambridge University Press, 2009.

Behler, Ernst. "The Theory of Irony in German Romanticism." In *Romantic Irony*, edited by Frederick Garber, 43–81. Budapest: Akadémiai Kiadó, 1988.

Berg, Edgardo H. *Poéticas en suspenso: Migraciones narrativas en Ricardo Piglia, Andrés Rivera y Juan José Saer*. Buenos Aires: Editorial Biblos, 2002.

Bergsten, Gunilla. *Thomas Mann's Doctor Faustus: The Sources and Structure of the Novel*. Translated by Krishna Winston. Chicago: University of Chicago Press, 1969.

Berry, Ellen E., and Carol Siegel. "Rhizomes, Newness, and the Condition of Our Postmodernity: Editorial and a Dialogue." *Rhizomes: Cultural Studies in Emerging Knowledge* 1 (Fall 2000). http://www.rhizomes.net/issue1/newness1.html.

Best, Steven, and Douglas Kellner. *The Postmodern Turn*. New York: Guilford Press, 1997.

Black, Joel. "Newtonian Mechanics and the Romantic Rebellion: Introduction." In *Beyond the Two Cultures: Essays on Science, Technology, and Literature*, edited by Joseph W Slade and Judith Yaross Lee. Ames: Iowa State University Press, 1990.

———. "Probing a Post-Romantic Paleontology: Thomas Pynchon's Gravity's Rainbow." *boundary 2* 8, no. 2 (1980): 229–54.

Bloch, Ernst. *The Principle of Hope*. Translated by Neville Plaice, Stephen Plaice, and Paul Knight. 3 vols. Oxford: Blackwell, 1986.

Bohm, David. *On Creativity*. Edited by Lee Nichol. London and New York: Routledge, 1998.

Borges, Jorge Luis. "El Aleph." In *El Aleph*, 155–74. Buenos Aires: Emecé, 1971.

———. "El Zahir." In *El Aleph*, 105–16. Buenos Aires: Emecé, 1971.

Bouveresse, Jacques. *Prodigios y vértigos de la analogía: Sobre el abuso de la literatura en el pensamiento*. Translated by Helena Alapin. Buenos Aires: Libros del Zorzal, 2005.

Bracamonte, Jorge. "Futuros potenciales en mundos contemporáneos. O James Ballard en la poética extraña de Marcelo Cohen." *Revista Iberoamericana* 78, no. 238–39 (June 2012): 209–23.

Braidotti, Rosi. *Metamorphoses: Towards a Materialist Theory of Becoming*. Cambridge, UK; Malden, MA: Polity, 2002.

Brochoud, Francisco Alí. "El hombre amable" [interview with Marcelo Cohen]. *El Territorio*, July 4, 1999, sec. Suplemento SED. http://marcelocohen.8m.net/sed.htm.

Bronner, Stephen Eric. "Utopian Projections: In Memory of Ernst Bloch." In *Not Yet: Reconsidering Ernst Bloch*, edited by Jamie Owen Daniel and Tom Moylan, 165–74. London; New York: Verso, 1997.

Brown, J. Andrew. *Cyborgs in Latin America*. New York: Palgrave Macmillan, 2010.

———. *Test Tube Envy: Science and Power in Argentine Narrative*. Lewisburg, PA: Bucknell University Press, 2005.

Bruni, John. "Thermodynamics." In *The Routledge Companion to Literature and Science*, edited by Bruce Clarke and Manuela Rossini, 226–37. New York: Routledge, 2011.

Byron, George Gordon. "Manfred." In *The Complete Poetical Works*, edited by Jerome J. McGann, 4:50–102. Oxford: Clarendon Press, 1986.

Calvino, Italo. "Cybernetics and Ghosts." In *The Uses of Literature: Essays*, translated by Patrick Creagh, 3–27. San Diego: Harcourt Brace Jovanovich, 1986.
———. *Six Memos for the Next Millennium*. Translated by Patrick Creagh. London: Penguin Classics, 2009.
———. *The Castle of Crossed Destinies*. Translated by William Weaver. London: Vintage, 1998.
Capek, Milic. *Bergson and Modern Physics: A Reinterpretation and Re-Evaluation*. Dordrecht: Reidel, 1971.
Carroll, Joseph. "The Science Wars in a Long View: Putting the Human in its Place." In *Interdisciplinary Essays on Darwinism in Hispanic Literature and Film: The Intersection of Science and the Humanities*, edited by Jerry Hoeg and Kevin S. Larsen, 19–33. Lewiston, NY: Edwin Mellen Press, 2009.
Cavaillès, Jean. "On Logic and the Theory of Science." In *Phenomenology and the Natural Sciences: Essays and Translations*, edited by Joseph J. Kockelmans and Theodore J. Kisiel, 353–409. Evanston: Northwestern University Press, 1970.
Changeux, Jean-Pierre, and Alain Connes. *Conversations on Mind, Matter, and Mathematics*. Edited by M. B. DeBevoise. Translated by M. B. DeBevoise. Princeton, NJ: Princeton University Press, 1995.
Cid, Claudio. "Hacia una nueva novela policial argentina: Guillermo Martínez y Pablo De Santis" (2008). http://guillermo-martinez.net/notas/Hacia_una_nueva_novela_policial.../Cid.
Cittadini, Fernando. "Historia y ficción en *Respiración artificial*." In *La novela argentina de los años 80*, edited by Roland Spiller, 37–46. Frankfurt: Vervuert Verlag, 1991.
Clemens, Justin. *The Romanticism of Contemporary Theory: Institution, Aesthetics, Nihilism*. Aldershot, UK: Ashgate, 2003.
Cohen, Marcelo. *¡Realmente fantástico! y otros ensayos*. Buenos Aires: Norma, 2003.
———. "Aspectos de la vida de Enzatti." In *El fin de lo mismo*, 150–77. Buenos Aires: Alianza, 1992.
———. *Buda*. Barcelona: Lumen, 1990.
———. *Donde yo no estaba*. Buenos Aires: Norma, 2006.
———. "El fin de lo mismo." In *El fin de lo mismo*, 121–49. Buenos Aires: Alianza, 1992.
———. "El reencantamiento del mundo." *La Nación*, January 16, 2010, sec. ADN Cultura.
———. *El testamento de O'Jaral*. Buenos Aires: Alianza Editorial, 1995.
———. "La ilusión monarca." In *El fin de lo mismo*, 9–120. Buenos Aires: Alianza, 1992.
———. "Lydia en el canal." In *El fin de lo mismo*, 207–73. Buenos Aires: Alianza, 1992.
———. "Un hombre amable." In *Hombres amables*, 143–316. Buenos Aires: Norma, 1998.
———. "Unas palabras." In *La solución parcial*, 9–12. Madrid: Páginas de Espuma, 2003.
———. "Volubilidad." In *El fin de lo mismo*, 178–206. Buenos Aires: Alianza, 1992.
Colás, Santiago. *Postmodernity in Latin America: The Argentine Paradigm*. Durham, NC: Duke University Press, 1994.
Colebrook, Claire. *Gilles Deleuze*. London and New York: Routledge, 2001.

Coleridge, Samuel Taylor. *Biographia Literaria*. Edited by Nigel Leask. London: Everyman, 1997.
Connor, Steven. "Topologies: Michel Serres and the Shapes of Thought" (2002). http://www.bbk.ac.uk/english/skc/topologies/.
Cortázar, Julio. *Rayuela*. Madrid: Punto de Lectura, 2001.
———. "Teoría del túnel." In *Obra Crítica 1*, 31–137. Edited by Saúl Yurkievich. Madrid: Alfaguara, 1994.
Costa, Flavia. "Inolvidables veladas de la ficción [entrevista a Marcelo Cohen]." *Clarín*, June 3, 2001, sec. Revista Ñ. http://old.clarin.com/suplementos/cultura/2001/06/03/u-00311.htm.
Curtis, James M. "Bergson and Russian Formalism." *Comparative Literature* 28, no. 2 (April 1, 1976): 109–21.
Dalmaroni, Miguel. "El fin de lo otro y la disolución del fantástico en un relato de Marcelo Cohen." *Cuadernos Angers-La Plata* 4, no. 4 (March 2001): 83–96.
Dapía, Silvia G. "Transgresiones, subjetividad y postmodernismo la búsqueda de una lógica no binaria en *Acerca de Roderer* de Guillermo Martínez." In *Pasajes: Homenaje a Christian Wentzlaff-Eggebert*, edited by Susanne Grunwald, 413–24. Seville: Universidad de Sevilla, 2004.
Deleuze, Gilles, and Félix Guattari. *A Thousand Plateaus: Capitalism and Schizophrenia*. Translated by Brian Massumi. London and New York: Continuum, 2004.
———. *Anti-Oedipus: Capitalism and Schizophrenia*. Translated by Robert Hurley, Mark Seem, and Helen R. Lane. London and New York: Continuum, 2004.
———. *Kafka: Toward a Minor Literature*. Minneapolis: University of Minnesota Press, 1986.
———. *What Is Philosophy?* Translated by Graham Burchell and Hugh Tomlinson. London: Verso, 1994.
Deleuze, Gilles. "Literature and Life." Translated by Daniel W. Smith and Michael A. Greco. *Critical Inquiry* 23, no. 2 (January 1, 1997): 225–30.
Deleuze, Gilles, and Claire Parnet. *Dialogues II*. London: Continuum, 2006.
Demaría, Laura. "Rodolfo Walsh, Ricardo Piglia, la tranquera de Macedonio y el difícil oficio de escribir." *Revista iberoamericana* 67, no. 194 (2001): 135–44.
Doggett, Frank A. *Stevens' Poetry of Thought*. Baltimore: Johns Hopkins University Press, 1966.
Echavarren, Roberto. "La literariedad: *Respiración artificial*, de Ricardo Piglia." *Revista Iberoamericana* 49 (1983): 997–1008.
Eichenbaum, Boris M. "The Theory of the Formal Method." In *Readings in Russian Poetics: Formalist and Structuralist Views*, edited by Ladislav Matějka and Krystyna Pomorska, 3–37. Cambridge, MA: MIT Press, 1971.
Eichner, Hans. *Friedrich Schlegel*. New York: Twayne, 1970.
———. "The Rise of Modern Science and the Genesis of Romanticism." *PMLA* 97, no. 1 (January 1, 1982): 8–30.

"El rock me acompaña desde siempre" [interview with Marcelo Cohen], November 29, 2007. http://elmedium.mforos.com/1807311/9173140-29-11-07-marcelo-cohen.

Erlich, Victor. *Russian Formalism: History - Doctrine*. The Hague: Mouton, 1955.

Federman, Raymond. "Imagination as Plagiarism [An Unfinished Paper…]." *New Literary History* 7, no. 3 (April 1, 1976): 563–78.

Foucault, Michel. "Nietzsche, Genealogy, History." In *The Foucault Reader*, edited by Paul Rabinow, 76–100. New York: Pantheon, 1984.

———. *The Order of Things*. London and New York: Routledge, 1970.

———. "What is an Author?" In *The Foucault Reader*, edited by Paul Rabinow, 101–20. New York: Pantheon, 1984.

Freese, Peter. *From Apocalypse to Entropy and Beyond: The Second Law of Thermodynamics in Post-War American Fiction*. Essen: Die Blaue Eule, 1997.

Frye, Northrop. *Anatomy of Criticism: Four Essays*. Princeton, NJ: Princeton University Press, 1957.

Fuchs, Christian. "Dialectical Philosophy and Self-Organisation." In *Causality, Emergence, Self-Organisation*, edited by Vladimir Arshinov and Christian Fuchs, 195–244. Moscow: NIA-Priroda, 2003. http://fuchs.uti.at/wp-content/uploads/causalityemergenceselforganisation.pdf.

Furst, Lilian R. *Fictions of Romantic Irony in European Narrative, 1760–1857*. London: Macmillan, 1984.

———. "Romantic Irony and Narrative Stance." In *Romantic Irony*, edited by Frederick Garber, 293–321. Budapest: Akadémiai Kiadó, 1988.

Garber, Frederick. "Sterne: Arabesques and Fictionality." In *Romantic Irony*, edited by Frederick Garber, 33–40. Budapest: Akadémiai Kiadó, 1988.

Garrett, Victoria, and Rachel VanWieren. "A Conversation with Andrew Brown: Mashing Up Latin American Literature, Science, Technology, and the Post-human." *Mester* 39, no. 1 (July 7, 2010): 149–60.

Gnutzmann, Rita. "La mirada histórica de Piglia en *Respiración artificial*." *Río de la Plata* 11–12 (1990): 271–77.

Goldstein, Jeffrey. "Emergence as a Construct: History and Issues." *Emergence* 1, no. 1 (1999): 49–72.

González Echeverría, Roberto. *Myth and Archive: A Theory of Latin American Narrative*. Cambridge: Cambridge University Press, 1990.

Gross, Paul R., and Norman Levitt. *Higher Superstition: The Academic Left and Its Quarrels With Science*. Baltimore: Johns Hopkins University Press, 1997.

Gunter, P.A.Y. *Bergson and the Evolution of Physics*. Knoxville: University of Tennessee Press, 1969.

Hamilton, Paul. "From Sublimity to Indeterminacy: New World Order or Aftermath of Romantic Ideology." In *Romanticism and Postmodernism*, edited by Edward Larrissy, 13–28. Cambridge: Cambridge University Press, 1999.

———. "The Romanticism of Contemporary Ideology." In *Intersections: Nineteenth-Century Philosophy and Contemporary Theory*, edited by Tilottama Rajan and David L. Clark, 302–21. Albany: State University of New York Press, 1995.
Harari, Josué V., and David F. Bell. "Introduction: Journal à plusieurs voies." In *Hermes: Literature, Science, Philosophy*, edited by Josué V. Harari and David F. Bell, by Michel Serres, ix–xl. Baltimore: Johns Hopkins University Press, 1982.
Hardy, G. H. *A Mathematician's Apology*. Cambridge: Cambridge University Press, 1940.
Hayles, N. Katherine. *How We Became Posthuman: Virtual Bodies in Cybernetics, Literature, and Informatics*. Chicago: University of Chicago Press, 1999.
———. "Introduction: Complex Dynamics in Literature and Science." In *Chaos and Order: Complex Dynamics in Literature and Science*, edited by Hayles, 1–33. Chicago: University of Chicago Press, 1991.
———. *The Cosmic Web: Scientific Field Models and Literary Strategies in the Twentieth Century*. Ithaca, NY: Cornell University Press, 1984.
Hayles, N. Katherine, ed. *Chaos and Order: Complex Dynamics in Literature and Science*. Chicago: University of Chicago Press, 1991.
Haywood Ferreira, *The Emergence of Latin American Science Fiction*. Middletown, CT: Wesleyan University Press, 2011.
Heffernan, Julián Jiménez. "Ironic distance in Thomas Pynchon's 'Entropy'." *Contemporary Literature* 52, no. 2 (2011): 298–329.
Hegel, Georg Wilhelm Friedrich. *Aesthetics: Lectures on Fine Art*. Translated by T. M. Knox. Oxford: Clarendon Press, 1975.
Heidegger, Martin. *The Principle of Reason*. Translated by Reginald Lilly. Bloomington: Indiana University Press, 1991.
Hofstadter, Douglas R. *Gödel, Escher, Bach: An Eternal Golden Braid*. London: Penguin, 1979.
———. *I Am a Strange Loop*. New York: Basic, 2007.
Hutcheon, Linda. *A Theory of Parody: The Teachings of Twentieth-Century Art Forms*. Urbana: University of Illinois Press, 2000.
James, Henry. *The Figure in the Carpet*. London: Martin Secker, 1916.
James, William. *Pragmatism: A New Name for Some Old Ways of Thinking; the Meaning of Truth: A Sequel to Pragmatism*. Cambridge, MA: Harvard University Press, 1978.
Jameson, Fredric. *The Prison-House of Language: A Critical Account of Structuralism and Russian Formalism*. Princeton, NJ: Princeton University Press, 1972.
———. *The Seeds of Time*. New York: Columbia University Press, 1994.
Jantsch, Erich. *The Self-Organizing Universe: Scientific and Human Implications of the Emerging Paradigm of Evolution*. Oxford: Pergamon Press, 1980.
Kaplan, Edward K. *Michelet's Poetic Vision: A Romantic Philosophy of Nature, Man, and Woman*. Amherst: University of Massachusetts Press, 1977.
Kellner, Douglas. "Ernst Bloch, Utopia, and Ideology Critique." In *Not Yet: Reconsidering Ernst Bloch*, edited by Jamie Owen Daniel and Tom Moylan, 80–95. London; New York: Verso, 1997.

Kenevan, Phyllis Berdt. "Nietzsche and the Creative Consciousness." *Man and World* 15, no. 4 (1982): 383–94.
Lacoue-Labarthe, Philippe, and Jean-Luc Nancy. *The Literary Absolute: The Theory of Literature in German Romanticism*. Translated by Philip Barnard and Cheryl Lester. Albany: State University of New York Press, 1988.
LaGuardia, David M. *Advance on Chaos: The Sanctifying Imagination of Wallace Stevens*. Hanover, NH: University Press of New England, 1983.
Latour, Bruno. "The Politics of Explanation: An Alternative." In *Knowledge and Reflexivity: New Frontiers in the Sociology of Knowledge*, edited by Steve Woolgar, 155–76. London: Sage, 1988.
Livingston, Ira. *Between Science and Literature: An Introduction to Autopoetics*. Urbana and Chicago: University of Illinois Press, 2006.
Lynch, Michael. "Against Reflexivity as an Academic Virtue and Source of Privileged Knowledge." *Theory, Culture & Society* 17, no. 3 (2000): 26–54.
Madrazo, Jorge Ariel. "Entrevista a Ricardo Piglia." *Atenea: Revista de ciencia, arte y literatura de la Universidad de Concepción* 473 (June 1996): 95–109.
de Man, Paul. *Romanticism and Contemporary Criticism: The Gauss Seminar and Other Papers*. Edited by E. S Burt, Kevin Newmark, and Andrzej Warminski. Baltimore: Johns Hopkins University Press, 1993.
Mann, Thomas. *Doctor Faustus*. Translated by John E. Woods. New York: Vintage, 1999.
———. *The Genesis of a Novel*. Translated by Richard Winston and Clara Winston. London: Secker & Warburg, 1961.
Marks, John. *Deleuze and Science*. Edinburgh: Edinburgh University Press, 2006.
Martínez, Guillermo. *Acerca de Roderer*. Buenos Aires: Booket, 1992.
———. *Borges y la matemática*. Buenos Aires: Seix Barral, 2006.
———. "Consideraciones de un ex político." *Blog de Guillermo Martínez*, 1994. http://guillermomartinezweb.blogspot.com/2011/06/consideraciones-de-un-ex-politico.html.
———. *Crímenes imperceptibles*. Buenos Aires: Booket, 2009.
———. "El lector y sus criterios." *Blog de Guillermo Martínez*, 2008. http://guillermomartinezweb.blogspot.com/2011/06/el-lector-y-sus-criterios.html.
———. "Eterna Cadencia, 2009." *Blog de Guillermo Martínez*, 2009. http://guillermomartinezweb.blogspot.com/2011/06/eterna-cadencia-2009.html.
———. *La fórmula de la inmortalidad*. Buenos Aires: Planeta, 2005.
———. "La irresistible elegancia de un teorema." *La Nación*, May 23, 2009, sec. Cultura. http://www.lanacion.com.ar/nota.asp?nota_id+1129718.
———. "La literatura argentina y un chiste de Aira." *Blog de Guillermo Martínez*, 2011. http://guillermomartinezweb.blogspot.com/2011/06/mitologia-y-cliche-en-las-discusiones.html.
———. *La muerte lenta de Luciana B.* Barcelona: Destino, 2009.
———. *La mujer del maestro*. Buenos Aires: Planeta, 1998.

———. "Lo que repito tres veces." *Blog de Guillermo Martínez*, 2011. http://guillermomartinezweb.blogspot.com/2011/06/lo-que-repito-tres-veces.html.
———. "Teoremas asesinos." *La Nación*, November 9, 2003, sec. Cultura. http://www.lanacion.com.ar/543270-teoremas-asesinos.
———. "Un plan a futuro." *Blog de Guillermo Martínez*, 2008. http://guillermomartinezweb.blogspot.com/2011/06/un-plan-futuro.html.
Martínez, Guillermo, and Gustavo Piñeiro. *Gödel (para todos)*. Buenos Aires: Seix Barral, 2009.
Massman, Stefanie. "La ficción acosada por la realidad: Narrar la historia en *Respiración artificial* de Ricardo Piglia." *Taller de letras: Revista de la Facultad de la Pontificia Universidad Católica de Chile* 34 (2004): 97–104.
McCarthy, John A. *Remapping Reality: Chaos and Creativity in Science and Literature (Goethe, Nietzsche, Grass)*. Amsterdam; New York: Rodopi, 2006.
McMullin, Ernan. "Is the Progress of Science Dialectical?" In *Hegel and the Sciences*, edited by Robert S. Cohen and Marx W. Wartofsky, 215–39. Boston Studies in the Philosophy of Science. Dordrecht: Reidel, 1984.
Michelet, Jules. *The Sea*. Translated by Unknown. London: T. Nelson and Sons, 1875.
Moledo, Leonardo. "Crimen, cálculo y castigo" [interview with Guillermo Martínez]. *Página/12*, December 7, 2003, sec. Radar. http://www.pagina12.com.ar/diario/suplementos/radar/9-1104-2003-12-10.html.
Morello-Frosch, Marta. "The Opulent *Facundo*: Sarmiento and Modern Argentine Fiction." In *Sarmiento, Author of a Nation*, edited by Tulio Halperín Donghi, 347–57. Berkeley: University of California Press, 1994.
Moscardi, Matías Eduardo. "El mito del crimen perfecto" (n.d.). http://guillermo-martinez.net/notas/1/3_El_mito_del_crimen_perfecto_/Moscardi.
de Mul, Jos. *Romantic Desire in (Post)modern Art and Philosophy*. Albany: State University of New York Press, 1999.
Nietzsche, Friedrich Wilhelm. "On Truth and Lying in a Non-Moral Sense." In *The Birth of Tragedy and Other Writings*, edited by Raymond Geuss and Ronald Speirs, translated by Ronald Speirs, 141–53. Cambridge: Cambridge University Press, 1999.
———. *The Birth of Tragedy and Other Writings*. Edited by Raymond Geuss and Ronald Speirs. Translated by Ronald Speirs. Cambridge: Cambridge University Press, 1999.
———. *The Gay Science*. Translated by Thomas Common. Mineola, NY: Dover, 2006.
———. *The Will to Power*. Translated by Walter Arnold Kaufmann and R. J. Hollingdale. New York: Vintage, 1968.
———. *Thus Spake Zarathustra*. Translated by Thomas Common. Ware, Hertfordshire: Wordsworth, n.d.
———. *Twilight of the Idols*. Translated by R. J. Hollingdale. Harmondsworth: Penguin, 1990.

Nouzeilles, Gabriela. *Ficciones somáticas. Naturalismo, nacionalismo y políticas médicas del cuerpo (Argentina 1880–1910)*. Rosario: Beatriz Viterbo, 2000.
Oeyen, Annelies. "Imágenes de la barbarie en 'La ilusión monarca' de Marcelo Cohen." In *Los imaginarios apocalípticos en la literatura hispanoamericana contemporánea*, edited by Geneviève Fabry, Ilse Logie, and Pablo Decock, 257–67. Oxford; New York: Peter Lang, 2010.
Orr, John C. "Adams, Henry Brooks." In *The Dictionary of Modern American Philosophers*, edited by John R. Shook and Richard T. Hull, Vol. I, A-C:12–18. Bristol: Thoemmes, 2005.
Ortiz, Carmen. *Cortázar el mago*. Buenos Aires: Diada, 2010.
Papanicolaou, Andrew C., and P.A.Y. Gunter, eds. *Bergson and Modern Thought: Towards a Unified Science*. New York: Harwood Academic, 1987.
Paulson, William R.. "Literature, Complexity, Interdisciplinarity." In *Chaos and Order: Complex Dynamics in Literature and Science*, edited by N. Katherine Hayles, 37–53. Chicago: University of Chicago Press, 1991.
———. *The Noise of Culture: Literary Texts in a World of Information*. Ithaca, NY: Cornell University Press, 1988.
Penrose, Roger. *Shadows of the Mind: A Search for the Missing Science of Consciousness*. Oxford: Oxford University Press, 1994.
———. *The Emperor's New Mind: Concerning Computers, Minds, and the Laws of Physics*. Oxford: Oxford University Press, 1989.
Piglia, Ricardo. *Blanco nocturno*. Barcelona: Editorial Anagrama, 2010.
———. *Crítica y ficción*. Buenos Aires: Planeta/Seix Barral, 1990.
———. "El fluir de la vida." In *Prisión perpetua*, 65–78. Barcelona: Anagrama, 2007.
———. "El último cuento de Borges." In *Formas breves*, 59–68. Buenos Aires: Temas, 1999.
———. *El último lector*. Buenos Aires: Anagrama, 2005.
———. "En otro país." In *Prisión perpetua*, 13–63. Barcelona: Anagrama, 2007.
———. "Encuentro en Saint-Nazaire." In *Prisión perpetua*, 81–147. Barcelona: Anagrama, 2007.
———. "Hoy es imposible en la Argentina hacer literatura desvinculada de la política. Reportaje de Ricardo Piglia a Rodolfo Walsh (Marzo de 1970)." In *Un oscuro día de justicia*, by Rodolfo Walsh, 53–69. Buenos Aires: Ediciones de la Flor, 2006.
———. *La ciudad ausente*. Buenos Aires: Espasa Calpe/Seix Barral, 1995.
———. "La loca y el relato del crimen." In *Cuentos morales: Antología (1961–1990)*, 122–31. Buenos Aires: Espasa Calpe, 1995.
———. *Respiración artificial*. Buenos Aires: Sudamericana, 1988.
———. "Rodolfo Walsh y el lugar de la verdad." *Nuevo Texto Crítico* 6 (1993-1994): 13–15.
———. "Tesis sobre el cuento." In *Formas breves*, 89–100. Buenos Aires: Temas, 1999.
———. *Tres propuestas para el próximo milenio (y cinco dificultades)*. Buenos Aires: Fondo de Cultura Económica, 2001.

Plant, Sadie. "The Virtual Complexity of Culture." In *Futurenatural: Nature, Science, Culture*, edited by George Robertson, Melinda Mash, Lisa Tickner, Jon Bird, Barry Curtis, and Tim Putnam, 203–17. London; New York: Routledge, 1996.

Plotnitsky, A. "Chaosmologies: Quantum Field Theory, Chaos and Thought in Deleuze and Guattari's What is Philosophy?" *Paragraph: A Journal of Modern Critical Theory* 29, no. 2 (2006): 40–56.

Pope, Rob. *Creativity: Theory, History, Practice*. New ed. London and New York: Routledge, 2005.

Porush, David. "Prigogine, Chaos, and Contemporary Science Fiction." *Science Fiction Studies* 18, no. 3 (November 1991): 367–86.

———. *The Soft Machine: Cybernetic Fiction*. New York: Methuen, 1985.

Prigogine, Ilya. *The End of Certainty: Time, Chaos, and the New Laws of Nature*. 1st ed. New York: Free Press, 1997.

Protevi, John. "Deleuze, Guattari, and Emergence." *Paragraph: A Journal of Modern Critical Theory* 29, no. 2 (July 2006): 19–39.

Pynchon, Thomas. "Entropy." In *Slow Learner: Early Stories*, 81–98. London: Vintage, 2000.

———. *Gravity's Rainbow*. London: Vintage, 1995.

———. "Introduction." In *Slow Learner: Early Stories*, 3–23. London: Vintage, 2000.

———. *The Crying of Lot 49*. London: Vintage, 2000.

Ryle, Gilbert. *The Concept of Mind*. London: Hutchinson, 1949.

Saavedra, Guillermo. "Los espacios imaginarios del narrador" [interview with Marcelo Cohen]. In *La curiosidad impertinente: entrevistas con narradores argentinos*, 79–93. Rosario: Beatriz Viterbo, 1993.

Sarlo, Beatriz. *La imaginación técnica: Sueños modernos de la cultura argentina*. Buenos Aires: Nueva Visión, 1992.

Sarmiento, Alicia Inés. "*Acerca de Roderer* de Guillermo Martínez: El *mysterium iniquitatis* en el fin de siglo literario." *Cuadernos del CILHA: Revista del Centro Interdisciplinario de Literatura Hispanoamericana* 7 (2005-2006): 267–79.

du Sautoy, Marcus. *The Music of the Primes: Why an Unsolved Problem in Mathematics Matters*. London: Harper Perennial, 2004.

Schachterle, Lance. "The Metaphorical Allure of Modern Physics: Introduction." In *Beyond the Two Cultures: Essays on Science, Technology, and Literature*, edited by Joseph W Slade and Judith Yaross Lee, 177–84. Ames: Iowa State University Press, 1990.

Schaub, Thomas. "'A Gentle Chill, An Ambiguity': *The Crying of Lot 49*." In *Critical Essays on Thomas Pynchon*, edited by Richard Pearce, 51–68. Boston: G.K. Hall, 1981.

Schlegel, Friedrich von. *Dialogue on Poetry and Literary Aphorisms*. Translated by Ernst Behler and Roman Struc. University Park: Pennsylvania State University Press, 1968.

———. *Friedrich Schlegel's Lucinde and the Fragments*. Translated by Peter Firchow. Minneapolis: University of Minnesota Press, 1971.

———. *Kritische Ausgabe*. Translated by Ernst Behler, Jean-Jacques Anstett, and Hans Eichner. 18th ed. Paderborn: Verlag Ferdinand Schöningh, 1958.

Schmidt, James. "Mephistopheles in Hollywood: Adorno, Mann, and Schoenberg." In *The Cambridge Companion to Adorno*, edited by Tom Huhn, 148–80. Cambridge: Cambridge University Press, 2004.

Schrödinger, Erwin. *What Is Life?: The Physical Aspect of the Living Cell & Mind and Matter*. Cambridge: Cambridge University Press, 1967.

Schweighauser, Philipp. "The Desire for Unity and Its Failure: Reading Henry Adams through Michel Serres." In *Mapping Michel Serres*, edited by Niran B. Abbas, 136–52. Ann Arbor: University of Michigan Press, 2005.

Serra, Laura. "La fórmula de Guillermo Martínez" [interview]. *Educar: El portal educativo del Estado argentino*, n.d. http://portal.educ.ar/noticias/entrevistas/la-formula-de-guillermo-martin.php.

Serres, Michel. *The Birth of Physics*. Edited by David Webb. Translated by Jack Hawkes. Manchester: Clinamen Press, 2000.

———. *Genesis*. Ann Arbor: University of Michigan Press, 1995.

———. *Hermes V: Le Passage Du Nord-ouest*. Paris: Éditions de Minuit, 1980.

———. *Hermes: Literature, Science, Philosophy*. Edited by Josué V. Harari and David F. Bell. Baltimore: Johns Hopkins University Press, 1982.

Serres, Michel, and Bruno Latour. *Conversations on Science, Culture, and Time*. Translated by Roxanne Lapidus. Ann Arbor: University of Michigan Press, 1995.

Sheldrake, Rupert. *The Presence of the Past: Morphic Resonance and the Habits of Nature*. London: Collins, 1988.

Shiner, Lewis. *Deserted Cities of the Heart*. London: Abacus, 1988.

Shklovsky, Viktor. "Art as Technique." In *Literary Theory: An Anthology*, edited by Julie Rivkin and Michael Ryan, 17–23. Oxford: Blackwell, 1998.

———. "The Mystery Novel: Dickens's Little Dorrit." In *Readings in Russian Poetics: Formalist and Structuralist Views*, edited by Ladislav Matějka and Krystyna Pomorska, 220–26. Cambridge, MA: MIT Press, 1971.

———. "The Resurrection of the Word." In *Russian Formalism: A Collection of Articles and Texts in Translation*, edited by Stephen Bann and John E. Bowlt, 41–47. Edinburgh: Scottish Academic Press, 1973.

———. *Theory of Prose*. Translated by Benjamin Sher. Champaign, IL: Dalkey Archive Press, 1990.

Sifrim, Mónica. "Literatura a la hora de la siesta" [interview with Marcelo Cohen]. *Clarín*, November 8, 1998, sec. Cultura. http://edant.clarin.com/suplementos/cultura/1998/11/08/e-00801d.htm.

Snow, Charles Percy. *The Two Cultures*. Cambridge: Cambridge University Press, 1993.

Sokal, Alan D. *Beyond the Hoax: Science, Philosophy, and Culture*. Oxford: Oxford University Press, 2008.

———. "Transgressing the Boundaries: Toward a Transformative Hermeneutics of Quantum Gravity." *Social Text* 46/47 (1996): 217–52.

Sokal, Alan, and Jean Bricmont. *Intellectual Impostures: Postmodern Philosophers' Abuse of Science*. London: Profile Books, 1998.

Sontag, Susan. *Against Interpretation and Other Essays*. London: Penguin, 2009.
Steiner, Peter. "Russian Formalism." In *The Cambridge History of Literary Criticism, Vol. 8: From Formalism to Poststructuralism*, edited by Raman Selden, 8:1–29. Cambridge: Cambridge University Press, 1995.
Stevens, Wallace. "Adagia." In *Opus Posthumous*, edited by Samuel French Morse, 157–80. London: Faber and Faber, 1957.
———. *Adagia*. Translated by Marcelo Cohen. Barcelona: Península, 1987.
———. "An Ordinary Evening in New Haven." In *The Collected Poems of Wallace Stevens*, 465–89. London: Faber and Faber, 1984.
———. "July Mountain." In *Opus Posthumous*, edited by Samuel French Morse, 114–15. London: Faber and Faber, 1957.
———. "Landscape with Boat." In *The Collected Poems of Wallace Stevens*, 241–43. London: Faber and Faber, 1984.
———. "On the Road Home." In *The Collected Poems of Wallace Stevens*, 203–4. London: Faber and Faber, 1984.
———. "The Auroras of Autumn." In *The Collected Poems of Wallace Stevens*, 411–21. London: Faber and Faber, 1984.
Stewart, Susan. *On Longing: Narratives of the Miniature, the Gigantic, the Souvenir, the Collection*. Baltimore: Johns Hopkins University Press, 1984.
Stoicheff, Peter. "The Chaos of Metafiction." In *Chaos and Order: Complex Dynamics in Literature and Science*, edited by N. Katherine Hayles, 85–99. Chicago: University of Chicago Press, 1991.
Striedter, Jurij. *Literary Structure, Evolution, and Value: Russian Formalism and Czech Structuralism Reconsidered*. Cambridge, MA: Harvard University Press, 1989.
Tanner, Tony. *Scenes of Nature, Signs of Men*. Cambridge: Cambridge University Press, 1987.
Tasić, Vladimir. *Mathematics and the Roots of Postmodern Thought*. Oxford: Oxford University Press, 2001.
———. *Una lectura matemática del pensamiento posmoderno*. Translated by Guillermo Martínez. Buenos Aires: Colihue, 2001.
Terán, Oscar. *Vida intelectual en el Buenos Aires de fin-de-siglo (1880–1910): Derivas de la cultura científica*. Buenos Aires: Fondo de Cultura Económica, 2000.
Todorov, Tzvetan. *The Poetics of Prose*. Translated by Richard Howard. Oxford: Blackwell, 1977.
Tomasi, Alessandro. "Nihilism and Creativity in the Philosophy of Nietzsche." *Minerva: An Internet Journal of Philosophy* 11 (2007): 153–83.
Tynyanov, Yury. "On Literary Evolution." In *Readings in Russian Poetics: Formalist and Structuralist Views*, edited by Ladislav Matějka and Krystyna Pomorska, 66–78. Cambridge, MA: MIT Press, 1971.
———. "The Literary Fact." In *Modern Genre Theory*, edited by David Duff, 29–49. Harlow, UK: Longman, 1999.
Venegas, José Luis. "El 'Principio de Incertidumbre' de Heisenberg y la narración intersticial de 'Axolotl' de Julio Cortázar." *Hispanic Journal* 28, no. 2 (2007): 79–93.

Viereck, Roberto. "De la tradición a las formas de la experiencia: Entrevista a Ricardo Piglia." *Revista Chilena de Literatura* 40 (1992): 129–38.
Villalonga, María Eugenia. "Creo en las novelas y en sus posibilidades de metamorfosis permanentes" [interview with Marcelo Cohen]. *Tiempo argentino*, April 7, 2013, sec. Suplemento Cultura. http://tiempo.infonews.com/2013/04/07/suplemento-cultura-99619-creo-en-las-novelas-y-en-sus-posibilidades-de-metamorfosis-permanentes.php.
Villani, Arnaud. *La guêpe et l'orchidée: essai sur Gilles Deleuze*. Paris: Belin, 1999.
Webster, Joseph. "Establishing the 'Truth' of the Matter: Confessional Reflexivity as Introspection and Avowal." *Psychology & Society* 1, no. 2 (2008): 65–76.
Wellek, René. "Russian Formalism." *Arcadia: International Journal for Literary Studies* 6 (1971): 175–86.
Whiting, Anthony. *The Never-Resting Mind: Wallace Stevens' Romantic Irony*. Ann Arbor: University of Michigan Press, 1996.
Wiener, Norbert. *The Human Use of Human Beings: Cybernetics and Society*. London: Eyre and Spottiswoode, 1954.
Wittgenstein, Ludwig. *Philosophical Investigations*. Translated by G.E.M. Anscombe. New York: Macmillan, 1968.
Young, Edward. *Conjectures on Original Composition*. Leeds, UK: Scolar Press, 1966.
Zencey, Eric. "Entropy as Root Metaphor." In *Beyond the Two Cultures: Essays on Science, Technology, and Literature*, edited by Joseph W Slade and Judith Yaross Lee, 185–200. Ames: Iowa State University Press, 1990.

Notes

INTRODUCTION

1. Eichner, "The Rise of Modern Science and the Genesis of Romanticism," 8.
2. See Sokal, "Transgressing the Boundaries"; the article is reprinted in Sokal, *Beyond the Hoax*, 5–91.
3. Gross and Levitt, *Higher Superstition*, 73–74.
4. Ibid., 74.
5. Best and Kellner, *The Postmodern Turn*, 226–44.
6. Livingston, *Between Science and Literature*, 7.
7. Ibid.
8. Snow, *The Two Cultures*.
9. Best and Kellner, *The Postmodern Turn*, 19, 196.
10. Ibid., 19.
11. Sokal and Bricmont, *Intellectual Impostures*, 136.
12. Hayles, "Introduction: Complex Dynamics in Literature and Science," 4.
13. Best and Kellner, *The Postmodern Turn*, 219.
14. Ibid., 195.
15. Ibid., 19.
16. McCarthy, *Remapping Reality*, 17.
17. Hamilton, "From Sublimity to Indeterminacy: New World Order or Aftermath of Romantic Ideology," 14.
18. Schachterle, "The Metaphorical Allure of Modern Physics: Introduction," 177.
19. Beer, *Darwin's Plots: Evolutionary Narrative in Darwin, George Eliot and Nineteenth-Century Fiction*, 5.
20. Martínez and Piñeiro, *Gödel (para todos)*, 42.
21. Ibid., 44. All translations into English from original texts in Spanish (or French) are my own.
22. Ibid.
23. Bauman, *Intimations of Postmodernity*, ix.
24. Best and Kellner, *The Postmodern Turn*, 133.
25. Ibid.
26. Berry and Siegel, "Rhizomes, Newness, and the Condition of Our Postmodernity: Editorial and a Dialogue."
27. Barth, *The Literature of Exhaustion and the Literature of Replenishment*, 10–11.
28. Hamilton, "The Romanticism of Contemporary Ideology," 304.

259

29 Federman, "Imagination as Plagiarism [An Unfinished Paper...]," 572.
30 Ibid., 569–70.
31 Pope, *Creativity*, 235.
32 Ibid., 70.
33 See, for example, Hayles, *Chaos and Order*; *The Cosmic Web*; Livingston, *Between Science and Literature*; Paulson, *The Noise of Culture*; Porush, *The Soft Machine*.
34 González Echevarría, *Myth and Archive: A Theory of Latin American Narrative*, 110–25.
35 Brown, *Test Tube Envy: Science and Power in Argentine Narrative*, 28–54.
36 Ibid., 55–83.
37 Ibid., 74.
38 Nouzeilles, *Ficciones somáticas. Naturalismo, nacionalismo y políticas médicas del cuerpo (Argentina 1880–1910)*, 21–22.
39 Haywood Ferreira, *The Emergence of Latin American Science Fiction*, 36.
40 Published under the pseudonym Víctor Gálvez.
41 Terán, *Vida intelectual en el Buenos Aires de fin-de-siglo (1880–1910): Derivas de la cultura científica*, 20.
42 Sarlo, *La imaginación técnica: Sueños modernos de la cultura argentina*, 38.
43 Ibid., 57.
44 Ibid.
45 Brown, *Test Tube Envy*, 26.
46 Hayles, *The Cosmic Web*, 15–23, 27.
47 Brown, *Test Tube Envy*, 219–20.
48 Villalonga, "Creo en las novelas y en sus posibilidades de metamorfosis permanentes" [interview with Marcelo Cohen].
49 Piglia, *Crítica y ficción*, 14.
50 See, for example: Brown, *Test Tube Envy*, 160–88; Ortiz, *Cortázar el mago*; Venegas, "El 'Principio de Incertidumbre' de Heisenberg y la narración intersticial de 'Axolotl' de Julio Cortázar."
51 These references include a mention of Morelli reading Heisenberg in Chapter 98 of *Rayuela* (559–60), a short description of the universe as explained by quantum mechanics in Chapter 71 of the same novel – in which "todo vibra y tiembla" (everything vibrates and trembles, 482) – and a brief comment in "Teoría del túnel" listing "la indeterminación en las ciencias físicas" (indeterminacy in the physical sciences, 107) as part of the Surrealist movement, alongside Cubism, Futurism, and Freudianism and other influences.
52 Brown, *Test Tube Envy*, 113–14.
53 Wiener, *The Human Use of Human Beings: Cybernetics and Society*, 36.
54 Hayles, *The Cosmic Web*, 17.
55 See Cohen, "El reencantamiento del mundo", discussed further in the Conclusion.
56 Black, "Newtonian Mechanics and the Romantic Rebellion: Introduction," 137.
57 Ibid.
58 Ibid., 138.
59 Stoicheff, "The Chaos of Metafiction," 85.
60 Bohm, *On Creativity*, 10.
61 Jantsch, *The Self-Organizing Universe*, 286.
62 Plant, "The Virtual Complexity of Culture," 213.
63 Garrett and VanWieren, "A Conversation with Andrew Brown," 159–60.
64 Ibid.

1 | THE SCIENCE OF LITERARY EVOLUTION: BETWEEN ROMANTICISM AND FORMALISM

1. Frye, *Anatomy of Criticism: Four Essays*, 132.
2. Martínez, "Lo que repito tres veces."
3. Erlich, *Russian Formalism*, 226.
4. Martínez, *La mujer del maestro*, 50–51.
5. Ibid., 126.
6. Ibid., 50.
7. Ibid., 120.
8. Ibid., 138.
9. Ibid., 92.
10. Ibid., 155.
11. Ibid., 123.
12. Barth, *The Literature of Exhaustion and the Literature of Replenishment*, 8.
13. Byron, "Manfred," 63 (Act I, scene ii, ll. 40–41).
14. Ibid. (Act I, scene ii, ll. 41, 43–45).
15. Martínez, *La mujer del maestro*, 121–22.
16. Ibid., 121.
17. Martínez, *Borges y la matemática*, 162.
18. Ibid., 164–65.
19. Aira, "La nueva escritura."
20. Martínez, "La literatura argentina y un chiste de Aira."
21. Martínez, *Borges y la matemática*, 166.
22. Ibid., 165.
23. Martínez, "Lo que repito tres veces."
24. Martínez, "Consideraciones de un ex político."
25. Martínez, "Eterna Cadencia, 2009."
26. Ibid.
27. Wellek, "Russian Formalism," 182.
28. Frye, *Anatomy of Criticism: Four Essays*, 97 (my emphasis).
29. Martínez, "Un plan a futuro."
30. Serra, "La fórmula de Guillermo Martínez" [interview].
31. See, for example, Tynyanov, "On Literary Evolution."
32. Frye, *Anatomy of Criticism: Four Essays*, 132.
33. Tynyanov, *Dostoevskij and Gogol*, cit. Eichenbaum, "The Theory of the Formal Method," 31.
34. Frye, *Anatomy of Criticism: Four Essays*, 344.
35. Shklovsky, "The Resurrection of the Word," 46.
36. Piglia, *Respiración artificial*, 191.
37. Piglia, *Crítica y ficción*, 99.
38. Massman, "La ficción acosada por la realidad: Narrar la historia en *Respiración artificial* de Ricardo Piglia," 98.
39. Piglia, *Respiración artificial*, 209.
40. Antonelli, "La figuración de la historia nacional en la novela realista: Del árbol genealógico al archivo," 11–12.
41. Gnutzmann, "La mirada histórica de Piglia en *Respiración artificial*," 271.
42. Avelar, "Como respiran los ausentes," 419.
43. Ibid., 420.
44. Ibid., 423.
45. Ibid., 424.
46. Colás, *Postmodernity in Latin America*, 130–31.
47. Piglia, *Respiración artificial*, 83.
48. Ibid., 84.
49. Ibid.
50. Ibid., 32.
51. Ibid., 77.
52. Ibid., 31.
53. Ibid., 209 (my emphasis).
54. Ibid., 184.
55. Ibid., 18.

56 Ibid., 153.
57 Shklovsky, "Art as Technique," 21.
58 See, for example, Cittadini, "Historia y ficción en *Respiración artificial*," 42.
59 See, for example, Piglia, *Crítica y ficción*, 71–76; 191–243.
60 Ibid., 195.
61 Ibid. What interests Piglia most about Tynyanov's approaches is his revision of the earlier stages of Formalist thinking. According to Formalism's first hypotheses, it is an internal process of automatization, parody, and renovation that brings about a change in literary form, which is then subjected to the same process, producing a constant cycle of stagnation and innovation. Tynyanov revises this model by introducing the idea of function: in this way, literature becomes something more than the sum of its forms and processes. The change in function of certain literary forms cannot wholly be explained by the operation of an unmotivated, internal process but must be understood in the context of the relationship between literary evolution and social change (ibid., 73).
62 Viereck, "De la tradición a las formas de la experiencia: Entrevista a Ricardo Piglia," 130; original emphasis.
63 Piglia, *Respiración artificial*, 129.
64 Ibid., 130.
65 Renzi argues that Borges "exaspera y lleva al límite, clausura por medio de la parodia la línea de la erudición cosmopolita y fraudulenta que define y domina gran parte de la literatura argentina del XIX" (exacerbates and takes to the limit, brings to a close by means of parody, that line of cosmopolitan and fraudulent erudition that defines and dominates a large proportion of Argentine literature in the nineteenth century). He also, according to Renzi, refunctions another, entirely different, literary inheritance from the nineteenth century – the gauchesque – by appropriating "las flexiones, los ritmos, el léxico de la lengua oral" (the inflections, rhythms, and lexicon of oral language) in the composition of stories such as "Hombre de la esquina rosada" (ibid., 129).
66 Piglia, *La ciudad ausente*, 160.
67 Echavarren, "La literariedad: *Respiración artificial*, de Ricardo Piglia," 1004.
68 Ibid., 997–98.
69 Ibid., 999, 1001.
70 Ibid., 997.
71 Piglia, *Respiración artificial*, 19.
72 Shklovsky, *Theory of Prose*, 190.
73 Berg, *Poéticas en suspenso*, 59.
74 Morello-Frosch, "The Opulent *Facundo*: Sarmiento and Modern Argentine Fiction," 347.
75 Piglia, *Respiración artificial*, 83.
76 Ibid., 199.
77 Ibid., 18–19.
78 Piglia, *Crítica y ficción*, 98–99.
79 See Shklovsky, *Theory of Prose*, 190.
80 Piglia, *Crítica y ficción*, 98.
81 Shklovsky, "The Resurrection of the Word," 46.
82 Piglia, *Crítica y ficción*, 43.
83 Piglia, *Tres propuestas para el próximo milenio (y cinco dificultades)*, 22.
84 Piglia, *Respiración artificial*, 46.
85 Ibid., 53.
86 Serres and Latour, *Conversations on Science, Culture, and Time*, 60.
87 Ibid., 57.
88 Serres, *The Birth of Physics*, 162.
89 Ibid., 163.
90 Serres and Latour, *Conversations on Science, Culture, and Time*, 57.

91. Piglia, *Respiración artificial*, 46.
92. Serres, *The Birth of Physics*, 162.
93. Serres and Latour, *Conversations on Science, Culture, and Time*, 58.
94. Serres, *The Birth of Physics*, 162.
95. Piglia, *Respiración artificial*, 60.
96. Ibid., 64.
97. Serres, *The Birth of Physics*, 164.
98. Piglia, *Respiración artificial*, 65.
99. Connor, "Topologies: Michel Serres and the Shapes of Thought."
100. Piglia, *Respiración artificial*, 51.
101. Connor, "Topologies: Michel Serres and the Shapes of Thought."
102. Piglia, *Respiración artificial*, 69.
103. Tynyanov, "On Literary Evolution," 75.
104. Piglia, *Crítica y ficción*, 236–37.
105. Piglia, *Respiración artificial*, 30.
106. Ibid., 109.
107. Ibid., 160.
108. Piglia, "Rodolfo Walsh y el lugar de la verdad," 15.
109. Piglia, "Hoy es imposible en la Argentina hacer literatura desvinculada de la política. Reportaje de Ricardo Piglia a Rodolfo Walsh (marzo de 1970)," 62.
110. Ibid., 69.
111. Demaría, "Rodolfo Walsh, Ricardo Piglia, la tranquera de Macedonio y el difícil oficio de escribir," 138–40.
112. Piglia, *Crítica y ficción*, 130.
113. Ibid., 39.
114. Kellner, "Ernst Bloch, Utopia, and Ideology Critique," 82.
115. Bloch, *The Principle of Hope*, I, 154–55.
116. Ibid., I, 144.
117. Bronner, "Utopian Projections: In Memory of Ernst Bloch," 168.

2 | ALLEGORIES OF READING IN AN AGE OF IMMANENCE AND UNCERTAINTY

1. Nietzsche, *The Will to Power*, 272 (section 493).
2. Martínez, "Teoremas asesinos."
3. Martínez, *Crímenes imperceptibles*, 65–66.
4. Ibid., 42.
5. Ibid., 69.
6. Nietzsche, *The Gay Science*, 84.
7. Martínez, *Acerca de Roderer*, 80.
8. Martínez, *La muerte lenta de Luciana B.*, 149.
9. Ibid., 168.
10. Martínez, *Crímenes imperceptibles*, 116.
11. Moledo, "Crimen, cálculo y castigo" [interview with Guillermo Martínez].
12. Martínez, *La fórmula de la inmortalidad*, 213.
13. Wittgenstein, *Philosophical Investigations*, 74–77 (sections 185–90).
14. Ibid., 81 (section 201).
15. Cid, "Hacia una nueva novela policial argentina: Guillermo Martínez y Pablo De Santis."
16. James, *The Figure in the Carpet*, 33.
17. Ibid., 23.
18. Martínez, *Crímenes imperceptibles*, 230.
19. Martínez, *Borges y la matemática*, 92; see also Piglia, "Tesis sobre el cuento," 92–94.
20. Shklovsky, "The Mystery Novel: Dickens's Little Dorrit," 220–21.
21. Martínez, *Borges y la matemática*, 92.
22. See Borges's theorizations on the subject, published in his prologue to María Esther Vázquez, *Los nombres de la muerte*, cited in ibid., 61–62.

23. Martínez, *Crímenes imperceptibles*, 7.
24. Ibid., 32.
25. Ibid., 74.
26. Ibid., 134.
27. Borges, Prologue to María Esther Vázquez, *Los nombres de la muerte*, cit. Martínez, *Borges y la matemática*, 61.
28. Moscardi, "El mito del crimen perfecto."
29. Pynchon, *The Crying of Lot 49*, 125.
30. Cohen, *¡Realmente fantástico! y otros ensayos*, 111, 152.
31. Ibid., 110–11.
32. Pynchon, *Gravity's Rainbow*, 434; cit. Cohen, *¡Realmente fantástico! y otros ensayos*, 110.
33. Cohen, *El testamento de O'Jaral*, 93.
34. Ibid., 275.
35. Deleuze and Guattari, *A Thousand Plateaus*, 127.
36. Ibid., 126.
37. Cohen, *El testamento de O'Jaral*, 74.
38. Ibid., 76.
39. Ibid., 110.
40. Ibid., 95–96.
41. Ibid., 43.
42. Ibid., 210.
43. Ibid., 58.
44. Ibid., 18–19.
45. Ibid., 19.
46. Ibid., 157.
47. Ibid., 159.
48. Ibid., 156.
49. Ibid., 82.
50. Ibid., 160.
51. Black, "Probing a Post-Romantic Paleontology," 235.
52. Ibid., 248.
53. Alsen, *Romantic Postmodernism in American Fiction*, 174.
54. Ibid., 181.
55. Pynchon, *Gravity's Rainbow*, 590.
56. Cohen, *El testamento de O'Jaral*, 219.
57. Ibid., 275.
58. Ibid., 327.
59. Ibid., 162.
60. Ibid., 80.
61. Ibid., 26.
62. Ibid., 37.
63. Ibid., 268.
64. Deleuze and Guattari, *A Thousand Plateaus*, 5.
65. Piglia, *Crítica y ficción*, 14.
66. Piglia, *La ciudad ausente*, 126.
67. Ibid., 147.
68. Ibid., 126.
69. Ibid., 127.
70. Ibid., 132.
71. Ibid., 133.
72. Ibid., 132.
73. Piglia, *El último lector*, 16.
74. Stewart, *On Longing*, 172.
75. Ibid., 65.
76. Ibid., xi–xii.
77. Piglia, *El último lector*, 12.
78. Ibid., 13.
79. Ibid., 17.
80. Ibid., 13.
81. Borges, "El Aleph," 171.
82. Piglia, *El último lector*, 17.
83. Piglia, "Encuentro en Saint-Nazaire," 96.
84. Ibid., 98–99.
85. Ibid., 101.
86. Ibid., 87.
87. Ibid., 95–96.
88. Ibid., 95.
89. Ibid.
90. Ibid.

91 Prigogine, *The End of Certainty*, 189.
92 Ibid., 187–88.
93 Piglia, "Encuentro en Saint-Nazaire," 109.
94 Ibid., 137.
95 Ibid., 120–21.
96 Ibid., 143.
97 Ryle, The *Concept of Mind*, 18.
98 The passage to which Stevensen appears to make oblique reference is one in which Ryle describes the "official doctrine" that he will go on to challenge: "A person therefore lives through two collateral histories, one consisting of what happens in and to his body, the other consisting of what happens in and to his mind. The first is public, the second private." Ibid., 11.
99 Ibid., 15–16.
100 Ibid., 11–12.
101 Ibid., 172.
102 Ibid., 61.
103 Ibid.
104 Sontag, *Against Interpretation and Other Essays*, 5, 6–7.
105 Ibid., 14.
106 Piglia, "En otro país," 48.
107 Ibid., 49.
108 Ibid., 46.
109 See Piglia, *La ciudad ausente*, 99–100.
110 Piglia, "En otro país," 52.
111 Piglia, "Encuentro en Saint-Nazaire," 124.
112 Piglia, "En otro país," 41.
113 Piglia, "El fluir de la vida," 67–68.
114 Piglia, "En otro país," 30.
115 Ibid., 41.
116 Piglia, "El último cuento de Borges," 66.
117 Deleuze, "Literature and Life," 227; Deleuze and Guattari, *What Is Philosophy?*, 170–71.
118 Piglia, "El último cuento de Borges," 63.
119 Ibid., 64.
120 Ibid.
121 Ibid., 66.
122 Piglia, *La ciudad ausente*, 63.
123 Piglia, "En otro país," 54.
124 Piglia, *La ciudad ausente*, 154.
125 Piglia, *El último lector*, 153.
126 Piglia, "En otro país," 43.
127 Ibid., 44.
128 Piglia, "El fluir de la vida," 66.
129 Piglia, *El último lector*, 174.
130 Colebrook, *Gilles Deleuze*, 99.

3 | MATHEMATICS AND CREATIVITY

1 Schlegel, *Dialogue on Poetry and Literary Aphorisms*, 82.
2 Nietzsche, *Thus Spake Zarathustra*, 56.
3 Mann, *Doctor Faustus*, 459.
4 Martínez, "La irresistible elegancia de un teorema."
5 Martínez, *La fórmula de la inmortalidad*, 118.
6 Martínez, *Borges y la matemática*, 161–62.
7 Ibid., 161.
8 Martínez, *Crímenes imperceptibles*, 66.
9 Sokal and Bricmont, *Intellectual Impostures*, 130.
10 Tasić, *Una lectura matemática del pensamiento posmoderno*.
11 *Reductio ad absurdum* is a method of proof which assumes the negation of a proposition to be true and then shows that it leads to an absurdity, thereby demonstrating that it is false.
12 Martínez, *Acerca de Roderer*, 35.

13 Ibid., 78.
14 Ibid., 80–81.
15 Striedter, *Literary Structure, Evolution, and Value*, 64; Viktor Shklovsky, for example, considers that renewal often takes place through the recollection of a previously broken line, which lies dormant but then resurges to a dominant position. See Shklovsky, *Theory of Prose*, 189–90, and the more extensive discussion of this idea in relation to *Respiración artificial* in Chapter 1.
16 Martínez, *La fórmula de la inmortalidad*, 122–23.
17 Ibid., 116.
18 Nietzsche, *The Will to Power*, 279 (section 516).
19 Ibid., 280 (section 516).
20 Ibid., 3 (section 4).
21 Martínez, *Acerca de Roderer*, 92.
22 Nietzsche, *Thus Spake Zarathustra*, 22.
23 Ibid.
24 Nietzsche, *The Will to Power*, 23 (section 36).
25 Tomasi, "Nihilism and Creativity in the Philosophy of Nietzsche," 155.
26 Clemens, *The Romanticism of Contemporary Theory*, 83.
27 Kenevan, "Nietzsche and the Creative Consciousness," 388.
28 Nietzsche, *Twilight of the Idols*, 49.
29 Similarities between the two texts have been traced by several critics. See, for example, Sarmiento, "*Acerca de Roderer* de Guillermo Martínez: El *mysterium iniquitatis* en el fin de siglo literario," and for a more extended treatment of the novel's intertexts, Dapía, "Transgresiones, subjetividad y postmodernismo la búsqueda de una lógica no binaria en *Acerca de Roderer* de Guillermo Martínez."
30 Martínez, *Borges y la matemática*, 165.
31 Mann, *The Genesis of a Novel*, 130.
32 Ibid., 26.
33 Ibid., 124; for more details of the collaboration between Adorno and Mann, see Schmidt, "Mephistopheles in Hollywood: Adorno, Mann, and Schoenberg."
34 For a comparative analysis of the work of Mann and Mahler, see Michael Mann, "The Musical Symbolism in Thomas Mann's Novel *Doctor Faustus*."
35 Mann, *The Genesis of a Novel*, 55.
36 Ibid., 183.
37 Bergsten, *Thomas Mann's* Doctor Faustus, 173.
38 Mann, *Doctor Faustus*, 459.
39 Schmidt, "Mephistopheles in Hollywood: Adorno, Mann, and Schoenberg," 153.
40 Martínez, *Borges y la matemática*, 164.
41 Martínez, *Acerca de Roderer*, 57–58.
42 Mann, *Doctor Faustus*, 144.
43 Hutcheon, *A Theory of Parody*, 37.
44 Martínez, *Acerca de Roderer*, 56.
45 Hutcheon, *A Theory of Parody*, 38.
46 Bouveresse, *Prodigios y vértigos de la analogía*, 76.
47 Tasić, *Mathematics and the Roots of Postmodern Thought*, 4.
48 Ibid., 97.
49 Ibid., 58–59.
50 Ibid., 98.
51 Ibid., 85.
52 Cavaillès, "On Logic and the Theory of Science," 372, 409.
53 See Tasić, *Mathematics and the Roots of Postmodern Thought*, 90–97. Tasić is at pains to point out that there is a historical link between Cavaillès and Foucault via the historian of science, Georges Canguilhem, who

was a great admirer of the first and an acknowledged inspiration for the second.
54 Foucault, *The Order of Things*, 364; cit. Tasić, *Mathematics and the Roots of Postmodern Thought*, 94.
55 Tasić, *Mathematics and the Roots of Postmodern Thought*, 5–6.
56 Erlich, *Russian Formalism*, 221.
57 Tasić, *Mathematics and the Roots of Postmodern Thought*, 6.
58 Sokal and Bricmont, *Intellectual Impostures*, 177.
59 Martínez, *Borges y la matemática*, 166.
60 Hutcheon, *A Theory of Parody*, 20.
61 Stevens, "An Ordinary Evening in New Haven," 466.
62 Cohen, "Un hombre amable," 191.
63 du Sautoy, *The Music of the Primes: Why an Unsolved Problem in Mathematics Matters*, 5.
64 Hardy, *A Mathematician's Apology*, 130.
65 To give an example, aliens first communicate with the Earth using prime numbers in Carl Sagan's novel *Contact* (1985).
66 For a lively account of the remarkable encounter between the Indian clerk Ramanujan and the two Cambridge mathematicians Hardy and Littlewood, see du Sautoy, *The Music of the Primes: Why an Unsolved Problem in Mathematics Matters*, 132–47.
67 Cohen, "Un hombre amable," 148.
68 Ibid.
69 Ibid., 183.
70 Ibid., 243.
71 Ibid., 204.
72 Changeux and Connes, *Conversations on Mind, Matter, and Mathematics*, 31.
73 Cohen, "Un hombre amable," 204.
74 Ibid., 289.
75 Ibid., 149.
76 Ibid., 290.
77 Ibid., 149.
78 Cohen, *¡Realmente fantástico! y otros ensayos*, 148.
79 Cohen, "Un hombre amable," 305.
80 Schrödinger, *What Is Life?*, 137.
81 See, for example, Hayles, *The Cosmic Web*, 19.
82 Cohen, *Buda*, 73.
83 Schrödinger writes: "I myself also form part of this real material world around me." *What Is Life?*, 128.
84 Cohen, "Un hombre amable," 259.
85 Brochoud, "El hombre amable" [interview with Marcelo Cohen].
86 Stevens, *Adagia*.
87 LaGuardia, *Advance on Chaos*, 148.
88 Doggett, *Stevens' Poetry of Thought*, 33.
89 Stevens, "An Ordinary Evening in New Haven," 473.
90 Stevens, "July Mountain," 114–15.
91 Schlegel, *Friedrich Schlegel's Lucinde and the Fragments*, 175.
92 Stevens, "The Auroras of Autumn," 411.
93 Cohen, "Un hombre amable," 203.
94 Schlegel, *Friedrich Schlegel's Lucinde and the Fragments*, 268.
95 Ibid., 247.
96 Cohen, "Un hombre amable," 232.
97 Ibid., 306.
98 Ibid., 237.
99 Schlegel, *Kritische Ausgabe*, 18: 82; The English translation given here is cited from Behler, "The Theory of Irony in German Romanticism," 63.
100 Schlegel, *Friedrich Schlegel's Lucinde and the Fragments*, 176.
101 Ibid., 268.

102   Whiting, *The Never-Resting Mind*, 10–11.
103   Cohen, "Un hombre amable," 291.
104   Ibid., 216.
105   Schlegel, *Friedrich Schlegel's Lucinde and the Fragments*, 148.
106   Hegel, *Aesthetics*, 1: 66.
107   Furst, *Fictions of Romantic Irony in European Narrative, 1760–1857*, 301.
108   See, for example: Webster, "Establishing the 'Truth' of the Matter: Confessional Reflexivity as Introspection and Avowal"; Lynch, "Against Reflexivity as an Academic Virtue and Source of Privileged Knowledge"; Latour, "The Politics of Explanation: An Alternative."
109   Latour, "The Politics of Explanation: An Alternative," 173.
110   Schlegel, *Friedrich Schlegel's Lucinde and the Fragments*, 167.
111   Stevens, "Adagia," 163.
112   Cohen, "Un hombre amable," 228–29.
113   Ibid., 257–58.
114   Saavedra, "Los espacios imaginarios del narrador" [interview with Marcelo Cohen], 83.
115   Cohen, "Un hombre amable," 256–57.
116   Ibid., 259.
117   Ibid., 297.
118   Whiting, *The Never-Resting Mind*, 11. The English translation is cited from Eichner, *Friedrich Schlegel*, 71; the original quotation is from Schlegel, *Kritische Ausgabe*, 2: 131.
119   Brochoud, "*El hombre amable*" [interview with Marcelo Cohen].
120   Cohen, "Un hombre amable," 178.
121   Brochoud, "*El hombre amable*" [interview with Marcelo Cohen].
122   LaGuardia, *Advance on Chaos*, 11.
123   Stevens, "On the Road Home," 204.
124   James, *Pragmatism*, 38–39.
125   Schlegel, *Friedrich Schlegel's Lucinde and the Fragments*, 175.
126   Cohen, "Un hombre amable," 296.
127   Ibid., 297.
128   Borges, "El Zahir," 115.
129   Sifrim, "Literatura a la hora de la siesta" [interview with Marcelo Cohen].
130   Deleuze and Parnet, *Dialogues II*, 39.
131   Plant, "The Virtual Complexity of Culture," 214.
132   Cohen, "Un hombre amable," 186.
133   Ibid., 187–88.
134   Ibid., 189.
135   Ibid.
136   Goldstein, "Emergence as a Construct," 49.
137   Cohen, "Un hombre amable," 190.
138   Stevens, "Landscape with Boat," 242.
139   Stevens, "On the Road Home," 204.
140   Cohen, *¡Realmente fantástico! y otros ensayos*, 147.
141   See Sokal and Bricmont, *Intellectual Impostures*, and the Introduction to this book.
142   Cohen, *¡Realmente fantástico! y otros ensayos*, 144.
143   Schlegel, *Dialogue on Poetry and Literary Aphorisms*, 89, 86.
144   Cohen, *Un hombre amable*, 211.
145   "Gurubel" is one of Cohen's many neologisms; it appears to refer to a kind of song to which it is usual to dance.
146   Cohen, "Un hombre amable," 211.
147   Ibid.
148   Ibid.
149   Ibid., 290.
150   Garber, "Sterne: Arabesques and Fictionality," 38.

151 Sifrim, "Literatura a la hora de la siesta" [interview with Marcelo Cohen].

152 The correct title of Stevens' poem (published in *Opus Posthumous*) is actually "A Mythology Reflects its Region." However, Cohen's transposition does not betray the sense of the poem, which explores the close interaction between creating self, religion, and physical environment.

153 Saavedra, "Los espacios imaginarios del narrador" [interview with Marcelo Cohen], 87.

154 "El rock me acompaña desde siempre" [interview with Marcelo Cohen]. The interview was conducted for Babasónicos, an Argentine rock band for whom Cohen has written lyrics and a short fictional biography, and was originally published on www.babasonicos.com.

4 | MACHINES, METAPHORS AND MULTIPLICITY: CREATIVITY BEYOND THE INDIVIDUAL

1 Porush, *The Soft Machine*, 19.

2 See, for example, Stoicheff, "The Chaos of Metafiction"; Paulson, "Literature, Complexity, Interdisciplinarity."

3 Deleuze and Guattari, *Anti-Oedipus: Capitalism and Schizophrenia*, 45.

4 Cohen, *¡Realmente fantástico! y otros ensayos*, 144.

5 Deleuze and Guattari, *A Thousand Plateaus*, 4.

6 Piglia, *La ciudad ausente*, 156.

7 Brown, *Cyborgs in Latin America*, 29, 31.

8 The term "strange loop" was suggested by Douglas Hofstadter to describe a movement up or down through hierarchies which paradoxically leads back to the beginning. See *Gödel, Escher, Bach: An Eternal Golden Braid*; *I Am a Strange Loop*.

9 See Madrazo, "Entrevista a Ricardo Piglia," 104.

10 Piglia, *La ciudad ausente*, 147.

11 Ibid.

12 Alí, "La pasión escrituraria de Ricardo Piglia. *La ciudad ausente*: De la novela a la ópera," 4.

13 See Lacan's Seminar XIX, Class 6. The text is not commercially published, although a translation was carried out for the Escuela Freudiana de Buenos Aires, and the relevant extracts are quoted in Martínez and Piñeiro, *Gödel (para todos)*, 121–23.

14 Ibid., 123.

15 Piglia, "La loca y el relato del crimen," 129.

16 Piglia, *La ciudad ausente*, 86.

17 Ibid., 106.

18 Ibid., 97.

19 Piglia argues that "ciertas corrientes actuales de la crítica buscan en la parodia, en la intertextualidad, justamente un desvío para desocializar la literatura, verla como un simple juego de textos que se autorrepresentan y se vinculan especularmente unos a otros. Sin embargo esa relación entre los textos que en apariencia es el punto máximo de autonomía de la literatura está determinada de un modo directo y específico por las relaciones sociales" (certain current trends in criticism find in parody, in intertextuality, a kind of deflection that desocializes literature, that sees it as a simple game of texts that point only to themselves, forging specular relationships with each other. However, this relationship between texts that apparently

represents literature's maximum point of autonomy is determined, in a direct and specific manner, by social relations, *Crítica y ficción*, 75).

20 Hayles, *How We Became Posthuman*, 147.
21 Ibid., 155–56.
22 Livingston, *Between Science and Literature*, 70.
23 Jantsch, *The Self-Organizing Universe*, 10, 33.
24 Piglia, *La ciudad ausente*, 125, 103.
25 Ibid., 42.
26 Piglia, *El último lector*, 165.
27 Jameson, *The Prison-House of Language: A Critical Account of Structuralism and Russian Formalism*, 89.
28 Todorov, *The Poetics of Prose*, 66–70. This account of the relationship between narrative and characters in *The Arabian Nights* is given by Jameson: "in a series of striking articles Todorov shows that the very subject of such story-collections as the *Thousand and One Nights* must be seen as the act of storytelling itself, that the only constant of the psychology of the characters (or of the psychological presuppositions on which the work is founded) lies in the obsession with telling and listening to stories: what defines a character as a compositional unit is the fact of having a story to tell, and from the point of view of their ultimate destinies, 'narration equals life: the absence of narration, death'" (*The Prison-House of Language: A Critical Account of Structuralism and Russian Formalism*, 199).
29 Piglia, *El último lector*, 169–70.
30 Piglia, *Blanco nocturno*, 239, 242.
31 See Propp, *Morphology of the Folktale*.
32 Piglia, *Crítica y ficción*, 15.
33 Calvino, "Cybernetics and Ghosts," 3–4.
34 Piglia, *Blanco nocturno*, 240.
35 Piglia, *La ciudad ausente*, 140.
36 Ibid., 41–42.
37 Ibid., 42.
38 Ibid., 71.
39 Calvino, *The Castle of Crossed Destinies*, 126.
40 Calvino, "Cybernetics and Ghosts," 8.
41 Ibid., 7.
42 Piglia, *La ciudad ausente*, 97–98; see "Encuentro en Saint-Nazaire," 81–82.
43 Piglia, *La ciudad ausente*, 100.
44 Ibid., 142.
45 Foucault, "Nietzsche, Genealogy, History," 81.
46 Tynyanov, "The Literary Fact," 31, 38 (original emphasis).
47 Porush, *The Soft Machine*, 40.
48 Berg, *Poéticas en suspenso*, 33.
49 Piglia, *El último lector*, 28.
50 Coleridge, *Biographia Literaria*, I: 167–68.
51 Young, *Conjectures on Original Composition*, 12.
52 Piglia, *Blanco nocturno*, 246, original emphasis.
53 Piglia, *La ciudad ausente*, 28.
54 Piglia, *Blanco nocturno*, 265.
55 Martínez and Piñeiro, *Gödel (para todos)*, 33.
56 See Penrose, *The Emperor's New Mind*, 416–18; *Shadows of the Mind*, chapters 1–3.
57 Hofstadter, *Gödel, Escher, Bach: An Eternal Golden Braid*, 458.
58 Calvino, "Cybernetics and Ghosts," 11.
59 Piglia, *Blanco nocturno*, 241.
60 Ibid.

61. Deleuze and Parnet, *Dialogues II*, 77.
62. Colebrook, *Gilles Deleuze*, 57.
63. Foucault, "What is an Author?," 119.
64. Ibid., 119, 118.
65. Ibid., 102.
66. Avelar, *The Untimely Present*, 134.
67. Piglia, *La ciudad ausente*, 154.
68. Stewart, *On Longing*, 172.
69. Abrams, "How to Do Things with Texts," 436.
70. Tynyanov, *Archaisty*, cit. Steiner, "Russian Formalism," 21.
71. Eichenbaum, "The Theory of the Formal Method," 33.
72. Erlich, *Russian Formalism*, 221.
73. Brown, *Cyborgs in Latin America*, 32.
74. Porush, *The Soft Machine*, 15.
75. Serres, *Genesis*, 132.
76. Pynchon, "Introduction," 14.
77. Zencey, "Entropy as Root Metaphor," 193.
78. Bruni, "Thermodynamics," 227.
79. Jameson, *The Seeds of Time*, 15.
80. Ibid., 17.
81. Ibid., 20.
82. Pynchon, "Introduction," 13.
83. Pynchon, "Entropy," 83.
84. Ibid., 98.
85. Ibid., 88.
86. Ballard, *The Atrocity Exhibition*, 122.
87. Cohen, "Lydia en el canal," 220.
88. Ballard, *La exhibición de atrocidades*.
89. Ballard, *The Atrocity Exhibition*, 57.
90. Ibid., 81.
91. Cohen, "Lydia en el canal," 220.
92. Ibid., 227–28.
93. Pynchon, "Entropy," 88, 92.
94. Cohen, "Lydia en el canal," 252.
95. Ibid.
96. Ballard, *The Atrocity Exhibition*, 46.
97. Ibid.
98. Ibid.
99. Deleuze and Guattari, *A Thousand Plateaus*, 38.
100. Ibid., 88.
101. Cohen, *Donde yo no estaba*, 382.
102. Deleuze and Guattari, *A Thousand Plateaus*, 93.
103. Cohen, "Lydia en el canal," 238.
104. Colebrook, *Gilles Deleuze*, 129.
105. Cohen, "El fin de lo mismo," 132–33.
106. Ibid., 133.
107. Ibid., 125.
108. Ibid., 128.
109. Dalmaroni, "El fin de lo otro y la disolución del fantástico en un relato de Marcelo Cohen," 86.
110. Cohen, "El fin de lo mismo," 148.
111. Cohen, *¡Realmente fantástico! y otros ensayos*, 144.
112. Prigogine, *The End of Certainty*, 158.
113. Cohen, *¡Realmente fantástico! y otros ensayos*, 146.
114. Serres, *Genesis*, 91.
115. Cohen, *¡Realmente fantástico! y otros ensayos*, 146.
116. Cohen, "Unas palabras," 12.
117. Ibid.
118. Cohen, "Aspectos de la vida de Enzatti," 150.
119. Ibid., 151.
120. Ibid., 152.
121. Ibid., 157.
122. Ibid., 152.
123. Ibid., 153.
124. Ibid.
125. Ibid., 155.
126. Ibid., 169.
127. Ibid., 153.

128 Ibid., 155–56.
129 Ibid., 167.
130 Cohen, ¡Realmente fantástico! y otros ensayos, 151.
131 Sheldrake, The Presence of the Past, 108.
132 Cohen, ¡Realmente fantástico! y otros ensayos, 151.
133 Ibid., 152.
134 Cohen, "Aspectos de la vida de Enzatti," 170.
135 Ibid., 177.
136 Ibid., 164.
137 Cohen, ¡Realmente fantástico! y otros ensayos, 148.
138 Ibid., 152.
139 Deleuze and Parnet, Dialogues II, 34.
140 Cohen, "Volubilidad," 190.
141 Ibid., 182.
142 Ibid., 190.
143 Ibid., 193.
144 Ibid., 202.
145 Ibid., 193–94.
146 Ibid., 195.
147 Cohen, ¡Realmente fantástico! y otros ensayos, 148.
148 Cohen, "Volubilidad," 183.
149 Cohen, Donde yo no estaba, 314.
150 Ibid., 13.
151 Deleuze, "Literature and Life," 225.
152 Colebrook, Gilles Deleuze, 132–33.
153 Deleuze, "Literature and Life," 227.
154 Oeyen, "Imágenes de la barbarie en 'La ilusión monarca' de Marcelo Cohen," 266.
155 Ibid., 259, 265–66.
156 Ibid., 265–66.
157 Ibid., 266.
158 Cohen, "La ilusión monarca," 30.
159 Ibid., 31.
160 Ibid., 66.
161 Ibid., 31.
162 Ibid., 118.
163 Ibid., 63.
164 Serres, Genesis, 7.
165 Nietzsche, "On Truth and Lying in a Non-Moral Sense," 146.
166 Michelet, The Sea, 25.
167 Ibid., 24.
168 Ibid.
169 Ibid., 31.
170 Ibid., 36, 87.
171 Cohen, "La ilusión monarca," 113.
172 Ibid., 18.
173 Kaplan, Michelet's Poetic Vision, 53.
174 Serres, Hermes: Literature, Science, Philosophy, 30.
175 Ibid., 33.
176 Ibid.
177 Ibid., 31.
178 Cohen, "La ilusión monarca," 114.
179 Ibid., 42.
180 Serres, Hermes: Literature, Science, Philosophy, 56, 61, 58.
181 Ibid., 62.
182 Ibid., 57.
183 Cohen, "La ilusión monarca," 18.
184 Ibid., 42.
185 Nietzsche, The Will to Power, 550 (section 1067).
186 Ibid.
187 Nietzsche, The Birth of Tragedy and Other Writings, 17–18.
188 Ibid., 19.
189 Cohen, "La ilusión monarca," 109.
190 Nietzsche, The Birth of Tragedy and Other Writings, 80–81.
191 Cohen, "La ilusión monarca," 120.
192 Nietzsche, The Will to Power, 550 (section 1067).

193 Cohen, "La ilusión monarca," 78.
194 Ibid., 18, 17.
195 Cohen, ¡Realmente fantástico! y otros ensayos, 185.
196 Serres, Genesis, 109.
197 Ibid., 111.
198 Orr, "Adams, Henry Brooks," 17.
199 Tanner, Scenes of Nature, Signs of Men, 85–87.
200 Adams, The Education of Henry Adams, chapter 8.
201 Ibid., chapter 16.
202 Schweighauser, "The Desire for Unity and Its Failure: Reading Henry Adams through Michel Serres," 145.
203 Ibid., 143, 145; the citation is from Serres, Genesis, 25.
204 Harari and Bell, "Introduction: Journal à plusieurs voies," xxvii.
205 Heidegger, The Principle of Reason, 48.
206 Nietzsche, "On Truth and Lying in a Non-Moral Sense," 146.
207 Ibid., 150.
208 de Mul, Romantic Desire in (Post)modern Art and Philosophy, 53.
209 Nietzsche, "On Truth and Lying in a Non-Moral Sense," 151–52.
210 Cohen, ¡Realmente fantástico! y otros ensayos, 148.
211 Serres, Hermes: Literature, Science, Philosophy, 36.
212 Ibid., 37.
213 Ibid.
214 Ibid.
215 Ibid., 38.
216 Nietzsche, The Will to Power, 548 (section 1066).
217 Ibid., 419 (section 796).
218 Bracamonte, "Futuros potenciales en mundos contemporáneos. O James Ballard en la poética extraña de Marcelo Cohen," 209, 214.
219 Heffernan, "Ironic distance in Thomas Pynchon's 'Entropy'," 325.
220 Freese, From Apocalypse to Entropy and Beyond, 550.
221 Schaub, "'A Gentle Chill, An Ambiguity': The Crying of Lot 49," 51.
222 Pynchon, The Crying of Lot 49, 89.
223 Freese, From Apocalypse to Entropy and Beyond, 558.
224 Heffernan, "Ironic distance in Thomas Pynchon's 'Entropy'," 324.

CONCLUSION | LITERATURE AND SCIENCE, NEITHER ONE CULTURE NOR TWO

1 Freese, From Apocalypse to Entropy and Beyond, 405; also see Porush, "Prigogine, Chaos, and Contemporary Science Fiction."
2 Shiner, Deserted Cities of the Heart, 256, 126.
3 Deleuze and Guattari, What Is Philosophy?, 173.
4 Alazraki, Borges and the Kabbalah: And Other Essays on His Fiction and Poetry, 183.
5 Hayles, The Cosmic Web, 151–52.
6 Piglia, La ciudad ausente, 147.
7 Giardinelli, Equilibrio imposible, 8.
8 Brown, Test Tube Envy, 198–212.
9 Giardinelli, Equilibrio imposible, 119.
10 Plant, "The Virtual Complexity of Culture," 210.
11 De Man, Romanticism and Contemporary Criticism, 6.
12 Carroll, "The Science Wars in a Long View: Putting the Human in its Place," 30.
13 Colebrook, Gilles Deleuze, 128.
14 Braidotti, Metamorphoses, 226.
15 Ibid., 228–29.

16. Furst, "Romantic Irony and Narrative Stance," 301.
17. McMullin, "Is the Progress of Science Dialectical?," 215.
18. Ibid., 227.
19. Ibid., 220.
20. See, for example, Fuchs, "Dialectical Philosophy and Self-Organisation."
21. Deleuze and Guattari, *A Thousand Plateaus*, 20.
22. Cohen, *¡Realmente fantástico! y otros ensayos*, 151.
23. Colebrook, *Gilles Deleuze*, 94.
24. Cohen, "El reencantamiento del mundo."
25. Deleuze and Guattari, *Kafka*, 22.
26. Deleuze and Parnet, *Dialogues II*, 57.
27. Piglia, *Blanco nocturno*, 243.
28. Deleuze and Guattari, *What Is Philosophy?*, 175.
29. Tynyanov, "On Literary Evolution," 66.
30. Deleuze and Parnet, *Dialogues II*, 52.
31. Ibid., 29.
32. See, for example, ibid., 19–20, 27–30.
33. Curtis, "Bergson and Russian Formalism."
34. See, for example, Papanicolaou and Gunter, *Bergson and Modern Thought*; Capek, *Bergson and Modern Physics: A Reinterpretation and Re-Evaluation*; Gunter, *Bergson and the Evolution of Physics*.
35. Villani, *La guêpe et l'orchidée*, 130.
36. See, for example, Plotnitsky, "Chaosmologies"; Protevi, "Deleuze, Guattari, and Emergence"; Marks, *Deleuze and Science*.
37. Hayles, *The Cosmic Web*, 9–10.
38. Steiner, "Russian Formalism," 17.
39. Martínez, "El lector y sus criterios."
40. Costa, "Inolvidables veladas de la ficción [entrevista a Marcelo Cohen]."
41. Deleuze, "Literature and Life," 229.
42. Deleuze and Guattari, *Kafka*, 19.
43. Deleuze and Guattari, *What Is Philosophy?*, 176.
44. Cohen, *¡Realmente fantástico! y otros ensayos*, 131–32.
45. Deleuze and Parnet, *Dialogues II*, 32.
46. Ibid., 77.
47. Plant, "The Virtual Complexity of Culture," 203.
48. Ibid., 211, 212.
49. Ibid., 213–14.
50. Ibid., 214.
51. Serres, *Hermes V: Le Passage du Nord-ouest*, 18.
52. Serres and Latour, *Conversations on Science, Culture, and Time*, 122.
53. Ibid., 91.
54. Harari and Bell, "Introduction: Journal à plusieurs voies," xxix.
55. Calvino, *Six Memos for the Next Millennium*, 105.
56. Ibid., 112.
57. Cit. Erlich, *Russian Formalism*, 170.
58. Fuchs, "Dialectical Philosophy and Self-Organisation," 204.
59. Serres and Latour, *Conversations on Science, Culture, and Time*, 66.
60. Hayles, *The Cosmic Web*, 22.
61. Ibid., 23.
62. Lacoue-Labarthe and Nancy, *The Literary Absolute*, 83, 12.
63. Ibid., 16.
64. Ibid.

Index

A

Acerca de Roderer, 17, 73–74, 115–33, 148, 225, 228, 230
"Adagia," 145
Adams, Henry, 186
    The Education of Henry Adams, 217
Adorno, Theodor, 125, 266n33
Aira, César, 14, 35–36, 226–27
    El congreso de literatura, 14
    El juego de los mundos, 14
    Los misterios de Rosario, 14
Arabian Nights, The, 38, 171, 181, 270n28
"Aspectos de la vida de Enzatti," 197–202
Atrocity Exhibition, The, 188–91, 220
"Auroras of Autumn, The," 140
autopoiesis, 16, 21, 25, 162–63, 168–70, 240, 242, 244
Avelar, Idelber, 44–45, 181–82

B

Ballard, J. G., 1, 19, 20, 159–60, 162, 185–86, 192, 195–96, 223
    The Atrocity Exhibition, 188–91, 220
    Crash, 220
Barth, John, 9, 33
Baudrillard, Jean, 3, 5, 7
Bergson, Henri, 236, 243
"biblioteca de Babel, La," 225

Blanco nocturno, 16, 162, 164, 172–74, 178–79, 180, 234
Blaustein, Eduardo, 14
Bloch, Ernst, 65–66, 95, 113, 243
Bohm, David, 25, 138
Borges, Jorge Luis, 13, 16–19, 33, 51, 71, 80, 112, 177, 224–25, 227, 262n65
    "El Aleph," 101
    "La biblioteca de Babel," 225
    "El jardín de senderos que se bifurcan," 26
    "La lotería en Babilonia," 112–13, 225
    "La muerte y la brújula," 72–73, 76, 79
    "Las ruinas circulares," 150–51, 182
    "Tlön, Uqbar, Orbis Tertius," 9
    "El Zahir," 151
Bouveresse, Jacques, 7, 117, 129
Braidotti, Rosi, 229
Brecht, Bertold, 49, 63
Bricmont, Jean, 5, 7, 117–18, 132
Brouwer, L. E. J., 121, 130–31
Brown, J. Andrew, 11–14, 18, 26, 164, 183, 225–26, 238
Buddhism, 91, 138–39, 243
Burroughs, William, 19–20, 111, 193
Byron, George Gordon, 120
    Manfred, 33

C

Calvino, Ítalo, 19, 173, 175, 179, 242
Cambaceres, Eugenio, 11
Casa de Ottro, 15, 160, 191–92
Cavaillès, Jean, 130–31, 266–67n53
chance, 5, 17, 27, 67, 69, 71–75, 83, 95, 102–4, 108–9, 127, 175–76, 204, 212
Changeux, Pierre, 136
chaos
    chaos theory, 1, 4–6, 13, 15, 19–20, 22, 61–62, 117–18, 130, 162, 195, 216, 220–21, 224, 227, 237, 240, 243
    chaotic (or non-linear, or non-equilibrium) systems, 59–60, 82, 85, 89–90, 95, 104, 117, 153–54, 157, 188–89, 162, 195–96, 216–17, 225–26
    Romantic understanding of, 115–16, 139–42, 155, 157–58
ciudad ausente, La, 16, 52, 59, 67, 95–98, 109, 111–12, 162–71, 174–84, 225
Cohen, Marcelo, 1–2, 10, 14–15, 17–26, 69–70, 81–83, 161, 223–34, 236–44
    "Aspectos de la vida de Enzatti," 197–202
    Casa de Ottro, 15, 160, 191–92
    Donde yo no estaba, 15, 160, 192, 205, 239
    Un hombre amable, 115–16, 134–60
    "La ilusión monarca," 192, 207–19, 234
    El fin de lo mismo, 162–63, 185–221
    "El fin de lo mismo," 193–96
    "Lydia en el canal," 188–93
    realismo inseguro (or *incierto*) in, 15, 82, 162–63, 197, 201, 204–5, 218–19, 238
    El testamento de O'Jaral, 83–94
    "Volubilidad," 202–6

complexity, 1, 5–6, 15, 17, 19–20, 25–26, 62, 82, 85, 89–90, 115, 134, 152–59, 161–62, 169–70, 193–98, 213–14, 220, 223–24, 226, 228, 237–38, 240–41, 243–44. *See* emergence; *see also* self-organization
congreso de literatura, El, 14
connectionism, 26, 240–41
constructivism, 115, 126, 135–36
Cortázar, Julio, 17–18, 224, 227, 260n51
Crash, 220
Crímenes imperceptibles, 17, 69–81, 117–18, 145, 230
cruz diablo, La, 14
Crying of Lot 49, The, 94, 221
"cuento como sistema lógico, El," 79
cybernetics, 17, 19, 161, 169, 179, 183
    cybernetic fiction, 161, 164, 183

D

Daedalus, 29, 36
Darwin, Charles, 12, 18, 175, 228
de Man, Paul, 228, 239–40
Debray, Régis, 6–7, 16
Deleuze, Gilles, 5, 7, 16, 23–24, 84, 95, 111, 113, 117, 130, 151–52, 161, 163–64, 180, 184, 191–93, 205–6, 224, 227–29, 231–37, 239–40, 243
Derrida, Jacques, 3, 130
Deserted Cities of the Heart, 223–24
dialectical evolution of thought, 5, 17, 21, 22, 27, 29, 35, 39, 41, 59, 81, 116, 118, 120–23, 126, 129, 143, 183, 228, 230–31, 243
Dick, Philip K., 20, 111, 113, 162, 185
Dionysian art. *See under* Nietzsche
dissipative structures, 15, 162–63, 187, 195–96, 201–2, 220, 223
Doctor Faustus, 123–29
Donde yo no estaba, 15, 160, 192, 205, 239

E

Education of Henry Adams, The, 217
Eichenbaum, Boris, 62, 171, 183, 235
emergence, 15, 20, 22, 61, 90, 115, 144, 152–58, 161, 193–95, 213–14, 223, 231, 237, 240–41, 243. See complexity; *see also* self-organization.
"Encuentro en Saint-Nazaire," 101–10, 175–76
En el siglo XXX, 12
"En otro país," 108–11, 113
entropy, 1, 5, 19–20, 25, 60, 82, 89–90, 162–63, 184–87, 189, 193–96, 202, 213–14, 219–21, 223–24
"Entropy" (Pynchon), 185–87, 189–91, 193
Equilibrio imposible, 225–26
evolution
   in biology, 5 18–19, 20, 164, 174–77, 228–29
   of literature, 2, 13, 17, 20, 28, 37–45, 51–56, 62–63, 116, 120, 131–32, 164, 174–77, 183, 223, 227–28, 234–35, 238, 240, 262n61
Ezcurra, Eduardo, 12

F

Facundo, 11, 64–65
Faust, 29, 32–33, 36, 115; *see under* Mann
Fernández, Macedonio, 64–65, 164, 166–67, 170
field model (or concept), 13, 22, 237–38, 244
Figure in the Carpet, The, 77–78
fin de lo mismo, El, 162–63, 185–221
"fin de lo mismo, El" 193–96
Finnegans Wake, 97–98, 170
"fluir de la vida, El," 109–10
Formalism
   mathematical formalism, 97, 130–31, 166, 179
   Russian Formalism, 2, 21, 22–23, 27–29, 37–45, 48–59, 62–63, 65, 79, 81, 115–16, 118, 120, 133, 170–71, 173, 176–77, 182–83, 227, 231, 234–36, 238–39, 243, 262n61
Foucault, Michel, 3, 131, 266n53
   "What is an Author?", 181
fractals, 15, 19, 130
Frege, Gottlob, 130
Freud, Sigmund. *See* psychoanalysis
Frye, Northrop, 28, 38–41
genetic recombination, 16, 18–19, 174–76, 78

G

Giardinelli, Mempo: *Equilibrio imposible*, 225–26
Gödel, Kurt: theorems of incompleteness, 1, 6–7, 19, 69, 72, 95, 104, 117, 164, 168–69
Gorodischer, Angélica, 14
Gravity's Rainbow, 82, 91
Guattari, Félix. *See* Deleuze

H

Hardy, G. H.: *A Mathematician's Apology*, 135
Hayles, N. Katherine, 5, 10, 13, 22, 26, 169, 225, 237–38, 244
Hegel, Georg Wilhelm Friedrich, 34, 41, 61–62, 143–44, 175, 230–31
Hilbert, David, 130
Holmberg, Eduardo, 12, 227
hombre amable, Un, 115–16, 134–60
Hutcheon, Linda, 128–29, 133

I

"ilusión monarca, La," 192, 207–19, 234
incompleteness, theorems of. *See* Gödel
information theory, 161, 195, 221
intuitionism, 130–31
"isla, La," 95–98

J

James, Henry, 19
   The Lesson of the Master, 77
   The Figure in the Carpet, 77–78
James, William, 150
Jameson, Fredric, 24, 171, 186
Jantsch, Eric, 25, 170
"jardín de senderos que se bifurcan, El," 26
Joyce, James, 109, 191
   Finnegans Wake, 97–98, 170
   Ulysses, 57, 170–71
juego de los mundos, El, 14
Jung, Carl. *See* psychoanalysis

K

Kafka, Franz, 48, 56, 226, 229, 233
Kristeva, Julia, 7, 16, 117

L

Lacan, Jacques, 7, 16, 167
Lacoue-Labarthe, Philippe, 10, 244
Latour, Bruno, 7, 144
Lem, Stanislaw: *Solaris*, 209–10
Lesson of the Master, The, 77
Livingston, Ira, 4, 10, 169
"loca y el relato del crimen, La," 167–68
"loteria en Babilonia, La," 112–13, 225
Lugones, Leopoldo (son), 52
Lugones, Leopoldo, 12, 17, 51–52, 170
"Lydia en el canal," 188–93
Lyotard, Jean-François, 3, 16, 117

M

Macedonio Fernández. *See* Fernández, Macedonio
machines, 21, 212, 229
   Deleuzean machines, 23–24, 161, 163–64, 180, 184, 235–36, 240
   "ghost in the machine," 106–7
   writing or storytelling machines in Piglia, 97, 112, 162–63, 162–84, 225, 238, 240
Mahler, Gustav, 125–26, 266n34
Manfred, 33
Mann, Thomas, 19, 117, 266n34
   Doctor Faustus, 123–29
Mansilla, Lucio V., 11, 17
Mármol, José, 11, 17
Martínez, Guillermo, 1–2, 7, 10, 14, 16–26, 167, 179, 223–25, 227–28, 230–32, 234, 236–40, 242–44
   Acerca de Roderer, 17, 73–74, 115–33, 148, 225, 228, 230
   Crímenes imperceptibles, 17, 69–81, 117–18, 145, 230
   "El cuento como sistema lógico," 79
   La mujer del maestro, 27–42, 77, 81, 225, 228, 230
   La muerte de Luciana B., 17, 74–75
Marxist approaches to literary criticism, 24, 66, 107, 206
Mathematician's Apology, A, 135
Mathematics of Postmodern Thought, The. *See under* postmodernism
Maturana, Humberto, 169. *See also* autopoiesis
memory implantation, 16, 70, 95, 110–12
Messiaen, Olivier, 157
Michelet, Jules: *The Sea*, 211–12, 219
misterios de Rosario, Los, 14
"mono ahorcado, El," 12
morphic resonance. *See* Sheldrake

mujer del maestro, La, 27–42, 77, 81, 225, 228, 230
muerte como efecto secundario, La, 14
muerte de Luciana B., La, 17, 74–75
"muerte y la brújula, La," 72–73, 76, 79
multiplicity, 163–64, 178, 187, 195, 200, 203–10, 215–18, 220–21, 231, 235–36, 237, 241–44

N

Nancy, Jean-Luc, 10, 244
New Wave of science fiction, 19, 184–86
Newton, Isaac: Newtonian science, 2, 4–5, 103–4, 140–238
Nietzsche, Friedrich, 70, 73–74, 116, 122–25, 162, 210–11, 213–16, 218, 220
  Dionysian art in, 213–15
non-equilibrium systems. *See under* chaos
non-linear systems. *See under* chaos
nondualism, 116, 138–39, 243
Novalis, 155

O

"On the Road Home," 150
"Ordinary Evening in New Haven, An," 133, 140
ostranenie, 38, 48–50, 65
Oulipo group, 38

P

Perec, George, 38
Piglia, Ricardo, 1–2, 10, 14, 15–28, 69–70, 113–14, 161, 223–34, 236–44
  Blanco nocturno, 16, 162, 164, 172–74, 178–79, 180, 234
  La ciudad ausente, 16, 52, 59, 67, 95–98, 109, 111–12, 162–71, 174–84, 225
  "Encuentro en Saint-Nazaire," 101–10, 175–76
  "En otro país," 108–11, 113
  "El fluir de la vida," 109–10
  "La isla," 95–98
  "La loca y el relato del crimen," 167–68
  Prisión perpetua, 101–11, 175–76
  Respiración artificial, 16, 22–23, 27–28, 42–67, 177, 183, 230–31, 239
  "Tesis sobre el cuento," 79
  "El último cuento de Borges," 96
  El último lector, 99–101, 113
Plant, Sadie, 26, 152, 228, 240–41
Poincaré, Henri, 130
Porush, David, 10, 161, 164, 176, 183–84, 223
postmodernism, 25, 32–33, 112, 138–39, 144, 162, 205, 207, 210–11, 220
  epistemological skepticism in, 1, 2, 34–36, 43, 69–70, 132, 142, 216, 223, 237
  exhaustion of artistic innovation in, 2, 8–10, 21, 28–29, 34–36, 123–24, 127–28, 132, 186, 237
  Mathematics and the Roots of Postmodern Thought, 118, 129–32
  representation of science in, 3–7, 11, 21, 22, 24, 117–18, 129, 132, 237
  Romantic and/or Formalist legacies in, 10, 23, 115, 121, 129, 135, 158, 227
pragmatism, 150, 154
Prigogine, Ilya, 15, 20, 104, 187, 195, 223–25
prime numbers, 134–35, 267n65
Prisión perpetua, 101–11, 175–76
Prometheus, 29–33, 36, 42, 228
Psychoanalysis
  Freudian, 84, 173
  Jungian, 172–74, 233